MISS ELIZABETH ARDEN

Alfred Allan Lewis *and*
Constance Woodworth

MISS ELIZABETH ARDEN

W. H. ALLEN
London & New York
A division of Howard & Wyndham Ltd.

© Alfred Allan Lewis and Constance Woodworth, 1972
First British edition, 1973
Reprinted, 1974
Printed in Great Britain by Fletcher & Son Ltd, Norwich
for the publishers W. H. Allen & Co. Ltd,
43 Essex Street, London WC2R 3JG
Bound by Richard Clay (The Chaucer Press) Ltd, Bungay, Suffolk

ISBN 0 491 01270 5

CONTENTS

Epilogue

ACKNOWLEDGMENTS

The authors wish to express particular gratitude for the assistance of Elizabeth Arden's niece and nephew, Patricia Young and John Graham. Among the countless people in the salons they visited, all of whom were cooperative, they wish to single out Gordon Yates, Eve St. John, Pablo Manzoni, Mary Blakely, Robin Schulte, Masha Magaloff, Elizabeth Hokstead, Bettie Hamilton, Natalie MacEwen, Lillian Macmillan, Paulette DuFault, Julia Brokaw Lowell, Lois McKinney, and Mary Yee. For their time and assistance, they also wish to thank Henry Sell, Wellington Cross, Charles James, Ferdinando Sarmi, Oscar de la Renta, Robert Sinclair, Serge Obolensky, Robert Kelley, Emmett Davis, Molly Collum, Florence Owens, Mildred Wedikind, Rose Mornay, Becky McGrevey, Mrs. Arnold Wilson, Grace DeMun, Bettie Wysor, Irene Hayes, Elinor McVickar, Nancy White, Lillia De Vendeuvre, Nicholai Remisoff, Mrs. K. Wennacott, Monica Smith, Carl Gardiner, Alan McGeehan, and Barbara DuBrul.

Most of all, they are grateful to the staffs of the New York Public Library, the San Francisco Public Library, the New York *Times*, the San Francisco *Chronicle*, the New York *Daily News*, the *Morning Telegraph,* the *Daily Racing Form*, Time, Inc., *Harper's Bazaar*, and *Maclean's* Magazine, in Canada, as well as the staff of Coward, McCann & Geoghegan—especially their kind and patient editor, Peggy Brooks.

MISS ELIZABETH ARDEN

PROLOGUE

Despite gloomy forecasts, the spell of bad weather had broken. The dawning of Friday, October 21, 1966, had blessed New York City with one of those clear, crystalline mornings on which the hard silhouette of Manhattan stands out in relief against a cloudless, silky sky. On such a morning, the simple act of getting up makes one feel good to be alive. It couldn't have been a better day for a funeral.

And on that particular Friday, there were two excellent ones from which the great and small citizens were able to make their choices. The gawking ghouls, celebrity watchers, and autograph hounds had to decide on whether to take up their positions in front of St. Patrick's or St. James'.

There was something to be said for either choice. The very glamorous mayor would almost certainly be at St. Pat's. But then again, you could catch him at any Broadway opening or race riot.

The horsey set would be very much in evidence at the elegant church farther uptown. And you couldn't get them without hitching a ride out to Belmont on the day of an important race.

Only a mile separated the two sacred edifices. A ten minute bus ride and a lucky break in timing would enable one to attend both affairs. But the celebrity watchers and autograph hounds knew better than to depend upon luck. The selection had to be made.

To propound the quandary, there was a rumor that Elizabeth Taylor and Richard Burton were at the Plaza. They found it best not

:[11]:

to think about that for the moment. If it were true, they could always wait upon the far from star-crossed lovers later in the afternoon.

St. Patrick's Cathedral offered twelve firemen, killed in the line of duty during one of the worst blazes in recent memory, down at Broadway and 23rd Street. It was sure to be a memorable event. The firemen collectively had left behind twelve widows and thirty-two children.

Also in St. Pat's favor was the size and number of entrances to the building. There was the improbable but still possible chance of being able to crash. At St. James' Episcopal Church, the stellar attraction was Elizabeth Arden. Any serious funeral goer will tell you that one star will outdraw twelve good supporting players.

There was the very real expectation that Miss Arden's good friend, Mamie Eisenhower, would turn up. After all, Miss Arden had once turned her Maine Chance beauty farm upside down in order to receive her properly.

The problems emanating from Elizabeth Arden's interment did not belong exclusively to the professional funeral watchers. They touched almost everybody associated with her. The reason for this was that the lady had simply refused to believe in her own mortality. Consequently, death was one of the few things in her life for which she was totally unprepared.

So was everybody else.

The streets were a mushroom patch of umbrellas that completely obliterated a skyline already partially obscured by gray clouds and billows of rain. That Monday morning gave no hint of the sort of autumn in New York of which songsters lyrically boasted. Nevertheless, Monica Smith was humming one of the hit songs from *Cabaret* on her way to work.

Despite the weather, it had been a smashing weekend. Probably because she knew that both were very temporary conditions, Monica enjoyed her life in New York, and she enjoyed the job that was very much a part of it. One day soon, she would return to her home in England and to a very different kind of life. Every so often, the caprices of her employer made it necessary to remind herself of that.

Monica knew that Miss Arden liked her. She was English, and she was well born. That appealed to her employer's very pronounced streak of snobbery. Monica was a very good secretary. That appealed to her practical streak. She knew about and adored horses. And that appealed to the part of the old lady that came closest to an expression of real love.

The business day always began in Miss Arden's bedroom. She liked having breakfast in bed and going through her morning rituals, while seeing to those items of business that required uninterrupted attention. It no longer surprised Monica to find that a letter might be dictated while the lady was standing on her head, doing her yoga exercises, massaging her face with one of her creams, or mixing the colors of her makeup and expertly applying it. There was no part of the treatments given in her salons, that Miss Arden could not and did not execute by herself and on herself morning and night. She genuinely believed in their beneficial qualities and was totally uninhibited about practicing them.

Elizabeth went through her beauty routines no matter who was present. She had no reason to be modest or retiring. Aside from the good that she felt they did for her, they were part of her business—a business that grossed an estimated $60,000,000 a year.

Monica shook out her umbrella, folded it, and left it in the handsome stand beside the door. The penthouse was an eclectic mélange of late eighteenth-century French and early 1930's moderne. There were floral arrangements everywhere one looked. Pink horses and feathers muraled the walls. Purple satin sofas vied with yellow velvet chairs, and all was suffused in shades of pink, a color so identified with Elizabeth Arden that the lady could smile whimsically at Schiaparelli's futile attempt to capture it for herself in a pink called Shocking. As she commented at the time, "When people think pink, dear, they think Arden."

Objectively, the apartment was a decorative disaster area, but it managed to provide the perfect background for its doll-like owner. The look was so much a logical extension of the look she had foisted upon the world that, when Miss Arden passed through the rooms, disbelief was willingly suspended, and they became lovely. Such was the astonishing personal magnetism of the deceptively un-prepossessing-looking chatelaine.

When Monica entered the bedroom, Pat Young was seated beside her aunt's bed. Tall, large-boned, handsome, and with a shy, almost timid nature, Pat was the precise antithesis of Elizabeth.

Miss Arden's bed was all pink frills and silk. It was feminine almost to the point of caricature. Its mate in the room provided as much contrast as the niece did to the aunt. It was piled high with racing forms, advertising layouts, samples, brochures, magazines, and books. These things had been its only occupant since 1943, when Miss Arden's last husband had been forcibly ejected.

Pat had just returned from a visit to the Arden Maine Chance horse farm in Kentucky. She was relating the latest gossip about what was going on in the neighboring stables. "I ran into Mr. Kleberg. He told me that Buffles is desperately ill. He isn't expected to last much longer."

Miss Arden laid down the hand mirror into which she had been gazing critically. She wrinkled her brow, a thing she told other women never to do on pain of excommunication from her temples of Venus, and sighed. "The poor little darling."

Miss Arden turned to the door and smiled warmly at Monica. "Good morning, dear. Did you have a pleasant weekend?"

"Fine, thank you." Ordinarily, the girl was filled with questions about the horses but, on that morning, she only made her brief, polite reply and kept quiet. She did not like the way Miss Arden looked. She had spent the entire previous week at home, but the rest had not done her any good. Her face was drawn and sallow.

How old was she, Monica wondered. Depending upon whom you believed, she was eighty plus one, or four, or seven. It did not matter. She usually looked sixty, had the energy of thirty, and seemed indestructible. This was one of the few times that Monica was aware of the woman's considerable age. She asked, "How are you feeling?"

"A little under the weather. It's this awful cold, dear. I didn't sleep well. Perhaps you'd better call and cancel that meeting I scheduled for this morning.''

Pat said, ''I think that's a good idea. You shouldn't get over-tired.''

For a moment, Miss Arden looked as if she was going to refute this, but then she slowly nodded her head and said crossly, ''If there's anything I don't need, it's a lot of stupid men lounging around here, saying—'Yes, Miss Arden. Yes, Miss Arden.' The only time they'll say—'No, Miss Arden'—is when there *is* no Miss Arden.''

There were three phones in the room. One was for outgoing calls, another for incoming calls, and a third was a direct tie-line to the office and salon some three-quarters of a mile south on Fifth Avenue.

Monica picked up the direct line and informed the firm's general manager, Carl W. Gardiner, that the meeting was canceled. He asked if anything was the matter and, when informed that all was well, asked no farther. Gardiner had been with the firm for over twenty years. To last over twenty minutes, one had to learn to ask no farther about any of Miss Arden's decisions.

It was only a short time later, while in the middle of dictating a letter, that she suddenly wrapped her arms around her chest and winced painfully. ''Pat,'' she wheezed. ''Pat!''

Pat was already racing for one of the phones. ''I'm going to send for the doctor immediately.''

''Not the doctor,'' the old woman cried. ''Only a bad cold. Not the doctor. Come here. Help me walk around the room.'' She began to plead in a childish tone, ''Please. A tiny walk around the little room.''

It was one of the few times in her life, that Pat had disregarded her aunt's orders and done as she thought best. After completing her call, she came back to the side of the bed. ''Is it very bad? Are you in much pain?''

Miss Arden was undoubtedly in great pain, but still greater than her pain was her fury at not being obeyed. She somehow managed to gather some of the characteristic old strength into her voice. She commanded imperiously, "You just walk me around this room, damn it! Walk me!"

Pat looked helplessly at Monica. The tone left no doubt in either of their minds. They had often heard it before. Each supporting her by an arm, they slowly walked the frail, but indomitable, old woman back and forth across the room.

Elizabeth was painfully walking away from death. She was walking toward life. She would win. She had to win. There was no alternative. If she did not win, what would become of the rest of them? Walking . . . Away from death . . . Walking . . . Walking . . . .

"What in God's name do you think you're doing? Get that woman into bed." The doctor's voice shot across the room.

"No," she cried, trying to pull away from them. "No!" The bed had become her enemy, but she did not have the energy to resist. Over her feeble protests, they managed to get her back between the covers. Once there, the brave show of force ebbed away. She weakly rolled her head from side to side and unsuccessfully tried to find her voice.

They sent for an oxygen tent. The old fight would return, and retreat, and return again only once more to desert her. It became too much for them to handle at home, and they were forced to call for an ambulance, knowing how much she hated hospitals. As they were carrying her out of the room, she sobbed, "Buffles. Just like Buffles."

The hospital corridor resembled a displaced persons' camp. It was filled with desperate people waiting to learn their fates. All of the company top brass was there, as well as a group of very special old-timers.

The nurse came out of the room, and they crowded around her. "She's putting up a great fight. There's nothing more any of us can do for her right now. She's resting quietly. The doctor wants you all to go home." She looked around at the cluster of uncomprehending faces. "Please. There's a good chance that she'll pull through this. Now, please—go home."

It was still raining when Monica left the hospital. She glanced at her watch. It felt like midnight, but it was only seven.

The city was awakening. From the brightly illuminated buildings of Park Avenue, shimmering shafts of light pierced the hazy damp evening. Elegantly attired people waited under canopies for taxis and cars. The new night's pleasures stretched before them. The season had begun. New plays, new restaurants, new operas, new concerts, new ballets, new parties beckoned from a night in which a million electric bulbs more than compensated for the obscured stars.

Monica dashed across the street to join one of the taxi queues. She discreetly studied the other women in the line. Their hair and freshly applied makeup glowed in the dim light. Even the homeliest and most timid of them felt a little more confident, a little less plain, thanks to the protective illusion of cosmetics.

Elizabeth Arden had done that for them. It was her victory. She couldn't die now. Surely, she would pull through triumphantly. She always had before.

She was dead. Dear God—dead! One of the treatment girls blurted out, "But it's so unlike her!"

When they'd arrived at work that Tuesday morning, Mr. Gardiner had solemnly announced that she was dead, and that they would be closed on the day of the funeral. Until then, it was business as usual. As the dear departed had been fond of saying—the show must go on!

In the salon, they were weeping. Even the new girls, who had scarcely known her, were weeping. Even the few, who had fervently wished more than once that she'd drop dead, were weeping.

They were discovering that it was possible to weep for the loss of something one hated, as well as the loss of something one loved. There had been great security in hatred, especially hatred of a boss like Miss Arden. Personal vindication for more than one career that went nowhere, could go nowhere, had been found in the awfulness of working for her. Now, they would have to seek out somebody else for whom it would be as easy to fail as it had been for her.

Upstairs in the executive offices, failure was the last thing on Carl Gardiner's mind. As general manager of the company, he had not failed Elizabeth, and he would not fail her successor. He wondered who that would be. It had been, for so long, a one-woman operation. She had not trained any single successor but had, instead, shrewdly delegated authority among many executives, playing one off against the other to get the best from all. The new head might come from within the family as had happened at Rubinstein but, knowing Elizabeth, he doubted it. It was true that her sister, the Vicomtesse de Maublanc, had headed the Paris salon and French company from their very inception, but he didn't think she would enjoy America. She loved her life in France too much. She was also far too old for the job. The niece, Patricia Young, had lived for years with Miss Arden. But genius is not contagious. You don't catch it by getting close to it. Moreover, Mrs. Young had never evinced any real interest in working in the firm. That left the nephew, John Graham. He might be the only male heir, but mere masculinity had never been a sufficient recommendation to Elizabeth. She'd never shown any genuine enthusiasm for that gender, except when it belonged to a race horse.

The family was out. Gardiner wondered if she'd left any instructions in her will. The lady had been capable of being capricious and whimsical. She had often thought of herself as a monarch—but hers had not been a Louis XV *"Après moi le deluge"* attitude. She must have wanted the business to go on. She must have wanted the name to live—even if the business no longer belonged to her.

Who would take charge of the vast Arden holdings? Gardiner knew that he was capable of it. There were many below him who thought that he was already thinking of himself as g-Ardin-er.

Gardiner decided that he had better have a long talk with Elizabeth's attorney, J. Howard Carter. Fortuitously, Carter was having the same thought about Carl Gardiner.

What a time for the old girl to pop off! The man in the accounting department buried his head in his hands. If she had only listened to some advice—if she'd only given them some warning—they could have started cleaning up the mess. Now, it was going to take years. For Christ's sake, by the time it was all sorted out, they'd owe the government over $40,000,000 in taxes!

Serge Obolensky unthinkingly screwed a flower into the lapel of his immaculately cut suit and sat down to stare vacantly into the space in front of his desk. It was incredible. Only the night before she'd been stricken, they had dined together in her apartment. She had spoken animatedly about the publicity campaign for the next collection. They had made plans extending into the following year, with neither of them feeling the slightest doubt that Elizabeth would be around to carry them through. And she was dead.

Obolensky was a White Russian. He had witnessed the downfall of a great empire and had been revolted by the wanton destruction that followed. He suspected that he was about to witness the downfall of another one. There was a slim chance of preventing it. He thought that, with his backing, Pat Young could take over. He doubted that she would try. The woman was far more interested in horses than empire.

Thomas Jenkins Lewis wondered if he could take any satisfaction in the fact that he had outlived her. Was longevity a form of revenge? To Elizabeth, it might well be.

The queen is dead. Long live—he shrugged. He would go to the funeral. He owed that much to himself and, he supposed, to her. She had been cruel to him. She had cheated him of what was rightfully his. She had been unjust beyond measure. But she had also given him the most exciting fifteen years that any man could desire, fifteen years that had held more exhilaration and fulfillment than any of the other men he knew had experienced in a lifetime.

Between them, Florence Nightingale Graham and he had created Elizabeth Arden and invented a billion-dollar industry.

When they asked Pablo, who was makeup director of Elizabeth

:[19]:

Arden at that time, he became terrified. He did not want to see Miss Arden that way. He did not like the dead. He did not want to touch them. He was a makeup artist for the living. He called his lawyer to find out if he had to do it under the terms of his contract. The attorney assured him that there was no clause to that effect, and suggested that he refuse on the grounds of religious scruples.

They had to find somebody else. All the more popular artists backed away from the assignment. They had all had terrible times making her up while she was alive—having to endure hearing her call them stupid and fools and know-nothings and worse. They did not want to touch her in death. It was almost as if they feared the corpse would sit up and once again hurl imprecations at them.

The request went out to all the better makeup artists in all the Arden salons across the country. Some were ill. Some were too grief-stricken. Some had bookings with important clients that could not be canceled. The excuses were manifold, the reply—a constant no.

Somebody had to do it. They could not leave the final maquillage of Elizabeth Arden to a mortician. It would be too mortifying.

Miss Harris had been with the salon for over forty years. Miss Arden had personally trained her as a treatment girl. She was due to retire very shortly and was considered too old for any but her own clients of many years standing.

But she adored Miss Arden. After the fruitless, frantic search, she said, "If nobody else wants to do it, I will."

On Wednesday morning, a small staff from the salon started uptown. The group included a hairdresser, a fitter, and Miss Harris. Their first stop was the apartment of their late employer, where they were asked to wait in the drawing room. At the sight of the Augustus John portrait, one of the girls began to sob. Another muttered dryly, "She doesn't have to worry. Harris will paint a prettier picture than that one."

A sniffling maid came in, carrying a small suitcase and a pink tea gown on a hanger. A few years earlier, Oscar de la Renta had designed and made it especially for Miss Arden. The enigmatic lady had always felt, what seemed to many, an uncharacteristic sentimental affection for it. Handing over the frock, the maid warned, "I just pressed it. You see you don't get it wrinkled. She'd have a fit!"

By the time the cortege of cosmeticians arrived, enormous floral tributes were already beginning to crowd the chapel at the Frank E. Campbell Funeral Home at Madison Avenue and Eighty-first Street. It was decidedly the establishment where one would expect to find Miss Arden laid out. In the matter of status, Campbell's was to embalming the dead what the Arden salon was to embalming the living.

One of the directors showed them into a plain back room. The abrasive odor of formaldehyde seemed to ooze from the bare walls. "Remember," their guide said, "this makeup job isn't for a one-night stand. It's got to last two, three days. Now you people make it snappy. She goes on display at one o'clock sharp. And our clients are never late to their own funerals. That's a house rule."

She lay on a slab shrouded in a sheet. The director pulled back the cover to reveal a thing that looked more like a pale blue effigy of Miss Arden than it resembled the lady they had all known and feared and loved. As baby blue was her second favorite color, it could have been worse.

The director looked at the tea gown and shook his head. "Pink. All those pink flowers, too. Why don't people ask first? Pink is not the best color for the Williamsburg Room. Ecru is."

Resembling the rosy sleeping beauty of some Walt Disney epic, Elizabeth Arden slumbered in splendor in an African mahogany coffin. There were so many flowers that they spilled into the hallway leading to the Williamsburg Room. It would later take four cars to transport them to the family burial ground at Sleepy Hollow Cemetery, in Westchester County, and there would still be so many left over, St. James' would feel obliged to charge a fee for disposing of them.

It never occurred to any of the people involved in the preparations for the funeral to ask that, instead of flowers, donations be sent, in

:[21   ]:

Miss Arden's name, to charity. They knew that she would not have liked that. They knew that she would have wanted to die as she had lived—in a blaze of aromatic pink glory.

On Wednesday evening, two fashion magazine editors were viewing the remains. "My God. The last time I was here was for Rubinstein. It's a year and a half already."

"It's probably the only time Miss Arden didn't mind Madame Rubinstein getting ahead of her."

The other tittered. "Who was Monsieur Rubinstein?"

"An alias for Mr. Graham." They both gazed down at the corpse and howled with laughter.

Late on Thursday afternoon, one of her hairdressers stood in a queue to bid a final farewell to his employer. He looked around at the somber, rather musty Williamsburg Room and gasped, "If Arden could get a load of this place, she'd drop dead!"

On Friday morning, Prince Michael Evlanoff dressed carefully in what was later described as "somewhat seedy splendor." When Miss Arden married him, a few years after Mme. Rubinstein had married her Prince Gourielli, a rather vapid *Vogue* editor made a fleeting reputation as a wit by commenting, "These days, it's only peasants who can afford Princes."

Evlanoff's floral tribute to his former wife was three red roses, the Russian symbol for the cross, delivered each day after her death. They totaled an even dozen. An even number of flowers was something about which, everybody close to her knew, she was superstitious. Her bouquets had to contain eleven or thirteen, but never an even dozen; twenty-three or twenty-five, but never an even two dozen.

Still and all, as one friend kindly remarked, "It was very generous of him. On the settlement he got out of Elizabeth, a dozen roses was a great extravagance."

Elizabeth Arden had once boasted to an interviewer, "There's only one Elizabeth like me, and that's the queen."

She would not have been displeased by the stately column of Rolls-Royces, Mercedes-Benzes, and Cadillacs, all with liveried chauffeurs, that started to pull up at the portals to St. James' Episcopal Church at about ten forty-five that morning. Always one who knew how to play to the grandstands, she would have relished the more than a thousand people who crowded the street to gape at the invited guests.

It was truly a royal sendoff. There were television cameras to record the great event for a posterity that extended unto the eleventh hour news.

Suitably clad in black and sorrowfully leaning on the arm of her son, Estée Lauder was very much in attendance. With Arden and Rubinstein out of the way, she had every right to think of herself as heiress apparent to their titles. After all, it was extremely doubtful that Charles Revson would enjoy being called ''The Queen of the Cosmetics Industry.''

Mrs. Lauder underscored this opinion by leaning still more heavily on her son and telling the television audience, ''A great era has passed, leaving just us to carry on the fine tradition that Elizabeth leaves to us.''

If she could have heard her, it would doubtless have been the one occasion on which Miss Arden would have totally agreed with Mme. Rubinstein, who had once said of Estée, ''What chutzpah!''

One could only wonder if Mrs. Lauder had so easily forgotten an event that took place barely two months before in the Arden Paris salon.

''Get her out of here! She's here to spy on me. That's what she's here for!'' Miss Arden had screamed, when she heard that Estée was sitting cozily under one of the dryers and calmly munching on a steak and salad. She dispatched her decorator, Tony Duquette, to pose as a lawyer and insist that Mrs. Lauder depart under threat of court action.

Mrs. Lauder simply stared at him. Her own hairdresser was out of town for his August holiday, and she had a dinner engagement with the Duke and Duchess of Windsor. Neither heaven nor the hell of

Miss Arden's wrath was going to prevent her from looking her best. But Miss Arden did. She had her discreetly removed.

The men responsible for the funeral arrangements were scattered through the handsome church. They looked around at the prominent assemblage. If they caught each other's eye, it was with a wink of mutual congratulations. They had pulled it off brilliantly. Elizabeth would have enjoyed it. It was her kind of party.

Carl W. Gardiner and John A. Treat were the only Arden employees who had been asked to serve as honorary pall bearers. The rest of the list was composed of: Charles M. Bliss, Spruille Braden, John C. Clark, Clarence Gifford, Walter Hoving, John D. Lodge, Alexander H. McLanahan, and Henry Sell. Elizabeth would have adored being escorted anywhere by these gentlemen—even out of this world.

Some of the fashionable ladies among the mourners were Miss Margaret Chase, Mrs. Clare Boothe Luce, Mrs. Ambrose Diehl, and Mrs. Charles S. Payson. If these, or any of the other ladies in attendance, felt irritation, it was not directed at being in church in the middle of a beautiful autumn morning.

It was directed at the same gentlemen who were congratulating themselves for having got them there. They had ordered the salon closed for the day of the funeral. This had forced the ladies to scrounge around elsewhere for early hair appointments. They had wanted to look their best. It was the least they could do for poor Elizabeth.

As she was entering the church, one of these perfectly coiffed heads had whispered to her escort, ''Arden's was always so cosy. But at ten in the morning, let me tell you, Bergdorf's is a bloody bore.''

The Reverend Dr. Arthur Lee Kinsolving was eloquently intoning a simple prayer. His rich, ripe, resonant voice rattled through the vaulted chamber.

''We thank Thee for the spark of creative imagination in Thy servant, Elizabeth, as for her ingenuity, energy, and enterprise. We thank Thee for her keen perception and her love of beauty, of flowers and of animals, for her wide ranging human interests and broad humanity, for her flair for life and vitality in living it, for her many friends and kindnesses along life's way.''

On most of these points, the good doctor could not be faulted. Elizabeth had many of the qualities mentioned in abundance. She was just as richly endowed with several of a very different nature. It would definitely have not been seemly to mention those in that sacred place at that solemn hour.

After the benediction, the coffin was lifted and carried slowly up the center aisle. She was starting on her last journey away from her adopted city that had given her so much wealth and fame. Elizabeth always got more than her fair share from places and things. It was with people that she had her difficulties.

In one way, her life was a dream come true—an American dream. One could only marvel that a poor Canadian truck farmer's daughter, named Florence Nightingale Graham, had dared to dream it.

CHAPTER ONE

The Richest Little Woman in the World

The child was born on December 31, 1878. She was later to regret that she had been in such a hurry to greet the world. By her own perverse logic, one day's delay would have made her a year younger. She remedied this by deducting a few years every now and again until, aside from official records, nobody including herself could be certain of her true age. Whenever anybody got close enough to have the temerity to ask about it, she would reply, "Dear, I've lied about it so often, that I'm not sure how old I really am."

William Graham kissed the tiny red face that peeked out from amid the blankets. He glanced tenderly at his wife. " 'Tis a new year, my darlin'. A new year and a new bairn. Oh, I tell ye, Susan, I've a feeling—such a feeling!"

Susan turned aside and closed her eyes. Willie was forever having feelings, like tips from some great tout, but always on the wrong horse.

What was the result of this great event with which they had heralded still another year? Another child. Another mouth to feed. And not a pin between them and perdition. Her fourth baby and only one son in the lot—only one on which to say a prayer.

A girl child. What good were they? She had brought three of the useless creatures into this world. They were only a drain. Dolls, and dresses, and dowries. They could provide none of it. Didn't God understand that? They had nothing—nothing—except useless girls.

The cough came on her again, sending bolts of wretched pain to tear at her chest. Would she never be free of these damnable colds? Winter and summer, they were upon her. More for warmth than love, she hugged the soft bundle of baby to her breast. It began to cry. Using only one finger, she gently smoothed the frowning brow. "Hush. Poor darling girl. Poor useless girl."

From the doorway of the shabby room, two large sets of eyes stared at her and began to edge with tears. "My little dears," she called. "Come have a look at your new baby sister."

Chris and Lollie ran to the bedside and gazed down at the tiny, wrinkled face. Lollie removed the thumb from her mouth long enough to say, "She looks like an old lady."

Chris asked, "What will we call her?"

Willie knelt between his two daughters, placing protective arms around their shoulders. "Yes. What shall we name her?"

Susan thought for a moment. No name like those of the other two. Not a Lillian or a Christine. Not another pretty, meaningless name. A name for a doer. A name with which to march out into the world. And not Victoria. In every corner of the vast empire, there were already too many Victorias. Besides, the queen didn't march out into the world. The world marched in on her. If this babe were to wait for that, it would be doomsday before anything happened to her.

Suddenly, it was clear. She knew the right name. It was that of her idol as a child and adult, the only woman who had ever managed to get anything accomplished on her own. "Florence!" she exclaimed. "Florence Nightingale."

Will laughed and said for the first time, what he was often to repeat in the years to come. "Poor tyke. What a monicker to live up to. Florence Nightingale Graham."

But she did not remain Florence for long. In the Graham family, names were quickly reduced to terms of endearment. Florence rapidly became Flo as, before her, Christine had become Chris or Chrissie and Lillian, Lollie, and the two Williams, father and son, Will or Willie. Only Susan remained Susan, the strong focal point, the center

:[27]:

of the household, the provider of the affection that shielded it against the harsh wind that blew down from the North.

She was soon over her resentment at giving birth to another female. The child became just another creature to love. Love was all she had. From the moment when she first laid eyes on William Graham, it had been her salvation and her ruin.

She took pleasure in recounting to the children how it had all begun between their parents. It had started at a country fair. With the coming of the mild spring weather, fairs blossomed in her native Cornwall as surely as the cultivated green shoots of the hillsides and fields. All winter long, the natives were a dour lot, grimly hardening themselves against the ravages of the cold and stormy sea that broke upon the rocky promontories of the coast. They were a people tempered by the weather, who turned jolly and expansive with the coming of the warmer months. The fairs were an outgrowth of an ancient Arthurian festival (Cornish Tintagel had been the birthplace of King Arthur) that gave pagan thanks for the early sprouting of the new crops.

Some of these fairs were famous for their horse races, and men came from all over the British Isles to compete for the handsome prizes. William Graham was such a man. For generations, the Scottish Grahams had worked the lands of the local laird, and Willie, an excellent horseman, had journeyed down in quest of a prize that might buy him his freedom and a place of his own.

It was a few days before the race that William met Susan Tadd. He knew immediately that, prize or no prize, he never wanted to go home. This was where he wanted to be—this or any other place where he might be with her. From the beginning, it had been love for both of them.

Love was not the emotion that Willie inspired in her family. The Tadds were very well-to-do, with large local landholdings and a fleet of seagoing boats. Susan never let her children forget that. They came of good and prosperous stock. Poverty did not humble the pride that she instilled in them.

Her parents were looking for an advantageous marriage for their

A family photograph of the Tadd family showing Florence Nightingale Graham's mother, Susan Tadd Graham, standing at right rear and her grandparents, Samuel and Jane Tadd, seated. Others are Emma Tadd Borst, Jane Tadd Forbes, and Samuel Tadd, Jr.

Schooner Bedwelly of Fowey. Samuel Tadd Master. Entering the Port of Marseilles 11th Dec

Samuel Tadd, Elizabeth's grandfather, was the master of a schooner, *Bedwelty of Fowey.*

pretty and intelligent young daughter. They could not understand what she saw in Graham, and forbade her ever to see him again. But he was what she wanted and see him, she would—and marry him—and if must be, go away with him—and live happily ever after.

Even when Willie became a bit of a local celebrity by winning the race, the Tadds would not change their minds about him. He was not the man that they wanted for their daughter.

The only hope for the young lovers was to elope. Between the price he got for selling his horse and his winnings, Willie had enough money to buy two steerage tickets to Canada and to get them started in the new world. He promised her that it would be their world, that they would conquer it. Another generation would have to pass, before one of the useless daughters miraculously fulfilled that promise.

The newlyweds settled in Toronto. Like many another country boy, Willie felt that he could find his fortune in the streets of the big city, but if those golden pavements really existed, they remained obscured behind a thickness of mud that he could never pierce.

He moved from menial job to menial job. At best, they could keep no more than one foot ahead of the bill collectors and, indeed, often drew apace and still more frequently fell behind. Christine was born and Lillian was on her way, before they were finally forced to admit that the city was no place for them. They were country people and should go back to the land.

After looking around, Willie found a tenant farm that he could lease in the little town of Woodbridge, some fourteen miles north of Toronto. If he ever felt any resentment at having journeyed thousands of miles just to till another man's field as his father had before him, he never showed it.

Graham borrowed some money to buy a horse. When he brought home the mangy animal, Susan was very dubious about him. Willie reassured her that he was not just any horse. This colt had the blood of great winning thoroughbreds in him. But the Tadds had always owned fine horses. Susan had grown up with them and, despite what he said, one look and she knew this one was no winner.

Susan Tadd Graham — Elizabeth Arden's mother.

It was at the farm that Lollie was born, and then young Will and Flo and, after her, Gladys. With the same regularity that Susan became pregnant, Willie bought horses—bad horses that had nothing to recommend them but their lineages. He might go out all set to buy a cow, but he returned with a mare. Florence was later to say, "I was born with a whinney in my ear."

Willie's justification for each purchase was predictably the same. He could not afford to pass up a horse by so-and-so out of such-and-such. Unfortunately, they were all too finely bred to make good work horses. Willie attempted to give purpose to their existences by explaining that he would breed them and sire a champion. Because of this dream, the family had to work like horses to keep the horses living like royalty with the finest feed money could buy.

Susan's health rapidly deteriorated after the birth of her youngest child. The cough became a frightening and unbearable presence, keeping them up long into the night and awakening them too early in the morning. Over her protests, Willie insisted on taking her into Toronto to consult a specialist.

It was as she had feared. She had a severe case of tuberculosis. If she wanted to live, a sanitarium was the only proper place for her but, with five small children to rear and no money, that was out of the question.

Susan went to great lengths to make certain that the youngsters would never be afflicted by the disease of which she was slowly but surely dying. Whatever precautions she had to take for herself, she also took for them. So thoroughly did she inculcate them with the necessity for these anodynes that, until the end of her life, Florence was stuffing folded newspaper into her elegant and expensive, hand-made shoes.

As their mother started to spend more and more time in bed, the children had to assume the responsibilities of people far in advance of their ages. Chris and Lollie took over the running of the house, looking after all the cooking, cleaning, and mending. Young Willie helped his father with all of the farm chores. Because she loved them so much, Flo was put in charge of feeding, watering, and exercising the horses. She very soon had much more the manner of an accomplished stableboy than that of a six-year-old little girl. Susan kept reassuring herself that the child would outgrow her coltish behavior. Susan was wrong. She never did.

Gladys preferred tagging after Florence to anything in this world, but her mother was not about to lose a second daughter to the ponies. She insisted that all of the older children take turns looking after the baby. One afternoon, young Willie rebelled. He wanted to go fishing in the nearby Humber River. He whined, ''Let Flor take care of her. I don't want to keep an eye on any dang kid.'' ·

Susan slapped him soundly. To his astonishment, it was not because of his refusal to care for his youngest sister. It was because of his language. She said, ''My children can say damn, if they must, but if I catch any of you saying dang, I'll box your ears.''

It was an admonition that Florence would always remember. Through the years, she was often heard shouting—damn!—but never once even whispering—dang.

The dying young mother's illness was complicated by deep concern over what would happen to her children, once she was gone. They had to have educations, if they were ever to be able to climb out of Woodbridge. She knew that Willie Graham was basically a good father, but that he would much rather buy another horse than send his children to school.

She overcame her pride and wrote to a wealthy Tadd aunt, in Cornwall, explaining her condition. The aunt had always been very fond of her and responded favorably. She promised to send a monthly allowance to be used for the children's schooling.

Willie was furious when he heard what she had done. How could she lower herself and humiliate him in front of a member of the family that had turned its back on her? It did not matter. She felt that she could die in peace, now that she knew they would be looked after. She exacted a deathbed promise, that the money would be spent on his children and not on his horses.

Florence was six when her mother died. She could not understand why it had happened. If mama was good, and kind, and loving, and loved, why should she die? It made no sense.

On market days, Florence would often accompany her father to sell his produce in York. She very quickly developed into a precociously shrewd salesgirl. She learned that if she used a babyish voice and acted cute, people would fawn and fuss and buy anything she tried to sell them. When she was not busy herself, she would watch the women haggling over pennies, trying to, as she would say, ''jew down'' her father on the price of the vegetables that they had worked so hard to cultivate.

It was a curious thing, but the richer and prettier they were, the more obsequious Willie became, the more apt he was to let them get away with cheating him out of his just profits. And gradually, she made a discovery. It was an answer to the question that had been bothering her ever since the death of her mother.

Love was not enough. It could even hurt you. It could make a drudge out of you and kill you. The only things that were really important were to be rich and to be beautiful. Then you were free. Then you could do anything you wanted to in the whole wide world. It was a lesson well learned. It would ultimately bring her everything that she had ever dreamed of having—everything in the whole wide world—everything except that insufficient love.

Because they had so few toys, the Graham children amused themselves by inventing verbal games. One of them was to say what you wanted to be when you grew up. Chris wanted to be a housewife and Lollie, a painter, and young Willie, just about everything from cop to Casanova. When it was Flo's turn, she replied, ''I want to be the richest little woman in the world.''

Gladys quickly added, ''Me, too.'' Whatever Florence wanted, Gladys wanted. That was the way it was going to be for as long as they both lived.

Competitiveness and a will to win were something a girl learned early, when she was one of four handsome and high-spirited sisters. The can-can was the scandalous rage of the day and, in the seclusion of the barn, skirts flounced wildly, as the Graham girls did their own interpretations of the dance. Flo was determined to be best and kick higher than any of the others. With one breathtaking fling, she succeeded—in throwing a hip out of joint. From then on, she was to stand at the same angle to the ground, as a listing ship to the sea.

Although Florence was an intelligent and promising student, she never finished high school. The Tadd aunt died, and the money stopped. The disappointment was tremendous, for she had a great thirst for knowledge and a genuine respect for those who really had it. It was only with people, who did not know what they attempted to fool her into thinking they knew, that she had no patience. She did not suffer fools easily.

Women were beginning to enter the universities. She longed to be among them, but it was out of the question. To support herself and help support the others, she would have to learn a trade.

Whenever one of the horses or children got ill, Flo played the family doctor. She began to believe that she had a gift for healing, and decided to follow in the footsteps of her illustrious namesake.

It was not long after entering nurses' training school that she discovered that she had made a terrible mistake. There was a very big difference between being a nurse and having a gift for healing. That difference consisted of a stomach for the uglier aspects of illness. Florence did not have it, and she did not remain to finish her first semester. She explained, ''I found I didn't really like looking at sick people. I want to keep people well, and young, and beautiful.''

Two things did always remain with her from that early hospital experience. The first was a morbid curiosity about illness coupled with a conviction that she had superior knowledge of how to cope with it. No sooner did she hear that somebody was laid up, than Florence had to know all the details of the ailment and how it was being treated. She was available for consultation on everything from a splinter to a spastic colon.

For those in hospital, care packages and flowers were dispatched in great profusion. Prescriptions were written in little notes. Advice was given by the yard over the telephone. The only thing that she would almost never do was to visit the patient. She adored everything about illness except the physical look of it.

The other important thing that came out of the nursing business was a chance meeting with a biochemist. He was employed in the hospital laboratory trying to discover some sort of cream that would help to cure skin blemishes. His interest was strictly medical but Florence, looking over his shoulder, had other thoughts about his experiments. If such a cream could be devised, why couldn't it be used cosmetically to beautify as well as pharmaceutically to cure?

The Graham sisters were very lucky girls. They had inherited their mother's glorious English complexion and coloring. In those pre-makeup and plastic surgery days, a good skin was essential to good looks, for there was no way to hide a bad one. What a boon the cream she had in mind would be to all of the women who were not similarly blessed.

After resigning from nursing, Florence returned to Woodbridge in very high spirits, which her father did not share. He worried about what was to become of the girl if she had no trade.

She told him to stop fretting. She had the solution to all of their problems. She was going to make them rich. Not only that, she would not have to leave home to do it. She would be there, and they would have the money to breed great horses together. The girls would all have gorgeous clothes and handsome dowries. Young Will would be able to go to the university or do anything else he fancied.

When he asked how she was going to arrange this avalanche of wealth, she replied that she was going into the mail-order business. She was going to make a cream that women all over the world would want, for it would make them beautiful. The only thing standing in her way was that she had not perfected it yet but, with Gladys' help, she would.

Her father simply shook his head and said, ''You're an ass. Go to grass.''

Old Will was wrong. Although she did eventually go to Grasse, Florence was no ass. She was a goat—a Capricorn and typical of those born under that sign. One doesn't have to believe in astrology to see

Florence Nightingale Graham, before she became Elizabeth Arden,
photographed in the rustic setting of her home in Canada.

certain striking similarities between the traits of her personality and those attributed to the characteristic Capricorn.

She was a determined careerist. She was adept at using feminine wiles to mask a steely determination. She had a very strong ambition and hated criticism. She could look as harmless as a feather quilt and be as tough as nails. She was always seeking to improve herself and get ahead, get to the top of the mountain. She was a social climber as well as a mountain climber. She knew where she was going and what she wanted and could take any punishment, any setback that came her way, without ever deviating from her goal. She lived by the rules of success as well as morality, and expected those around her to live by the same rules. She was not an actress playing a part, she was the whole play, doubling in any role necessary to ensure a triumphant performance.

With Gladys' fervid assistance, Florence began to use the wood-burning kitchen stove to experiment at cooking up a batch of instant beauty. The smell was so frightful that it often drove the entire family, including Florence, out of the house. No threats from the others, no imprecations, no pleas could deter her. She stubbornly continued to do what she knew she had to do—until the day that the minister came to call.

The good clergyman looked at her with compassion. He sighed sympathetically and thrust a basket of eggs into her hands. When she looked completely baffled, he explained, ''My child, you shouldn't have been too proud to ask for help.''

Her expression of bewilderment persisted, and he continued, pressing a handkerchief delicately to his nose, saying that the neighbors had reported the smell of rotten eggs coming from their kitchen and were convinced that they were in a very bad way. He added, sniffing into his linen, ''I fear they were absolutely right.''

It was the cream. If the kindly Samaritan had known that what she actually was cooking was a cosmetic, the gift would not have been eggs. It would have been fire and brimstone.

Florence began to giggle. No matter how hard she tried, she could not restrain the rush of laughter. She blurted out a thank-you and raced back into the kitchen, slamming the door in the bewildered man's face. Amid spasms of hysterical mirth, she told Gladys what had happened. The two girls clutched at each other and shrieked with laughter, until the tears rolled down their faces.

When the incident was reported to their father, he was definitely not amused. "That does it, Flo. I'll not have the entire village thinking I'm in such a bad way, that I have to feed my family rotten eggs. No more of this face cream nonsense. You'll either get married or get back to Toronto and find a good, honest job."

With the image of her mother's life clearly in mind, she opted for returning to the city and seeking employment.

It was not long before she found another job. It might have been honest, but it was hardly what Flo could consider good. She went to work as a receptionist for a manufacturer of trusses and athletic supports. It was about as far as you could get from face creams.

When she no longer could stand it, she went on to a dreary succession of positions, including that of bank teller and secretary in a real estate company. The latter was the only job from which she was ever fired. Convinced that she could conquer anything, she was nevertheless defeated by the mechanical child of Mr. Remington's conception—born the same year that she was—the shift-key typewriting machine. She never did get the hang of it. In later years, the letters, carefully typed by her secretaries, had handwritten addenda of P.S.'s that generally went on for pages longer than the original message.

The years began to pass swiftly. Chris got married. Bill emigrated to New York City in search of a better life. Lollie went to work for a milliner. Gladys had a series of beaus and proposals. But there were no beaus, proposals, marriages, or betterment for Florence. She discouraged the first three, and the fourth constantly seemed to elude her.

A new century had rolled in. The world was changing so rapidly that one had to race to keep step with it. Automobiles were no longer a laughable novelty in the streets of Toronto. The gleeful shouts of "Get a horse" were stilled, as people started saving to get a motorcar. Nickelodeons were providing the breathtaking thrills of motion pictures. Spliced with signs requesting ladies to remove their hats and gentlemen to refrain from smoking, great train robbers were pursued by Keystone Kops, while elegant drawing rooms distilled an atmosphere of sophisticated sin. Florence adored the movies and would go as often as the bills changed, seeking some thrilling escape from her dreary and monotonous life.

Everywhere other women were becoming defiant. They were beginning to agitate for the right to vote. They were getting better jobs and better educations. Some were even daring openly to paint their faces, though these, of course, could no longer be considered ladies. Only Florence was standing still, watching the shadowy images of somebody else's life flash upon a screen.

By 1907 she was working as an assistant to a dentist. The job paid better than anything she'd had up to that point. When she wasn't handing him his instruments, she was taking care of his books. One look at his accounts, and she knew that the position would not last long unless she did something about drumming up some new business. She hit upon an idea that was very daring in its time.

Florence bombarded his patients with letters graphically describing what would surely happen to their teeth, if they didn't come to see the dentist very soon. His business doubled within a year. It was her crude first stab at what one day would be called her genius for public relations.

But once again, she became restless and discontented. There had to be more to life than this. She felt the lassitude of time passing. Something had to happen, and quickly, or it would be too late.

On a visit home, she slipped into the lisping child's voice that she thought people found irresistible. Who could deny anything to such a cute little girl? "Daddy, dear, I've decided to go to New York and join Willie."

Far from beguiled, her father was shocked and completely forbade it. Toronto was bad enough, but no daughter of his was going to expose herself to the wickedness of life in New York City. They had all those Jews, and Niggers, and Chinks, and white slavery, and opium dens, and Lord knew what else.

If the little girl was not to be given her way, the woman would demand it. Her voice hardened. ''It's no use, Father. You can't stop me. But don't worry. Nothing's going to happen to me. I'm nearly thirty years old. If I haven't been wicked until now, I'm not likely to start at my age. Who'd be interested?''

What Florence refused to recognize was that she was the only one who would *not* be interested. Her features belied her age. Approaching thirty, she looked like a girl just turning twenty, and a very pretty one at that, with auburn hair, and bright blue eyes, and even features, and a fair, smooth, fresh complexion.

Her figure was de la mode of the period. Although only a petite five feet two, she possessed an ample, firm bosom, tiny waist, and full, rounded hips. Delicate ankles above dainty, beautifully shaped feet would do full justice to the approaching fashion of shorter skirts.

Her hands were the only features that did not indicate a charming feminine helplessness. They were square, with spatulate fingers, and gave the impression of being very strong and competent.

And so, armed only with her native shrewdness, her pretty looks, her inviolate virtue, her carefully modulated voice, and her capable hands, Florence Nightingale Graham set forth to conquer the wickedest city in the Western world.

CHAPTER TWO

Enter Elizabeth Arden

Woodbridge was never like this. Not even Toronto was anything like it. Nothing in her entire experience had prepared Florence for New York City. It was a town on the make and on the way, aggressively banging on the doors of London, Paris, and the other great cities, demanding to be let in, pugnaciously demanding its right to be considered their peer if not, indeed, their superior.

Noise was the city's music. There were already traffic jams, as Pierce Arrows, and Packards, and Locomobiles, and Peerlesses chased the horse and carriage all the way uptown, above Fifty-seventh Street, to the relative safety of the quiet, almost suburban treelined streets of the Sixties, Seventies, and Eighties.

The cacophony of honking horns mingled with the sounds of construction to make a deafening din. Skyscrapers were going up with such a dizzying speed that, no sooner did one building announce itself the tallest in the world, than another was on its way to usurp its claim to the title. Since its founding in 1625, New York had been searching for an identity and had finally found it in a skyline. Mountains and castles perched ahigh had skylines, but never before in history did a city have one.

This was it. The real McCoy. This was where all the great action was. And Florence Nightingale Graham had never felt so comfortable in any other place in her whole life. It did not frighten her, as her family had predicted it would. It exhilarated her. She was tireless in her efforts to sate her enormous appetite for the place.

There was so much to see, and she wanted to see it all. She walked endlessly, trying to explore every corner and crevice of home, for this was home as surely as there was a broken heart for every light on Broadway. But no heart of hers would break in New York. The place would be the making of her. She knew that the moment she hit the bright sunlight outside the old Grand Central Station.

She visited the shops, and theaters, and galleries, and nickelodeons, and restaurants, and hotels, and museums. Of all the places she went, she returned most frequently to those where the very fashionable ladies congregated. She gaped, and gawked, and envied, and memorized, and imitated. She redid all of the frocks that had seemed so smart in Toronto but were utterly hopeless in New York. She familiarized herself with a whole new language, until freshly minted terms, like "the four hundred" and "the smart set," slipped from her lips with the ease of one who had been using them all her life. Naturally, it was no great span of time before she ran out of money and had to seek employment.

The only job that even remotely appealed to her was a position as bookkeeper at E. R. Squibb and Sons. Later, some of her employees were to claim that she could not read a balance sheet. She promoted that notion, because it suited her purposes to let them think it. It was much less enervating than attempting to explain her private theory of economics. One spent money to make money. It was so easy, but she knew that most people were too stupid to comprehend its meaning and very clear logic.

The true estimation of her abilities with ledgers and figures can be found in her own characteristically modest observation. "I was a whiz at bookkeeping."

However, it was not the books that fascinated her at Squibb. It was the laboratory. As one of the country's leading manufacturers of chemo-pharmaceutical products, it had an extensive and completely up-to-date installation. The new bookkeeper was soon to be found there much more frequently than at her desk.

:[43]:

With a curiosity that found no justification in her own flawless complexion, she asked question after question about substances that might be good for the care of the skin. She wanted to discover every conceivable remedy for the treatment of blemishes. Little Florence had not at all given up her dream of perfecting a skin cream.

Florence was not long in the city before discovering the existence of a limited number of practitioners of a new skill. They called themselves beauty culturists and claimed to have mastered the science of rejuvenating the skin by massaging it with their special preparations. It was not the beauty parlor that was a new concept, the first having opened in Philadelphia ten years before her birth, but the scientific approach that was revolutionary.

With her intense interest in chemistry and limited but thoroughly absorbed education in nursing, this was obviously Flo's cup of cream. The moment she heard of an opening at one of the parlors, she switched jobs with a speed that would have made a champion out of one of her father's horses.

Eleanor Adair knew all there was to know about the new beauty business. She was a very clever Irish woman who had salons in Paris and London as well as her New York beauty culture parlor. Through a crafty manipulation of women's fears and vanities, she had made an enormous success in all three cities—but as shrewd as she undoubtedly was, she got much more than she bargained for in hiring Florence Graham as a cashier. Flo did not stay long at the till. Had Mrs. Adair really been watching it, she would have chained her to it.

The Adair treatment was tastefully advertised in the ladies' magazines as "a new facial method." The copy went on to extoll the virtues of the Ganesh muscle-strapping treatment.

Beauty was not yet an industry (that was not to happen until Florence grew a few years older in private and a few years younger in public), but it was already inventing its own vocabulary. "Ganesh" was not a word that any of the ladies could have found in their dictionaries. As far as they might be able to trace it, it derived from the French *ganache*, meaning lower jaw. This seemed likely, as it was the lower jaw that was strapped tightly shut against the rest of the skull before the treatment, thus depriving the clients of one of the few lasting benefits of a trip to the beauty parlor—gossip.

After the strapping, the copy told the prospective clients that Ganesh Diable skin tonic, muscle oil, creams, and other astonishing Ganesh beauty aids were tapped and patted in by "wonderfully magnetic hands." It was a bargain at $2.50 a treatment during an era when the average wage earner was happy with $7 a week.

It was those wonderful little products that Florence could not wait to get at, but in order to dip her hands into them, she first had to convince Mrs. Adair that her hands were truly "magnetic."

She got her way. More to shut her up than anything else, Mrs. Adair graciously consented to teach Florence how to be a treatment girl—at no raise in the salary she was earning as cashier. The magnanimity of her act can only be measured by the fact that the other treatment girls were making almost double what Florence was earning.

The injustice of her salary did not bother her. Money could wait. The only thing that mattered was that she had found her way. She knew where she was going. She also knew that, to get there, she had to learn everything Eleanor Adair could teach her, and a few more things that the wily woman would not willingly teach to anybody— like the formulas for her preparations.

It was not that Florence intended to steal the formulas and market them on her own. That was not in her mind at all. She did not have the slightest idea of how to go about merchandising this sort of ladies' product. If asked, she would have replied that it was impossible. There was no precedent for its commercial sale at any price necessary to make a profit.

Her naïve dream of a mail order business was ridiculous. The feminine goods sold in that fashion were such items as an ordinary crude cold cream costing 28 cents, Princess Tonic Hair Restorer at 57 cents, and La Bore's Bust Food Cream ("for developing the bust and making it firm and round") at 40 cents. The drug and department store over-the-counter trade were accustomed to paying a dime for a flask of rose and glycerin water or envelopes of talcum powder and *riz de poudre.*

All that Florence wanted and dreamed of was one day to be able to set herself up in a beauty parlor just like Mrs. Adair's. To this end, she listened very carefully and learned her lessons well. She also discovered that Mrs. Adair's products were next to useless. The important thing was the strapping and the very vigorous patting and massaging.

Medical men have since pointed out that her original estimation was right. Treatment benefits consist 90 percent in patting and 10 percent in cosmetics.

It was the hands that did the job, and Flo had a very good, strong pair of them. From the beginning, she had been accurate in her assessment of them. She truly did have "healing hands."

Within a matter of months, customers were asking for that nice Canadian girl, and that nice Canadian girl was asking for and getting a raise. In addition to that, she had begun to supplement her income by advertising as a manicurist in her after-work hours.

She could at last afford to buy herself some good clothes and to send a little money home, so that Gladys could get some decent things. She took a flat in a respectable but slightly run-down building at 321 West Ninety-fourth Street, right off Riverside Drive. It was then a very solid middle-class neighborhood.

Every morning she rode to work on the brand-new underground railroad. She loved the roar and excitement and speed of it. Years later she attended a very fashionable wedding. After the ceremony, her companions lost sight of her. They found her again at the very top of the receiving line. When they asked how she had managed to get there so quickly, Elizabeth smiled and replied, "Early subway training."

In those first years in New York, there were no romantic involvements. She discouraged them. There were only some casual beaus. Casual was exactly what she wanted her beaus to be and would

:[46]:

go on wanting them to be, on and off, for close to sixty years.

Life was not bad, but it was still not as good as she insisted that it could and would be. She was actually biding her time, waiting for the right moment to arrive—her moment—never doubting that it would arrive. And so it did, in the person of one Elizabeth Hubbard.

The New York beauty business was a very small, closely knit one. It was inevitable that Florence Nightingale Graham, who had healing hands and no formulas, would meet Mrs. Elizabeth Hubbard, who had ungifted hands but formulas that were an improvement on Mrs. Adair's.

That meeting took place late in the year of 1909. They were both born autocrats and would never have got along, from their very first encounter, were it not for the fact that each had something that the other wanted.

From the moment she tried Elizabeth Hubbard's products, Florence recognized their superiority to others on the market. At the same time, Mrs. Hubbard recognized that Florence was not only a gifted treatment girl, but also a brilliant saleswoman. Because their talents were so perfectly complementary, the girls decided to join forces and set up in business for themselves. What they did not take into account was that their temperaments were so alike that clashes were inevitable.

Before looking for quarters, Florence made certain that Mrs. Hubbard agreed to two vital business stipulations. The first was that the preparations were to be available to anybody who came in to ask for them, and not simply to very special customers, as had been the practice with Mrs. Adair.

The second was that they take over one point bodily from Eleanor Adair. In her advertisements, Mrs. Adair always underscored "Ladies only accepted." She informed her ladies that "beauty culture must be taken up by gentlewomen of social standing." She went on to boast that her European clients were "royalty and women of the highest social standing."

This link to high society was a completely new approach to the beauty business, and it immediately appealed to snobbish, social-climbing New York matrons. Loveliness and prestige, all in one package, were more than they could resist.

Until then, the prevalent attitude had been that helping nature along was not only not quite nice, but downright immoral. It was the sort of thing that might be expected of an actress or demimondaine but never of a lady. In Florence's capable hands, Mrs. Adair's point of view would eventually make cosmetics, in turn, fashionable, respectable, and an enormous industry.

The two new entrepreneurs set about finding headquarters for their establishment. They settled on the whole third floor of a brownstone at 509 Fifth Avenue, between Forty-second and Forty-third Streets. The rent was a formidable $75 a month, but they did not hesitate for a moment. It was an address that suited Florence so perfectly, that she was never to be located on any other street in New York City.

At the time that the ladies installed themselves there, Fifth Avenue was a thoroughfare in transition. It had only been a very few years since the only buildings above Forty-second Street were gentlemen's clubs and the townhouses of the very rich and very fashionable. This gold coast was the dream destination of anybody who wanted to be somebody and, most assuredly, Florence belonged in that category.

The avenue was a sight to behold. It most probably revolted knowledgeable architects, but the sham French chateaux and Tudor manors and Rhine castles and Swiss chalets and Georgian palaces, standing all in a row, dazzled a poor little girl from Woodbridge, Canada. The brass nameplates of Frick, Vanderbilt, Astor, Gould, and Carnegie were, in themselves, enough to cause a flutter in the heart of the impressionable Florence. Fortunately, it was not a fatal weakness, for she was never to recover from it, and she lived for a very long time.

Despite the fact that by 1910 the great families were residing above Forty-fifth Street, as commerce relentlessly marched uptown from Madison Square, Fifth Avenue above Thirty-fourth Street remained as it still is, the place to be if one wanted to elicit a smart clientele. The two new beauty culturists could not have found a better address.

They were directly across the street from Sherry's Restaurant and just a few steps below Delmonico's.

On one rainy afternoon shortly before they were to open, Florence was hanging drapes in the reception room. A drenched, bedraggled, and dispirited column of women were parading up the center of the street. From the pavements, jeering men were pelting them with eggs. They were the suffragettes. How ridiculous they were, Florence thought, to believe that the vote would bring liberation to members of their sex. They would never find her marching with them. There was only one road to freedom, the one upon which she was embarked. Fame, beauty, wealth, position—those were the only things that could ever emancipate a lady.

The two partners had their first big fight even before they opened their doors to the public. Elizabeth insisted that the name on the window and in the advertisements was to be Mrs. Elizabeth Hubbard. When Florence protested, it was pointed out to her that the name could not be Hubbard and Graham. That sounded too much like a haberdashery. Elizabeth Hubbard and Florence Nightingale Graham was simply too long. Moreover, the Florence Nightingale part would remind people of nurses and hospitals. It would discourage patronage. The clients would certainly not want to think of small repairs to their complexions in terms of going into a hospital. This was to be a beauty parlor, not an operating room.

Florence gave way. She was too anxious to get on with it to indulge in a large fight, but she did insist on one point. The place was not to be called a parlor. That reminded her of dingy little rooms in Toronto boardinghouses. It was to be a salon. That evoked images of Paris and graciousness and chic.

Before they could place their opening announcements, they had to find a name for their beauty products. Florence had always hated Ganesh. It was so guttural. She hit upon Grecian. She cried, "It has such purity. It's so classic. It evokes images of beauty, and passion, and wine dark seas."

Elizabeth Hubbard snorted, "It evokes images of ruins. I'd hardly call that inspired for a beauty product."

But she let Florence have her way—mostly because she could not come up with a better designation. The girls ambitiously announced in *Vogue* magazine that Mrs. Elizabeth Hubbard, at 509 Fifth Avenue, had opened a "beautifully appointed salon" serving "women socially prominent in the Metropolis and suburbs" and selling "the famous Grecian preparations"—Grecian Daphne skin tonic, muscle creams, and oils, as well as offering "a new method of face treatments" at $2 single and six for $10.

The price was also Florence's idea. It was sufficiently below Mrs. Adair's to lure away some of her old clients. It was one of the few times she ever undersold a rival. She much preferred overpricing, appealing to snobbery in advertising, selling less, and making a larger profit.

As for the vaunted "new method"—it was no more than the same old straps but with new gimmicks hanging onto them.

Florence had lost that first bout of the name. She was determined not to lose the next one. It was not long in coming. When the rent came due, Mrs. Hubbard announced to her startled partner that she must pay all of it. She patiently explained that as she slaved over making the creams, which were the mainstay of the business, it was not fair to ask her also to contribute to the rent. That could come out of Florence's tips as a treatment girl.

Florence could not understand the logic of that. The tips were not nearly sufficient to make up the necessary money, and Elizabeth Hubbard knew it. Florence protested that the creams were of no value without her to apply them. Mrs. Hubbard retaliated with the observation that she had seen her applications and was not impressed, to which Florence replied that she had used her creams and was equally unimpressed.

With that auspicious beginning, there was nothing to do but go on until there was not a shred of the character of each that by the other had not been thoroughly destroyed. By the time they had exhausted themselves and each other, the wreckage strewn around them included the bits and pieces of a collapsed partnership.

Mrs. Hubbard went directly to her lawyer, and Miss Graham went directly to the landlord. She paid the entire sum that she so recently had contested and received, in return, full and exclusive rights to the premises. She later explained, ''The dear little man always liked me better.''

A month later, Mrs. Elizabeth Hubbard announced her removal to new headquarters at 505 Fifth Avenue, which was then the tallest building north of Forty-second Street.

Mrs. Hubbard's position two doors away did not unduly disturb Florence. After all, their clients were generally coming downtown and would have to pass her place before arriving at the door of her rival.

The big problem was to find a new name. Her first notion was to return to Florence Nightingale, a name she still thought had a great deal of dignity to it. Unfortunately, she had to discard it when the venerable old lady with the lamp died at ninety, amid universal mourning. It was no longer an auspicious moment to dedicate a beauty salon to her. It would have been like writing a big, bold ''In memoriam'' over the entrance to a temple of Venus.

She then turned to the possibility of her own name, Florence Graham, but she ruled that out immediately. It had no real flair, no resonance.

While musing on the matter of names, she also remained very conscious of finances or, more specifically, the lack of them. She had taken on an estimable responsibility and had no idea of how she would meet it. To think about that was a waste of time. She would find the way later.

Mrs. Elizabeth Hubbard was already printed in brand new gold leaf on the window. It was an extravagance to discard the whole thing. There was nothing wrong with the Mrs. Elizabeth part. She rather liked the name—Elizabeth. It was so queenly-sounding. But Elizabeth what?

Elizabeth Graham? No. That was the name for a midwife, not a beauty expert. There was always her mother's maiden name. Elizabeth Tadd. It had possibilities, but it lacked that extra added something of names like Ethel Barrymore, or Consuelo Vanderbilt Churchill, or Elsie de Wolfe, or Edith Wharton. She had no way of knowing then that, one day soon, all those ladies would be her clients. Then they were no more than names on which to dream. What she was to be christened was the pressing problem of her waking hours.

One evening, when she was home alone, she picked up a volume of Tennyson's poems and started leafing through it. She came upon one that she had not read since school, *Enoch Arden.* It sounded so lovely and lyrical. If Enoch Arden, why not Elizabeth Arden? She wondered how it would look to somebody seeing it for the first time and sat down at her desk to write a note. It simply said—good luck. She stuck it into an envelope addressed to Mrs. Elizabeth Arden in care of the salon.

When she arrived at 509 Fifth Avenue the next morning, there it was, the one bright note in a pile of morning mail consisting of bills and advertising circulars. How much better it looked than the other envelopes addressed to Florence Graham and even Elizabeth Hubbard. She opened the note, taking care not to damage the face of its container.

"Good luck," it said in Florence Graham's scrawling handwriting. Yes, good luck, Elizabeth Arden. You'll need it. But don't fret about it—you'll have it.

Florence Nightingale and Florence Nightingale Graham passed away during the same year. It was the year that Marie Dressler opened on Broadway in a musical called *Tillie's Nightmare.* In the show, Miss Dressler sang a song that was an overnight sensation. Florence had an unflinching, almost religious belief in the sentiments expressed in its lyric, "Heaven Will Protect the Working Girl."

When the letterer had completed his work, she raced down the graceful front stoop into the street. She backed all the way to the edge of the curb and looked up at the third floor salon window. She smiled as if she had already won all the battles that were yet to come.

MRS. ELIZABETH ARDEN
Beauty Culture
By appointment only

CHAPTER THREE

First Little Steps

The newly baptized Elizabeth Arden was almost ready to make her debut. Thanks to Mrs. Adair, she had mastered the science of giving treatments. From Mrs. Hubbard she had learned the rudimentary formulas for beauty products. These preparations were only slightly better than those she had used at the Adair establishment. Even then, she was convinced that they could be made vastly better, but she had not yet the resources or knowledge to do it.

At that time, there was only one improvement that she could and did make. It was in the aroma. The creams and lotions had always smelled to her like a cross between a hospital ward and a house of ill repute. By using larger quantities of superior essences, she was able to move the products out of the whorehouse and into the boudoir.

The only thing that remained, was to find the proper designation for her new line. In later years, it would take her months to find precisely the right appellation for each product that she manufactured but, at the beginning, she did not have months, nor did she need them. The objective was to pick up a few customers through confusion with competitive lines. The name had to hint at their names, rather than at the romantic, or sentimental, or genteel, or exotic. As Mrs. Adair's Ganesh had become Mrs. Hubbard's Grecian, so Mrs. Hubbard's Grecian became Elizabeth Arden's Venetian.

Elizabeth had a name, she had a salon, she had a course of treatments, she had products. She was blessed with imagination, drive,

:[53]:

ambition, and energy. There was only one thing lacking. Capital. Her funds were so short that scraping together the next month's rent presented an enormous problem.

She appealed to her brother, Willie, who was starting to do rather well in New York. She told him her new name, which he thought was daft, and asked for $6,000, which he thought was dafter, but the combination of her determination and great gift for selling proved irresistible. Against his better judgment, William Graham wrote a check for the requested amount, endorsed to his spinster sister, Mrs. Elizabeth Arden.

Anybody else might have been expected to do the sensible thing and put aside some of the money as a cash reserve. Not Elizabeth. That was not the Arden way of doing things. While Florence Nightingale Graham continued to slave at giving manicures on West Ninety-fourth Street, Elizabeth Arden spent every last penny she had on the creation of the proper setting for her new emporium of beauty.

With the right ambience, she never for a moment doubted that she would be a great success. If she wanted to attract ladies to her salon, it had to be the sort of place to which they were accustomed and in which they would feel completely at home.

The first thing she did was to install an eye-catching red door and hang on it, in imitation of her fashionable neighbors farther up the avenue, a brass plate with her name spelled out in script. As it was ever to be, pink was then her passion. She paneled the walls with the most expensive pink damask, edged with a deeper pink braided satin ribbon. On the perfectly glorious Oriental carpet reposed rare French antique furniture as well as Venetian vitrines in which, suitably enough, were exhibited her Venetian products, while overhead an electrified Venetian crystal chandelier cast a bright glow over all. The three tiny treatment cubicles were done up like bon-bonesque powder rooms.

Only the small laboratory, in which she concocted her preparations, was Spartan and rather drab. If this surface elegance suggested a bit of charlatanism, it was also practical. The rooms to which her patrons were admitted had to be opulent to stimulate an obligation toward largesse in them. The room in which she alone worked, need only be efficient and devoid of any distracting loveliness.

There still remained a vacant rear parlor on her premises. In subletting it, she would not only make her one gesture of economy, she would also accidentally stumble upon a concept that was to revolutionize the beauty business. She would continually expand upon it in all the salons that she was ever to open.

It was the concept of total beauty. It was not only the face of a woman that required meticulous care, it was the woman as a complete entity from head to foot.

The body would have to wait a few years. In modest 1910, the only one permitted to make any improvements below the neck was the corsetiere. Anything else would have been considered the height of indecency. But there was more to the head than the face. Elizabeth already had a shrewd eye focused directly on the future.

Jessica and Clara Ogilvie were two of seven sisters. In a tiny room on Thirty-fourth Street, they had recently begun to give the hair and scalp treatments that would eventually make them both rich and famous. Elizabeth had been among their first clients. She had always had difficulties in managing her thin and bodiless hair.

The three young women had hit it off from their very first meeting. It was not long before Elizabeth noticed that Jessica and Clara had a very advantageous arrangement with Gladys, the oldest of the Ogilvie sisters.

Gladys was a fashionable milliner located a few doors away on Thirty-fourth Street. Her hats started at $45 each, and went up to a heaven of sheer profit. After selling a wealthy customer one of her creations, she would suggest that the hat would look smarter, if she did something about her hair. That something was to treat herself to a series of her sisters' extremely beneficial scalp treatments. In turn, Jessica and Clara would tell their patrons that their newly lustrous locks would look even better under one of Gladys' smart chapeaus.

It immediately occurred to Elizabeth that there was no reason why she should not be included in an extremely profitable triple parlay.

Why not form a triumvirate with the sisters that would offer a glowing complexion to go with the hat and hair?

The first step was to convince the hairdressing Ogilvies that they should move into the rear parlor at 509 Fifth Avenue. In combination with her remarkable gifts for selling, she offered several excellent inducements.

The city was moving uptown. If they remained in Thirty-fourth Street, they would soon find themselves in a somewhat less than smart backwater. It was a tribute to her persuasiveness that she got them to agree, despite the fact that their original location bordered on elegant Murray Hill and boasted the fashionable Waldorf-Astoria Hotel at the corner of Fifth Avenue (the current site of the Empire State Building). She clinched her argument with a direct appeal to economics. She pointed out that in addition to its other advantages, they would be saving some of their rent money by moving in with her.

The next step was to convince them that she should be allowed to share in their lucrative arrangement with Gladys. Her clients, she told them, were always asking for advice on what to do about their hair. It would be only natural to suggest that they have their tresses treated on the same day that they had their faces done. What could be more convenient than to ask them to step into the back room, before she set to work on them? Of course, it was only fair to expect the girls to return the favor—and Gladys, too.

The Ogilvies agreed, after exacting a promise that Elizabeth would give up selling shampoo and hair tonic. Although she made a great show of reluctance before acceding to this condition, it was actually not too great a sacrifice. She had never made or stocked either of the items.

On the day that the sisters moved in, Elizabeth welcomed them with a broad smile and wagging head. She clasped her hands, cooing, "You're so very fortunate. Just think—you'll be here to watch me take my first little steps."

The ladies did watch, and they marveled. Clara later exclaimed,

"The way she could sell! And the way she could train other girls to sell—it was astonishing!"

In addition to two treatment girls to help her, she hired a receptionist named Irene Delaney. Elizabeth called her Lanie. It was the start of a lifelong habit of giving nicknames to her favorites.

Lanie was to remain with Arden for over forty years. The treatment girls came and went amid thundering shouts of "God! How can you be so stupid?"

As they swiftly fled, the storm abated. Elizabeth would look at Lanie and, reverting to her helpless baby voice, sadly lisp, "Such untalented hands."

Lanie would nod her head, agreeing to she knew not what, and reply, "Yes, Miss Arden."

A pattern of employee-employer relations was started that would remain unchanged for all the years to come. Helpers were either hers forever, or they departed almost as quickly as they arrived. A later employee described working for Elizabeth Arden as "being caught in a revolving door."

Recollecting the early days, Lanie later admiringly said, "I used to marvel at her. She never thought she might run out of money. She never worried about anything. She just worked all the time, from morning till night."

And in between time, Florence Graham went on working as a manicurist.

Elizabeth's advertisements were placed regularly, even when she did not have the money to meet the payroll. When Fridays rolled around with no funds in the cash box, she just went next door to borrow it from the Ogilvies. She always paid it back at the beginning of the next week and then reborrowed at its end.

It never occurred to her that this system might have been imposing some hardship on the sisters. If anybody had dared to imply it, she would have been astounded at their utter stupidity. "What have they got to worry about? After all, there are only the two of them. They've got no payroll to meet."

Elizabeth was far more scrupulous about her debt to her brother. Money was regularly set aside for it, and within a half year, the entire $6,000 was repaid.

Elizabeth was a money maker from the start. From the first day that she opened her first red door, business was excellent. Unfortunately, she was also a money spender. There was always some expensive new little *objet d'art* that she just had to have for the salon. There were always new ingredients that had to be tested in her preparations. She thought nothing of spending vast sums on them and then completely discarding them, when they did not work out to her satisfaction. No matter how much money came in, there was always slightly more going out. She was completely true to her credo. "You've got to spend a little money to make a little money."

She was spending so fast that she could not afford a proper maid or porter. Beyond that, they seemed a foolish extravagance, while she still had a strong back and capable hands. She would simply come in earlier than any of the help and clean the tiny salon from top to bottom.

By the time the employees arrived at eight-thirty, the place was spotless. By the time the first client arrived at nine, Elizabeth was washed, combed, changed into a starched white coat, and ready to start giving treatments. She continued to work without stop until six in the evening, when the last client departed. Miss Delaney was afraid "the poor little thing" would break under the strain. She would chase her around with a glass of milk and sandwich which Elizabeth would impatiently wave aside.

A very important part of her day only began after she wished the girls a good evening and dismissed them at six-thirty. In the lonely, quiet hours of the evening, while the fashionable crowd were collecting in the theaters a few blocks west or at the neighboring Sherry's and Delmonico's, Elizabeth was hard at work in her laboratory.

It was only in the brief span of time between work and sleep, that the loneliness set in. Those were the hateful hours in which she was forced to realize that she was well over thirty and still alone, and likely to remain so for the rest of her life. At times, she could not stand the emptiness of her flat. With the passing years, it was becoming more difficult to people her life with dreams of glory.

She took to inviting Lanie, or one of the Ogilvies, or whichever treatment girl was her particular pet of the moment, to drop by for a light supper. She was her charming best during these visits, beguiling her guest with gossip and small talk about the clients and confidences about her future plans. It was such an entrancing performance, that nobody ever thought of leaving until long after her proper time for departure. Elizabeth would look at the clock in horror. Speaking in her little flirtatious voice, she would say, "You can't go home alone at this hour. It's too dangerous. You know, this is a wicked little city, dear."

From affection or fear or a combination of both, the guest usually agreed to stay. There was genuine admiration for the determined manner in which she unfailingly went through her nightly beauty ritual.

"No matter how tired she was," Miss Delaney recalled, "she always gave herself a little facial and put her hair up in curlers."

In short order, the ladies were safely bedded down and the lights extinguished. A strong, square hand stole across the bed, and a child's voice pleaded, "Please, hold my hand. Just until I fall asleep. Hold my hand."

During the first few years, Mrs. Elizabeth Arden and Mrs. Florence Graham were two separate entities. Even after they officially merged into one person, there was a part of the woman who was always Florence Graham looking on in awe at the wonderful exploits of Elizabeth Arden.

Until that merger was effected, Mrs. Arden was a mythical creature who traveled around England and the Continent gathering new and miraculous beauty secrets that Mrs. Florence Graham, her capable manageress, passed on to her fortunate clients. She felt that it was terribly important to be known as "Mrs."

"Clients have more confidence in married women," Elizabeth explained to the Ogilvies, who were struggling along with their own names and their legal titles of Miss.

On a sunny noon in 1912, an unprecedented event happened at the Elizabeth Arden salon. The Ogilvies, the treatment girls (there were three by then), and Lanie were completely flabbergasted, for it had never before happened in the two years that the establishment had been in operation.

The hardworking manageress removed her white coat, discreetly dusted her nose with some face powder, slipped into the jacket of a smart walking suit, put on a smashing Gladys Ogilvie original, replete with pink ostrich feathers, and announced that she would be out to lunch. As the trim figure daintily glided down the steps of the high stoop, a shapely pair of ankles, snugly buttoned into a pair of newspaperlined high shoes, was admired by more than one gentleman in the massive crowd that lined the avenue. Their number was estimated at a half-million on that pleasant afternoon.

Elizabeth stopped for her lunch at the corner of Forty-second Street. She purchased a hot sweet potato from a street vendor trying to hawk his wares above the shrill din of midday crosstown traffic. With meal in hand, she dashed over to the front of the handsome new public library building. She had watched them constructing it, and been among the spectators on the morning of its official opening almost a year to the day before. It was thrilling that the city had such an edifice and even more thrilling that it adorned "her" street.

In a voice that resembled nothing so much as a sergeant major's, a portly matron was shouting orders at the almost 15,000 women queueing in the middle of the avenue. Elizabeth proudly joined the marchers. She had become a suffragette.

This detour from her personal road to freedom was not brought about by any profound change in political convictions. The only compelling change was in the times. In the brief two years since 1910, suffrage had become fashionable. Mrs. O. H. P. Belmont, Lillian Russell, and Mrs. Otis Skinner would be leading the militant ladies on that afternoon. It was not so much the cause that Elizabeth admired as those who espoused it. Such a prestigious social aegis could only lend distinction to anybody who walked in its shadow. Elizabeth might have looked like a reformer, but she was actually only making another grab at the hem of the hobbled skirt of fashion.

She was not at all fazed by the fact that she had not yet made any effort to become an American citizen and, consequently, had no right to be meddling in American politics. It was but the first of many meddles to come. They were all motivated by the wish to advance her social position more than by any dedication to their tenets.

This first foray into the political arena did not improve her social standing, but it did give her credentials. She was later able to repudiate anybody who questioned her right to take a partisan position on public affairs. She would merely announce, ''I know what I'm talking about, dear. I've been taking an active part in politics ever since I joined the suffrage movement—when I was barely out of my teens.''

Aside from this one expedition into the great world outside her salon, Elizabeth was more than content to devote her time and herculean energies to the little world she was creating on her own premises. The business was growing beyond anybody's expectations but her own. Cosmetics and beauty treatments were beginning to find acceptance on all levels of society. Because she did not want to soil her hands on merely anybody's face, she did the one thing that would make certain that her clientele would remain exclusive. She raised her prices.

That year of 1912 proved a momentous one. For one thing, Florence Nightingale Graham retired from the manicuring business forever. For another, *Vogue* magazine stated that the discreet application of a little paint would enhance a lady's appearance.

That was all that Elizabeth needed to read. The midnight oil burned in both lamps and pots in her laboratory. She concocted a series of rouges and tinted powders and discovered, along the way, that she had a magnificent sense of color. It has been said that her ability to detect the most minuscule flaw, in the shade of any of her products, amounted to genius.

It was not long before she had a sufficient supply to start the new treatments. But she wasn't quite ready to try the makeup on her eminently respectable clients. She did not want them to look like painted dolls, harlots, or actresses. She had to master its proper application.

The Ogilvies, Lanie, and the treatment girls were pressed into service as guinea pigs. After the salon closed each night, they took turns in the treatment chairs, while Elizabeth painted and repainted their faces. She continued to refine the process of application, until the ladies had a lovely, natural-looking blush of high color that gave no evidence of having been painted on them. Once she had mastered the technique, she taught it to her treatment girls and was, at last, ready to accept customers who wanted to look a little lovelier, a little younger, for some important occasion.

It soon got around that the Elizabeth Arden salon was giving marvelously subtle and smart makeups. Clara Ogilvie described the start of her success with the daring new fashion. "Her clients would go to parties, and other women would ask them what they'd been doing, they looked so well. She got quite a few new clients that way."

By 1914 Florence Graham was convinced that Elizabeth Arden was sufficiently well known for Mrs. Graham to disappear from the business. She took advertisements announcing that Miss Elizabeth Arden, herself, was available for treatments and consultation.

She felt it permissible to tell the world of her maiden state, because she felt that the status of a married woman was no longer necessary in business. Women were beginning to question the value of being a man's chattel. They were casting off all the old mores to which they previously had been forced to adhere. They were immodestly displaying their legs in skirts that were gradually creeping up to the calf. They were openly smoking cigarettes and even demanding service in saloons and taprooms. There were over 10,000,000 single working women employed in all manner of positions that would have been denied to members of their sex as recently as the year before.

Elizabeth Arden was the right woman in the right business at the right time. Today cosmetics are considered, in some circles, one of the ways by which men enslave women. In those days it was considered one of the ways by which they liberated themselves.

With the advent of the new woman, the beauty business was on the march. Department stores were beginning to acknowledge the profits that could be made in cosmetics. They were devoting counter after counter to the sale of them. It was not long before Stern Brothers, an enormous store less than a block away from the salon, on West Forty-second Street, began stocking some of the Venetian products. They were rapidly followed by the fashionable Bonwit Teller store, which was located at the corner of Fifth and Thirty-eighth Street.

Elizabeth was exhilarated. One afternoon, she rushed back to the Ogilvies waving a fistful of mail. With breathless chirps of joy, she exclaimed, "Oh, I'm so excited! The orders I'm getting! Oh! If it goes on like this, my dears—marvelous! Oh, marvelous!"

Requests for the Venetian beauty line were pouring in from as far north as Boston, and as far south as Washington, D.C. She was not going to be able to fill them without initiating a program of expansion.

As usual, she was short of funds and would have to borrow the necessary capital. Her credit rating was so good that her brother was unnecessary. Elizabeth Arden had no outstanding debts. She owned her own business, free and clear, and even if she had no cash reserves, it was a good one that was getting better all the time.

She visited her bank and was directed to the desk of a minor official named Thomas Jenkins Lewis. Her first impression of the gentleman was not a good one. Mr. Lewis was slight in stature but exceedingly dapper and undoubtedly attractive with twinkling eyes and a fashionable mustache setting off a flashing, somewhat toothy smile, but he was also familiar to the point of flirtatiousness. Elizabeth did not know how to cope with it, and so she naturally did not like it.

As for Tom Lewis, he saw a very pretty woman who might be somewhere in her mid-to-late twenties (she was actually thirty-six), with whom it might be rather pleasant to have an after-hours relationship. Lewis enjoyed two things in equal measure—hard work and good-looking women. Although it seemed that she should fall in the latter category, she was actually very much in the former. No matter how much charm he exerted, she resisted it. She was all business. She requested and was granted her loan. As far as she was concerned, that was the end of Thomas Jenkins Lewis in her life. She was very much mistaken.

Elizabeth used part of the borrowed money to open her first branch salon, in July, 1914, in Washington, D.C. It consisted of one treatment room in the rear of a dress shop and was, predictably, a success from the very first day.

With the very able Irene Delaney installed as manageress of the New York salon, Elizabeth felt confident enough to contemplate her first European excursion. She booked a second-class passage on an ocean liner departing for France.

In those pre-air-conditioned days, summer crossings were most uncomfortably sultry, but that did not bother Elizabeth. She had a mission.

While her two cabinmates escaped to join in the above-deck festivities, the remote Miss Arden remained below in their tiny and stifling quarters, poring over a book of instructions on the intricacies of the French language. She was to experience one of her few failures and would never learn to speak the language properly—but it was not for want of trying.

It was a very strange time for a visit to Europe. Beginning on June 28, with the assassination at Sarajevo of the heir apparent to the Austrian throne, Archduke Franz Ferdinand, Europe had been rolling inexorably toward a war that would boom forth at the end of the very same month of August, that Elizabeth Arden first set foot in Cherbourg.

Although she was violently pro-British, she did not have the time to bother about a mere World War. Her interests lay in something larger and of greater endurance, the universal revolution in feminine beauty. Her mission was that of a master spy ferreting out the secrets that might be in the possession of her transatlantic rivals.

CHAPTER FOUR

A Shipboard Romance

Incredible as it may seem to those who today consider it the world's most beautiful city, Paris was even more beautiful at the dawn of World War I. The gilt and polish of the still comparatively new Belle Époque buildings sparkled in the sun. The quayside parks, along the Seine, had not yet been displaced by noisy, fume-scented highways. People strolled through them enjoying a fragrant, leafy respite from the late summer heat.

Despite the war, the city was comparatively empty, except for clusters of colorfully uniformed men arriving from all parts of the French empire. Not even the threat of holocaust could stem the outward flow of Parisians that took place annually during the August vacations. Elizabeth could walk unjostled through the broad boulevards and twisting, narrow streets. On days on which she felt particularly affluent, or a need for a lift in her spirits, she could take afternoon tea in the elegant shaded garden of the Ritz Hotel. In a more economical mood, she could have it in the cosy little tearoom above the English bookshop in the Rue de Rivoli.

There was nothing about Paris that did not delight her esthetically, but it was not her city. Despite the fame that she would one day enjoy there, as well as throughout the rest of France, it never would be. Every future visit would evoke the dreadful loneliness of that first summer.

Of all the places in the world, Paris is the least hospitable to solitary tourists. For the first time in her more than thirty-five years, she actually longed to lean on a strong, masculine arm. She longed for somebody with whom to laugh, and flirt, and perhaps even make love. She was building an empire based on feminine attractiveness and allure, on a quiet appeal to the need for sexual attractiveness. There was such irony in it that she was forced to smile bitterly. Like her famous namesake, she was a virgin queen at an age when most of the girls with whom she had grown up had children who were nearly grown up.

The evenings brought an almost unbearable feeling of isolation. Hampered by language, customs, and morality, she did not try to approach the French, and she was too shy to attempt communication with any of the other visitors, even with other spinster ladies who might also be yearning for some human contact.

She wanted to flee from Paris, but it was impossible. The hostilities had cut off all travel to Vienna and Berlin, and passage to London was prohibited to almost all but those with legitimate military reasons for being there. She had to remain or go home. She came to learn about European beauty techniques. She would not leave until she had accomplished that mission.

Elizabeth devoted all her energies to the task at hand. The days began to pass almost too rapidly. She discovered that Paris was far in advance of America in matters pertaining to her business. There was suddenly so much to do and so little time in which to do it.

She wanted to extend her visit, but she soon realized that, on the contrary, she would have to curtail it. The Parisians might be able to fool themselves into believing in a victory by Christmas, but Elizabeth read the English newspapers every morning, and they told a different story. The Germans were already in Belgium and would soon be within a half day's journey of the French capital. She did not relish the thought of being in a German-occupied city with an English-Canadian visa. They would surely intern her and, aside from anything else, she had much too much to do at home to put up with that kind of nonsense.

She redoubled her efforts, sometimes visiting as many as four salons in a day. After the treatments, she requested samples of every preparation that they used, on the pretext that she was an American and would not be able to obtain them in her own country. By evening she was too tired to be lonely. She had a light supper in some obscure bistro, returned to her modest hotel off the Rue de Rivoli, did her nightly facial, collapsed into an unyielding bed, and went directly to sleep.

Later, she would never admit it, but it is inconceivable that, in the course of her extensive investigation, she did not try the most talked-about salon of the day, Helena Rubinstein's new Maison de Beauté Velaze. Although herbs were never an important ingredient in Arden creams and oils, she must certainly have brought away the full line of Rubinstein herbal preparations. She later incorporated into her own products the most beneficial ingredients that she had found in their European counterparts, but she did not use herbs until she was in direct American competition with Madame Rubinstein.

In addition to the makeup and skin products, she bought every variety of French perfume that was on the market. Elizabeth adored scent. One of the things that people remembered most vividly about her was that she always smelled so refreshingly nice.

As her stay was drawing to a close, Elizabeth decided to treat herself to dinner at one of the smart restaurants. She felt that she had earned one memorable evening, and made a reservation at the very elegant Café de Paris.

That evening, she took a very long time over her toilette. She luxuriated in a hot, scented tub. She applied her best and most artful makeup and slipped into a very modish Callot Souers gown. It was the only Parisian frock that she had permitted herself.

As Elizabeth passed through the modest lobby of her hotel, the elderly concierge gave her an admiring salute. She was early and walked leisurely around the stately Place Vendôme, admiring the particular glow of the old stones in the lingering September sunset. Before entering the Rue de la Paix, she paused to commit to memory a vision of what must surely be one of the most magnificent squares in the world. She did not dream then that one day her name would be affixed to one of its most prominent landmarks, diagonally across the cobbled expanse from where she was standing.

At the Café de Paris, the maître d'hôtel looked skeptically at the unescorted woman. There was something so distinctly pure and genteel about her that he decided it would be all right to show her to one of the rear corner tables, generally reserved for lone male diners.

Elizabeth watched the gay crowd on the floor in the center of the room. They were enthusiastically executing the latest dance crazes, the Castle Walk and the foxtrot, both of which had been introduced to the world by the American dance team Vernon and Irene Castle in the same spot just two years before. How she envied the whirling couples. It was sad that somebody who loved to dance as much as she did should have so few opportunities to do it.

Many of the most dashingly turned-out women had a piquant glint to their eyes that baffled her. She studied their faces, trying to discern its source, and then she caught sight of her own reflection in one of the ornate mirrors. By comparison, she looked so pale and colorless. It puzzled her, for surely her makeup was as fine as theirs. Moreover, it had been applied by her own skilled and professional hands. It was definitely her eyes. They did not have the same vibrancy and sparkle as the others. Why was that, she wondered, when their bright China-blue color was often remarked upon as being particularly handsome?

She peered more closely at the vivacious eyes, and then she pulled back in a perplexed amalgam of admiration and horror. It could not be! And yet it must be, for there could be no other explanation.

They were wearing mascara and eye shadow. She had never seen them worn, except in the theater. Not even actresses wore them off stage. The astounding thing was that they had been applied so artfully, that it had taken all of this time to recognize them. She wondered if they were available commercially, or if they were the special trick of only one cosmetician. It took a great deal of self-restraint to keep from leaping up and asking one of the ladies about it.

Bright and early the next morning, Elizabeth bolted down her breakfast (English, by her insitence. Those little croissants couldn't compare with good, hard, dry toast). She raced to the excellent maquillage establishment that she had discovered around the corner from her hotel. In her agitation, the little French she knew completely departed, and it was with a great dumb show of batting lashes being painted by a trembling hand, that she was able to communicate what it was she wanted.

The woman brought out the little pots and brushes, and Elizabeth examined the contents carefully. They seemed completely wrong. The color of the shadow was much too intense, and the mascara only a powdery, theatrical kohl. She wondered how the women at the café had got those subtle effects. It had to be more than the restaurant's extremely flattering lights. There had to be some trick connected with the application.

She returned to the hotel with her purchases and started to experiment, blending rose-tinted rouge into the shadow to soften its tone. When she was satisfied that she had sufficiently muted the colors and added the proper degree of delicacy to the ingredients, she did what she always did with new products. She went in search of a guinea pig.

In the corridor, she pounced upon a terrified chambermaid, whose fear and suspicion were allayed by a handsome tip. She swathed the trembling girl in towels and sat her in a chair angled to catch the bright sunlight. Adjusting the ingredients and technique of application after each attempt, she did and redid the girl's eyes so often that her fear turned to boredom. It was only after endless experimenting that Elizabeth was even partially satisfied. She had captured the finesse of the ladies at the Café de Paris, and it was not nearly good enough. It had only seemed so because of the startling novelty and the soft light, but, with the proper laboratory adjustments, she was fairly certain that she could make a success of the product. What was more important, she would be the first to introduce eye makeup to America.

The dream of a future triumph made Elizabeth soften in her analysis and feel a little more kindly toward her efforts. She gestured toward the mirror and smugly indicated that the maid should view the transformation in her appearance. When the girl saw her reflection, she burst into floods of tears. Elizabeth thought, "God, she's stupid!"

It only took a moment for Elizabeth to discover something that she would never tell any of her clients or put in any of her advertisements. The girl's face had deep black stripes from eyes to chin. Before crying, it was obvious that one should remove one's mascara.

The more the girl cried, the more it ran. It took a large amount of cold cream and a larger tip to restore order, but Elizabeth rationalized the defect to her own satisfaction. It was no problem, because ladies did not cry in public, and all her clients were ladies.

It would take several years and a competitor to bring forth a mascara that did not run. Until then, it was advisable for women to remove their eye makeup before entering sad movies or funeral homes.

At the end of September, Elizabeth sailed for New York on the *Lusitania*. It was a British liner, and during the voyage, precautions against enemy attack were strictly enforced. All exterior lights were extinguished. Blackout curtains were hung in doorways, portholes, and windows. It was impossible to escape the ominous foreboding of danger encircling them, as surely as did the waters of the black ocean.

Elizabeth was not fond of fear. It made her cross. Nevertheless, the war at last impressed her as something that posed a personal threat. Why, those beastly little Germans could kill her and spoil all her plans.

There were extra berths in all the cabins, and every inch of space on the boat was taken by people fleeing to the safety of America. The overcrowding enforced an intimacy, for there was no place to which anybody could retreat and be alone. This pleased Elizabeth. She did not want to be alone. She'd had enough of loneliness in Paris.

The fear of sudden death lurked behind every conscious thought. In a brave attempt to obviate it, the passengers assumed an air of artificial gaiety and conviviality. They clung to each other, seeking a collective safety. Each individual sinner thought and prayed that he could escape God's wrath, for surely He would not punish these innocent companions just to get at one small transgressor.

On the first night out, an attractive man asked to join Elizabeth at the table for two that she was occupying by herself. The dining room was so filled that she could not possibly have refused, even had she wanted to—and she did not want to.

There was something familiar about him, but for the life of her, she could not place him. He smiled at her obvious bewilderment. It would have been an irritating smile, were it not such a contagious one.

Their pleasant little game of could it have been here that we met, or there, or the other place slid quite naturally into a flirtation. Of all the aspects of sex, flirting was the only one that Elizabeth truly enjoyed. She practiced it with great expertise, for the art of flirting was no more than an extension of her mastery of the art of selling.

After a half hour of this extremely pleasant occupation, he introduced himself as Tommy Lewis and reminded her that she had come to him for a bank loan. By then she was having such a good time that she completely disregarded her far from flattering first impression of him. Later in the evening, when she discovered that he was also a marvelous dancer, she was completely won over.

They took to spending every waking hour together. Whether she actually fell in love or merely fell out of loneliness, nobody—not even Elizabeth—would ever be able to say. The only important thing was that for the first time in her life, she truly felt as young and soft and pretty as she looked.

Her natural reticence, where men were concerned, might have made her suspect or disregard her personal reactions to Tommy, but there was one thing that she could not disregard. It played a very large part in the continuance of the affair. She was a complete loner in business but, where her private deportment was concerned, she could never disregard the opinions of those around her. They formed a mirror in which she beheld herself. It was consequently important to her that the other passengers found them an attractive and charming couple—and they did.

Tommy and Elizabeth were asked to participate in every activity. There were constant invitations to private parties and to the tables of the ship's officers. She had never before experienced that kind of popularity, and she was honest enough with herself to know that she was not responsible for it. Here, at last, was a strong arm on which to lean. Whether or not she would need to lean, or choose to lean, or even pretend to lean once they were back in New York, she did not know. It only mattered that, for the moment, it was exceedingly pleasing.

The night before they landed, Tommy pressed for some sort of avowal that she agreed with him in believing that theirs was more than a shipboard romance. He told her that his feelings for her were deep and true. He even indicated that marriage was already in his mind.

Elizabeth was too innocent to know how to handle it and did the worst possible thing. She was totally honest. A more experienced woman would have known how to practice a small deception and escaped safely into the relative security of being noncommittal.

She rambled on from a bad start to an impossible conclusion. Along the way, she told him that she did not know if she loved him and that, having seen what it had done to her mother, she was frightened of marriage. Had she stopped there, he could have given her some assurances that would have enabled her to retreat into evasiveness.

But she was relentless in her insistence upon telling all. She concluded by enumerating all the plans that she had for her business and flatly stating how little time she would have for anything beyond executing them. Tom Lewis was the sort of man who could understand doubt or fear in his beloved. Those qualities hinted at a charming feminine helplessness. What he could neither understand nor forgive was an overriding, almost masculine ambition. He turned and walked away.

Tears filled her eyes. Elizabeth would have preferred leaving the door ajar with the stop of friendship. She wanted to explain that she was thirty-six and he was thirty-eight, both very nearly middle-aged and that the sort of response he demanded was unseemly at their time of life. But it was impossible for her to do that. The truth was that she had played twenty-six throughout the journey, and now she was stuck with it.

Miss Arden did what she was always to do in moments of frustration and confusion. She buried her private setback in pursuit of professional advancement. Her first action was to rid herself of Florence Nightingale Graham by moving out on her. The City Directory for that year stated that Florence N. Graham continued to reside at the comparatively modest address of 321 West Ninety-fourth Street, while Elizabeth Arden was newly installed in much grander surroundings at 302 West Seventy-ninth Street.

The business of settling into a new apartment did not cause her to neglect the business at hand. She wanted to start adapting for her own purposes the best of the cosmetics and creams that she had brought back from Europe. She also wanted to start experimenting with an Elizabeth Arden perfume line.

Because of the war, the necessary raw materials would probably be difficult, if not impossible, to import. She would have to find domestic substitutes. To do this, there would have to be a thorough analysis of all the preparations. She did not have the knowledge to do this by herself, nor did she have the laboratory facilities for the quantity of manufacturing she was envisioning.

Miss Arden gathered together her treasures and went down to see the people at Parke, Davis, the chemical company from which she purchased her supplies. She explained that she not only wanted them to analyze the products, but she also wanted them to manufacture improved adaptations under her own imprint.

The war again thwarted her. It had created a great boom in the chemical field. There were big government contracts designed to prepare America in case of the eventuality of having to take up arms. It would have been both unpatriotic and unprofitable for Parke, Davis to devote time and space to filling Miss Arden's rather piddling order.

They suggested that she try Stillwell and Gladding, a smaller firm of analytical chemists. In light of what was about to happen in the cosmetics business, it was very shortsighted of them. Wars would come and go, but face creams would go on forever.

At Stillwell and Gladding, she met a man who was destined to become one of the two most important men in her life. A. Fabian Swanson was a partner in the company. The two hit it off immediately. He listened sympathetically to her requests. The enthusiasm with which she discussed her plans turned that sympathy into admiration. He told her that he was certain that something could be worked out, but that he would first have to discuss it with his partners. He was obviously a man of honor, and that served to strengthen her original high opinion of him. It was the quality she valued most in men. As far as Elizabeth was concerned, a man need not be intelligent, or handsome, or charming, or able, or physically desirable. All that really mattered was that he be honorable. She was born and reared during the reign of Victoria. In her lifetime, she would be largely responsible for a revolution that would forever destroy most of the old monarch's ideas of feminine decorum. But she would never relinquish her own adherence to the Victorian precept of an honorable man.

To Swanson's surprise, his partners were not as receptive to the cosmetics venture as he had been. When they did not succumb to his arguments, he insisted that they let him pursue the venture on his own.

In January, 1915, Elizabeth Arden and A. Fabian Swanson entered into a private agreement. He partitioned off a section of the Stillwell and Gladding laboratory and started to work on analyzing the items she had brought back from overseas and on developing new Arden preparations. When he was finished with his analysis, Swanson asked if she wanted him to start manufacturing similar products. He had asked merely as a matter of form, assuming that he would proceed as they had planned. Her answer was—*no.*

Her reply seemed capricious. Elizabeth often seemed capricious, but whimsy seldom played any part in her decisions. It was just that she never gave subordinates any idea of what was on her mind, until she had thought it out completely, and so her conclusions appeared to crystallize out of thin air, to be spur-of-the-moment flights of fancy. But there was nothing vague about the manner in which she reached them. They were the result of a thorough investigation of the problems. It was a very private process. If only she would think aloud, her associates would moan, then they would have some inkling of why they were agreeing and to what, for they always did agree. From the beginning, it was "Yes, Miss Arden!" "No" was the only two-letter dirty word in the language . . . except when she used it.

She told Swanson that she had reconsidered the European products. No matter how great an improvement they were on what was available in New York, they did not satisfy her. None of the creams of the day measured up to her idea of what they should be. They were all hard and greasy. She said, "I want a face cream that's light and fluffy—like—like whipped cream."

He shrugged and said that he would try. That was good enough for Elizabeth. Her request was a challenge, but one of the things that she had recognized immediately about Swanson was that he enjoyed a challenge. It was the foundation of most of their future successes. She would ask for the impossible, and he would reduce it to a reality.

Business in New York and Washington continued to grow at a very satisfactory rate. New treatment girls had to be added to the staff. One of them, Sally Bulkeley, was to remain with her for over forty years and play a large part in the future development of the firm. Another, Georgia Reed, was to stay just as long, and prove invaluable at both giving treatments and training others to do it.

There was initial client opposition to the eye makeup, but little Miss Arden was convinced that it was based on convention rather than esthetics. She persisted in her efforts to get ladies to try it. Among her patrons, there were some ladies who were socially secure enough to fly in the face of custom and who, indeed, enjoyed being slightly scandalous. She concentrated her attack upon them, prevailing upon them to try it at a big ball, promising to return the price of both treatment and makeup, if they did not create a sensation.

The refund never had to be made. As she had known from the first time she saw them used, mascara and eye shadow swiftly became the rage among those of her clients who thought of themselves as leaders of contemporary fashion.

One afternoon, Swanson burst into the salon crying, "I've done it! I've done it!"

He opened a jar and presented it to Elizabeth. It looked as if it were filled with beaten egg whites. It was velvety to the touch and went on the face with a liquid ease. It even had a light and pleasant aroma. In short, it was the cream that she had envisioned.

With her penchant for the Italianate, she christened it Venetian Cream Amoretta. In addition to its properties as a skin softener, it was the first powder base ever placed on the market. It was Swanson's invention, developed right in New York, but when Miss Arden advertised it, Cream Amoretta was "a famous French formula containing the perfume of delicate May flowers."

Elizabeth heaped congratulations upon the chemist and then casually added that the next thing he had to do was to develop a gentle new lotion as a companion to the cream. The tonics in use were so strong that ladies might as well be using pure wood alcohol on their faces.

Swanson celebrated his achievement by returning directly to his laboratory with a brand-new project that needed his immediate attention. The only festive note was that Miss Arden treated him to a taxicab—a generosity probably designed less as a reward for his accomplishment than as a way of getting him back to work by the fastest means available.

Swanson wasted no time in coming up with the lotion that Elizabeth had requested. She spent a great deal of time deciding what it was to be called. Even in those days, beauty products carried both the name of the manufacturer and that of the specific preparation. On the label, it was Elizabeth Arden's Venetian Cream Amoretta, or Eleanor Adair's Ganesh Cream, or Helena Rubinstein's Creme Valaze, but the public merely asked for Cream Amoretta and neglected to mention the name of its maker. Miss Arden did not like that. She was more important than any one of her products, because she was all of her products.

For the new lotion, she hit upon a happy solution. She called it Elizabeth Arden's Ardena Skin Tonic. It was another first, the first time a specific cosmetic was named for its maker. It was also a small stroke of promotional genius. It guaranteed that the purchaser could not forget the house that put out the item. From then on, her line was sprinkled with Ardenas. Many years later, her chauffeur, Charles Noble, even named his daughter Ardena. You may be sure that he was remembered most favorably in her will.

From their initial appearance, there was a heavy demand for the two products. Mr. Swanson had to bring them uptown from the laboratory to 509 Fifth Avenue on the Third Avenue elevated train. At first, he used gallon demijohns to transport them, but they were soon selling so well that two-gallon demijohns were needed. This not only placed a heavy burden on the strength of the slight and mild-mannered Mr. Swanson, but it also forced him into fights with El guards. He was obstructing the way of other passengers.

Swanson had no talent for fisticuffs. He was also devoting too much of his valuable time to toting creams, lotions, rouges, powders, and eye shadows. Presently, he told Miss Arden that she would get more out of him, if he did not have to interrupt his experiments to deliver the products. When she saw that she was cheating herself of full employment of his talents, she engaged a messenger. It was not long before the messenger proved insufficient, and she hired an ex-pressman.

With stock crowding them out of one of the treatment rooms, and an increasing number of clients demanding their services, Elizabeth decided that it was time to expand. She took larger quarters on the floor above at 509 Fifth Avenue. She named the new premises the Salon D'Oro and furnished them with what was becoming an habitual disregard for cost, when it came to creating an air of sumptuousness in her salons.

She did not give up the quarters that she shared with the Ogilvie sisters. She used part of them as a stockroom and, in the other part, took another step toward her total woman beauty concept. She was already taking care of the face and skin. The Ogilvies were in charge of hats and hair. There remained only the body, and Elizabeth Arden branched out into dressmaking.

Within a year, she retrenched and closed the branch. It was one of the very few failures she was ever to experience. Despite the defeat, her interest in clothes did not diminish, but another World War would start before she reentered the couture—and with very different results. The difference would be predicated on hiring the best designers available, instead of depending on her own limited sense of style which remained, throughout her life, a little suggestive of a Woodbridge farm girl going to a Sunday church social—all pink and bowed and ever so refined.

The end of 1914 and the beginning of 1915 was a period crowded with intense business activity and growth. The new salon was still more successful than its predecessor. The Arden advertisements touted it as being "where everything is so refreshingly different. And where the spirit of youth is so all pervading that you cannot leave without catching some of it."

When Elizabeth left in the evenings, it was without that contagious spirit of youth. All she went to bed with was the aching disease of loneliness. Aside from the Ogilvies and her employees, she had no real friends. Even the faithful few had lives of their own. She could not call upon them to fill all of the empty hours between salon and sleep. She looked around and seemed to be the one person in all the world who found fulfillment only in work.

She spent more and more time thinking of Tom Lewis, and of the happiness that she had found in his company. In the months since their return, their only contact had been discreet glances at the bank from which she had quickly turned away. How she wished that she could bring him back into her life, but it was impossible. The moral arbiters of the period ruled it beyond propriety for a lady to call upon a gentleman for other than a business transaction. She occasionally thought it a great misfortune to be doing so well, that she did not need another loan.

What actually did bring them back together was a tragedy of such monumental proportions that it precipitated America's entrance into the war. On May 8, Tommy telephoned Elizabeth at the salon. The *Lusitania* had been sunk off Ireland by a German U-boat. One thousand lives were lost, including 114 American citizens. He was extremely agitated. So was she—but for a different reason.

When he suggested that something should be rescued from the dear old ship—namely, their relationship—she heartily agreed. They began to see each other several nights a week. Although her reservations about marriage remained intact, there was no denying that her feeling for him had deepened during the months they had been apart.

Tommy found the right way to her heart. The romantic tête-à-têtes revolved around discussions of her business. As a bank official, he was not only aware of her progress, but he was also impressed by it. Here was a girl with everything, including a brain.

Even in peaceful, isolated America, there was no avoiding the war. It was everywhere, in the newspapers, in conversations, in the very air they breathed. The Atlantic had ebbed considerably, bringing Europe ever closer.

One morning, Tommy turned up at the salon in uniform. He had enlisted in one of the New York regiments, so that he could have a commission by the time America got into the fight. She was angry that he had not discussed the matter with her. A quarrel began, and she stormed into the back room, bolting it behind her. When his pounding got no reaction, he slipped a note under the door. She replied with a note, and they kept this up until one of his notes brought a gasp and a twittering oral response. "Don't go away, dear. I'll be right out."

It was a proposal. Seeing him in uniform had made her realize that she did, indeed, love him very much. But marriage? No, no. Marriage was not for her. She had to escape before she saw him, or she might weaken.

There was a fire escape outside the rear window. She clambered down three flights and raced up Fifth Avenue. At the corner of Forty-third Street, she suddenly stopped. Why was she running? She did love him. He was going off to war. If something were to happen to him—she mustn't think of that. Before he left, she owed it to her country to make him happy. If, in the process, she also made herself happy, that in no way lessened her patriotism.

Elizabeth retraced her steps and climbed up the front stairs of the building. When she appeared in the entrance, his back was to her. He was still facing the door to the other room, waiting for her to come out. She cried, "Yes, Tommy. Yes, yes, yes!"

On the day of the wedding, she continued to work until four o'clock, taking only enough time off to have one of the girls give her a quick facial and for the Ogilvies to run a hot curling iron through her hair. When the clock struck, she told Lanie that she was taking an hour off and said nothing about why or where she was going.

She returned precisely at five. She announced, "Well, I've done it," and went back to work until eight, when she was to join Tommy for their wedding supper.

The celebration and wedding night took place at the St. Regis. In years to come, she would adore the Ritz in Paris, and the St. Francis in San Francisco, and the Beverly Hills in Los Angeles, and Claridge's in London, but the St. Regis in New York was to remain her favorite hotel in all the world.

CHAPTER FIVE

War Finds Lizzie Arden

The year 1915 found Elizabeth Arden well ahead of her nearest competitors in the New York beauty mart. As New York was not only the largest but also the most sophisticated and fashion-conscious city in the United States, it was obvious that she was also leading the field in the entire country.

There were companies with a much larger gross volume of business, like Palmolive and Pond's, but they were primarily in the toiletries business. They were not beauty experts. In skin care and cosmetics, there were only two rivals who were worthy of any consideration—her former employer, Eleanor Adair, and the toast of the nineties, Lillian Russell.

Her former partner, Elizabeth Hubbard, was already out of the running completely. Her sparse rose-tint line could afford only an obscure classified advertisement in *Vogue*. Within a year, she was to retire from the scene forever.

Miss Russell had been a famous musical comedy star, whose gorgeous face, fulsome hourglass figure, and flawless complexion had made her the standard by which turn-of-the-century beauty was judged. Her products were allegedly her personal beauty secrets. Her appeal was to a fading nostalgia, and to those who persisted in wanting to emulate a style of looks that was already passe.

Mrs. Adair was still pushing the good old Ganesh treatments and products. In an attempt to keep up with the times, she had moved

:[81]:

from 21 West Thirty-eighth Street to 557 Fifth Avenue and had changed her directory listing from Massage to Toilet Products. In her advertisements, she tried to capture a new market by giving her line a touch of the glamor of the mysterious East. She completely repudiated the assumption that Ganesh had anything to do with the lower jaw. According to the copy, Ganesa was the Hindu god of wisdom, ''Near whose temple in India, Mrs. Adair first learned the secret of the now world-famous muscle cream.'' From a beauty point of view, she would have been better advised to stick with a Ganesh lower jaw, for Ganesa had an elephant head.

Nothing she did worked for the misfortunate lady. Her appeal remained limited to the aging members of the old guard who had long been faithful clients at her salons in New York, at 92 New Bond Street in London, and at 5 Rue Cambon, a short distance from the rear entrance to the Ritz, in Paris. Young women and leaders of the social set considered her hopelessly antiquated. They passed her by on their way to the up-to-date Arden Salon D'Oro. There was a great irony in this that could not have escaped Eleanor Adair. Miss Arden was still advertising and practicing the muscle-strapping treatment that she had stolen from her.

There was no doubt that Elizabeth was well on her way to fame and fortune. She already had two salons and was considering locations in several other cities and resorts. The formation of the Arden-Swanson alliance produced a steady flow of new products that were eagerly purchased by both her clients and customers in leading stores across the country. In addition to Cream Amoretta and Ardena Skin Tonic, the first year offered Venetian Cleansing Cream, Venetian Pore Cream for blackheads, Venetian Lille Lotion to prevent freckling and to keep the skin from darkening, Venetian Muscle Oil for wrinkles and hollows, Venetian Adona Cream for the neck and bust that might be losing firmness, the satiny emollient, Venetian Velva Cream, and a full line of rouges and tinted face powders. It was quite a leap forward for a woman who had started five years before with a line of two or three primitive, homemade products and a pair of capable, ''healing'' hands.

The Venetian flower powders came in Japanned metal cases that were so pretty that they were openly displayed, giving them the great advantage of being pieces of portable advertising. Her packaging was already becoming distinguished for the beauty that would remain their trademark for as long as she lived. She spent weeks poring over designs, before deciding upon the "right" little box or jar for a new item, and her decisions were infallible. Years later, Helena Rubinstein remarked, "With her packaging and my products, we could've ruled the world."

Miss Arden's *Vogue* advertisements were broadening in their scope. No longer were the salons the dominant feature. A typical quarter page in 1915 was headed by a drawing of an eighteenth-century beauty with teacup in hand and shocked expression on face. In large, bold type, the copy shouted, "My dear! She looks so much older!"

Beneath it, the story unwound in genteel beautyese. "Over the teacup! Those unkind remarks—unkind but frequently truthful. For a slight change in contour, a faint wrinkling or marking of the skin, a noticeable fading of the complexion—these add *years* to one's age, that is, in the eyes of one's friends. And there is really not an iota of an excuse for a woman of today to lose one bit of her youthful attractiveness. For every woman can do what hundreds of Miss Arden's clients have done for years, and keep the skin and complexion in the pink of condition, the facial contour firm, well-molded and youthful by devoting ten minutes each day to proper treatment with the Venetian products."

With very few modifications, the copy could appear in next month's magazines. Elizabeth Arden always supervised the wording of her advertisements, and in those days, she also wrote it. A comparison with Mrs. Adair's Hindu god indicates how far ahead of everybody else she was, even in this specialized area of her business.

Elizabeth could easily have been becoming secure, in the knowledge that her preeminent position in the cosmetics field would remain unchallenged. If this was the case, she was soon to learn that she was very much mistaken. At about the time Tommy Lewis appeared to threaten the peace of her private life, somebody else appeared to very nearly destroy the peace of her professional life.

Mrs. Edward Titus had decided that Europe at war was no place for her and hers. She packed up her husband, her sons, and her sister and came to New York. Her first observation of the females of that city presented a threat and an insult to Elizabeth Arden. "The first thing I noticed was the whiteness of the women's faces and the oddly grayish color of their lips. Only their noses, mauve with cold, seemed to stand out. . . . so I said to myself, here is not only a new country, but a huge market for my products."

Mrs. Titus was known professionally as Helena Rubinstein. As Elizabeth had tended to minimize the value of Mme. Rubinstein's Valaze products in Paris, so Helena tended to minimize the value of Miss Arden's Venetian products in New York. Their attitude toward formidable competition was but one of many characteristics that the ladies shared.

Physically, they were both short, had the constitutions of the healthy peasants that they basically were, and complexions that were better advertisements for their preparations than anything that any advertising or promotional genius could invent. They both missed being beautiful by so little that people were constantly wondering why they did not achieve it. Everything about each of them would have spelled beauty in almost any other woman. Perhaps, it was because their faces were shadowed by signs of the inner workings of those brilliant but devious minds.

Their facial features and coloring presented the only striking dissimilarities. Helena was dark with Semitic features, and Elizabeth was fair with Anglo-Saxon features. Those who knew both of them could not decide if they were diminutive, but large-breasted, versions of Rebecca and Rowena or merely feminine counterparts of the Katzenjammer Kids.

Both were born under the sign of Capricorn, in foreign countries, and had gained their American citizenships by marrying American natives. They married for the first time comparatively late in life, each at the age of thirty-seven, and more out of loneliness than from

Elizabeth Arden when she was Mrs. Thomas Jenkins Lewis.

Helena Rubinstein, known to all as ''Madame,'' but to Miss Arden she was always ''that woman down the street.''

any great sexual appetites. Both were much more comfortable with homosexuals, who doted on their imperiousness, than with heterosexuals, who might make physical demands upon them. Both were divorced and later remarried to impoverished Russian princes, chosen more for their titles than their masculinity. Mme. Rubinstein's prince once boasted, "I only had to sleep with her once."

It is quite possible that Miss Arden's prince beat that record.

From the evidence, it would appear that they were both totally frigid women. Although Helena did have sons, she was as indifferent to their personal desires as they seem to have been to hers. The fact that these two curiously unresponsive women invented the cosmetic look makes as strange a comment on twentieth-century standards of feminine beauty as does the fact that most dress designers are homosexual on twentieth-century standards of feminine taste.

In later years, their inverted maternal instincts were lavished on nieces, Pat Young and Mala Rubinstein. The girls acted as constant companions and attendants, to the possible detriment of their own private needs and lives.

Both women were given to professional nepotism. At one time or another, Arden employed two sisters, a brother, a husband, and three nieces. The score on Rubinstein relatives has never been fully tallied, but Helena was the more fortunate of the two. Many members of her family turned out to be efficient executives. With the exception of one sister and her husband, poor Elizabeth found very little business talent among those near and dear to her.

They were both autocratic, indifferent to the opinions of others, extremely vain, ruthless, ambitious, single-minded, dedicated careerists—and occasional charlatans.

The amazing thing was that, though these strikingly similar women moved in a tiny and restricted world, they were never to meet, even when they were in the same place at the same time, nor were they ever to refer to each other by name. To each, the other was simply "That woman" or "That dreadful woman."

Within a few months of her arrival in New York, Mme. Rubinstein took a full-page advertisement in *Vogue*, announcing the opening of her first American salon, the Maison de Beauté Valaze, at 15 East Forty-ninth Street. Elizabeth took this as a challenge. Although she had only recently moved into new quarters at 509 Fifth Avenue, upon reading of Mme. Rubinstein's proposed establishment, she decided that hers were inadequate.

Bergdorf Goodman was already at 616 Fifth Avenue, and there were new store fronts to be seen all the way up to Fifty-seventh Street. Commerce was definitely marching up Fifth Avenue, and Miss Arden marched with it. She took five rooms at 673 Fifth Avenue, with a private entrance on East Fifty-third Street, and planned to open a wholesale division at 665 Fifth. She convinced Mr. Swanson of the advisability of resigning from Stillwell and Gladding and moving into a new laboratory that would also be located at 665.

The new enterprise represented an enormous financial undertaking, and the Arden manageress, Irene Delaney, was frank to admit, "I was scared to death."

But the combination of war and changing mores brought a boom in the cosmetics business. Sally Bulkeley has described the first hectic months in the new salon. "We worked ourselves bowlegged getting ready for parties. Then, we grabbed a sandwich and trained new massage girls until midnight and on Sundays and holidays."

The battlelines were drawn. Tommy marched off to serve in a war that America would not enter for another two years. Elizabeth stayed home to engage in hostilities that had already begun.

From the moment that Rubinstein and Arden had opened their respective doors, they had both insisted upon glamor and opulence. Each felt that it was she who had done it first. Actually, they had both done it at approximately the same time, but in different countries.

The decorative difference in their salons provided an interesting insight into the differences in their social aspirations. Helena strove for the "artistic," with dramatic dark-blue velvet walls and red baseboards. Elizabeth wanted to capture the aura of the drawing rooms of the great mansions that lined upper Fifth Avenue. Consultations were held in the white-and-gold Oval Room. Treatment rooms were decorated in subdued pastels.

Helena's opening announcement gloried in recounting the great works of art to be found on her premises. Elizabeth merely stated that her new Salon D'Oro was "the largest and finest in the world."

The battle raged across the pages of the fashion magazines. These periodicals preached to those already converted to the cult of beauty. In those days, there were no laws governing advertising claims, and the ladies could cry havoc and let loose the cats of war. Printer's ink poured forth with the same deadly freedom as poison gas in Verdun and the valley of the Somme.

In one edition, Mme. Rubinstein would tout herself as "the greatest living beauty exponent." In the next, Miss Arden would state that she had "given her life to the study of this subject both here and abroad, in Paris, London, and Berlin."

It was quite a declaration for a lady who had spent no more than a total of six weeks abroad and only eight years, out of her thirty-eight, in the United States.

If Mme. Rubinstein stated that her massages offered what amounted to instant youth, Miss Arden took her to task by inferring that superficial massage was insufficient to the proper completion of the job.

Elizabeth Arden took an early lead in the number of products offered to the public. From 1915 through 1920, she introduced a larger number of preparations, of greater diversification of use, than any other cosmetics manufacturer in the world.

Mme. Rubinstein nosed ahead in the number of salons that she operated. By 1918, she had opened in Chicago, San Francisco, Philadelphia, New Orleans, and on the boardwalk in Atlantic City. Miss Arden was in Boston, Washington, San Francisco, Palm Beach, and Newport.

The racial prejudices of the day were subliminally stated in the locations of their respective establishments. Mme. Rubinstein limited herself to cities in which Jews had always been accepted. Miss Arden was in many places that not only were anti-Semitic, but actually boasted of their no-Jews-allowed policies.

Their respective religions played a large part in their later social aspirations, as well as in the locales of their salons. As a Jew, Helena knew that she would never find a place among the bigoted American socially "elite" and sought it in the superficially more tolerant world of the arts. She bought the works of all of the great artists of her day, but could not resist the impulse to, as Elizabeth might have put it, "Jew them down on their prices."

Elizabeth was what has since become known as WASP. Her maternal Cornish antecedents were better stock than could be claimed by a majority of those who were socially registered. She spent her life trying to enlarge the four hundred to four hundred-plus-one.

Anti-Semitism influenced the actions of both of them. Although she would seldom admit it, Helena was often the victim of it, and although she never realized it, Elizabeth often practiced it.

Whether it was an unwritten law dictated by the attitudes of some of her more influential clients or by her own convictions, Elizabeth Arden did not knowingly hire Jews until after the start of the Second World War. It must be added that there was never a law, written or unwritten, against Jews as customers.

Elizabeth once explained her personal biases to Ferdinando Sarmi. "To be Catholic or Jewish isn't chic. Chic is Episcopalian."

While the ladies engaged in their expensive advertising battle, new competitors, like Marie Earle and Dorothy Gray, were beginning to appear on the scene. Miss Gray went into business in 1916, when she listed herself in the directory as a Dermatologist, at 734 Fifth Avenue. It was not long before she was arousing an antipathy, in Elizabeth, that was almost comparable to what she felt for Mme. Rubinstein.

Dorothy Gray started to spread the word that she had been Elizabeth's original partner and that they had traveled to Europe together to learn massage from a French expert. The fact that the Gray products were often remarkably like the Arden products was attributed to the fact that both originated with Dorothy's father, who was a physician.

None of it was true, but the story spread so rapidly that Elizabeth found it necessary to deny it in a statement in *Vogue* which also took a side swing at some of her other competitors.

"In every city will be found one or more trading upon her [Ar-

:[89]:

den's] success by claiming to duplicate her methods. But no one but Elizabeth Arden, herself, knows the complete formulas for the Arden Venetian preparations.''

Their actual relationship was very close to the one Elizabeth had shared with Eleanor Adair. In 1915, Dorothy Gray worked in the Arden salon for a very brief period. She was employed as a custom cosmetologist, which was a high-toned way of saying that she was a treatment girl. When Miss Arden discovered that Miss Gray was living with a gentleman without benefit of clergy, she was so outraged that she fired her.

Before departing, Dorothy offered to double Georgia Reed's salary, if she would leave Arden and come to work for her. When Georgia told her employer, Elizabeth replied, ''If you stay with me, I promise to take care of you for the rest of your life.''

The girl elected to remain with Arden, where she continued to work for the next forty years, and Elizabeth was true to her word. After retiring, Georgie became ill and had to enter a nursing home. The Arden Company paid her bills. There was a special provision written into Elizabeth's will that stated, that Georgia Reed was to be taken care of for as long as she lived.

An armistice was signed, ending the World War on November 11, 1918. No such document ever existed between Elizabeth Arden and Helena Rubinstein. That remained a fight to the death. Even when other companies, like Avon and Revlon, far outdistanced them in sales, their personal emnity persisted. It created the headlines and provided the gossip that made the beauty business as consonant with excitement and glamor as the theater and cinema ever were or ever would be.

It was an equal contest between two giant personalities. Between them, they created an industry. There are now a multitude of giant corporations, all extravagantly competing for markets, but all run by rather small people whose largeness of spirit and imagination exists only in the minds of their public relations experts.

CHAPTER SIX

Galeries Lafayette,
We Are Here

By 1918 New York City was so filled with her family and Elizabeth so filled with plans that she rarely had time to be lonely and only thought fleetingly of her soldier husband. Those thoughts always made her apprehensive, and she did her best to push them out of her mind. She was superficially the brave war wife, but beneath the facade, she was relieved that the war had postponed the beginning of married life.

Until Tommy came marching home, she had family galore to fill the empty hours. There was brother William, his wife and three daughters, and Lillian, who had arrived in 1915, and Gladys. Only Christine remained in Canada.

Gladys had an infant son and was trying to find her way out of a bad marriage to a man named John Baraba. She was a restless, intelligent, courageous woman who, from the depths of her own unhappiness, looked at her sister's successful career and said exactly what she had always said as a child, "Me, too."

These two sisters adored each other but were profoundly different in their outlooks. There were some who liked one, and others who liked the second, but seldom were both liked by the same person. It was almost as if the two were born out of the separate cultural strains that made up the Canadian national character. Gladys spoke French beautifully and was an ardent Francophile. Elizabeth never mastered that language and was a devoted Anglophile. Problems constantly arose from these divergent points of view, but though they quarreled incessantly, their love and devotion never wavered.

Physically, they resembled each other, in that both were fair, blue-eyed, finely featured, and small-boned. While Elizabeth was superficially prettier, Gladys had a basic womanliness that made her capable of responding to men on a physical level. Elizabeth interpreted her sister's sensuality as flightiness, and spent a lifetime hoping that Gladys would outgrow it.

When Gladys announced that she had decided to leave her husband and enter the business, Elizabeth had a very mixed reaction. There was nothing that she would not have given "Sister" in the way of financial help or moral support, but her salons were something else again. They were hers alone. Hiring strangers to assist her was fine. She needed help—and you could always fire strangers. How could she fire Gladys? She was a part of her life.

There was another thing about Gladys that was most disquieting to her sister. Elizabeth had always sensed that, beneath the me-tooism, there was a stubborn strain of competitiveness. Given a chance, it might prove troublesome.

Elizabeth offered money, a nurse for the baby, anything, but Gladys would not accept charity. She wanted to work for her keep. Elizabeth only relented after she was convinced that it was not the salons that interested Sister. Gladys was fascinated by the unrealized potential for merchandising the products. Elizabeth did not understand what she meant. Orders were coming in to the tidy tune of $20,000 to $30,000 a year, and as far as she was concerned, it provided a very nice supplement, but it was the salons that were the backbone of the business.

Gladys argued that there were stores all over the country that had never heard of Elizabeth Arden. The preparations had to be displayed for and demonstrated to them.

Elizabeth became very angry. She spent a small fortune on advertising, and it was inconceivable that there was anybody who had not heard of her.

Realizing that she could never win a shouting contest with her sister, Gladys tried to calm down. She became terribly cool and logical. "Your money is spent in magazines like *Vogue*. There are thousands of shopkeepers who've never even heard of *Vogue*—let alone read it."

Elizabeth replied grandly, "I'm not interested in people who've never heard of *Vogue* They're simply not my kind of clients."

No matter what their journalistic tastes might be, not being interested in customers was too much for the shopkeeper in Gladys. She exploded, "You're an ass! Go to grass!"

The little couplet might well have adorned the crest Elizabeth later commissioned. It was the Graham family motto and, at the sound of it, both women shrieked with laughter, and the tension was broken.

If Elizabeth thought that was the end of it, she was reckoning without the persistence of Gladys. She kept at the subject, day after day, until Elizabeth was on the verge of commiting sororicide. Wherever she turned, Gladys materialized, asking the same questions. "Why are you content to sit back and wait for orders? Why don't you send somebody out to get them?"

Elizabeth tried to explain that there was a war on and that good salesmen were impossible to find. Gladys pounced. She quickly came to the point that had been in the back of her mind ever since the first discussion. "Let me go."

She would make a much better salesman than any mere male. She had learned how to give treatments and could demonstrate the products. She used them and could speak of their beneficial qualities from experience. "What's more, I've a very good complexion which makes the best kind of advertisement."

Elizabeth was horrified. A woman traveling alone all over the country, it was scandalous. It was also dangerous. There were corrupt men everywhere, who would try to molest her.

The differences in the sisters' response to the threat of sexual assault was indicative of their opposite views on sexual encounter. One completely discounted the possibility of it happening to her while the other thought that, given the right set of circumstances, she might consent.

When Father Graham had warned Elizabeth of the threat of licentiousness in the city, she had replied that she was too old for anybody to be interested. When Elizabeth warned her sister, Gladys airily responded that nothing was going to happen to her, that she did not want to happen to her. It was right, in the eyes of Victoria, versus light, in the eyes of Josephine.

A parade up Fifth Avenue was something that exasperated Elizabeth beyond all reason. She could never see why she should be forced to sacrifice an afternoon's business, just because some obscure saint had reputedly chased the snakes out of Ireland.

This parade was different. It was probably the only time that she was not upset by a stoppage of the midday business traffic. A flag was draped over her window, and she stood at it hurling streamers of colored paper, shouting as exuberantly as the crowd below her. It was Tommy's regiment returning from the war. She was soon to wonder what all that shouting had been about.

His repatriation was a particularly trying thing for Lewis. He was forty and did not share the optimism of his younger comrades-at-arms. All that he had in common with them was an indecision about where he fit into the world he had helped to make safe for democracy.

Tommy had very little money and would not be able to afford to do nothing for long. Even if he could, it would not have been for him. By nature, he was a worker who was happiest when employed at something that excited his imagination. It was the staid, stuffy steadiness, the lack of excitement, that made him not want to return to banking. His dilemma was deepened by the obvious fact that his wife was well on her way to becoming a wealthy woman. It looked very much as if Captain Lewis had reentered civilian life as Mr. Arden.

Had Elizabeth exhibited any compassion, it might have been easier for him, but how could she be expected to be compassionate when she did not even understand? He was the man of the house but, as she was not accustomed to having one around, she did not realize that she was expected to defer to him, if only in small things.

Three years had been cut out of Tommy's life, and he wanted to

:[94]:

make up for all the romance and passion he had missed. He wanted exactly those qualities that were most conspicuously missing from his wife's nature. For her part, she was in her fortieth year and much too old for that sort of nonsense. She was seeking justification for a lifelong pattern by citing an age that she would not admit to anybody but herself. For both of them, life would have been far less complicated if only he had been able to act like a beau instead of a husband. How foolish of him to have sought prerogatives where there were only pejoratives.

When he found that all of his other needs were unsatisfied, Tommy would have settled for understanding, but even that was beyond Elizabeth. She could not mask her irritation at seeing him still in his dressing gown when she left for work in the morning and lounging about, drink in hand, without a word about where he had been or what he had been up to in the intervening hours, when she got home in the evening.

Congress had just passed the Volstead Act, enforcing Prohibition. It created some unnecessary problems over obtaining alcohol for her preparations. She would point at his glass and scream, "I won't have you breaking the law in my house!"

Elizabeth seldom drank, but it had nothing to do with any scruples concerning the Eighteenth Amendment. She believed that alcohol was bad for the skin, except when mixed with perfumes and externally applied from a bottle bearing an Arden label.

The couple's only moments of true communication came when they were discussing her business affairs. She respected his acumen and, in those moments, became as open and feminine and appealingly helpless as the wife of his dreams.

It was clear to both of them that their future would be best served were he to become a part of the Arden Company. She was hesitant about broaching the subject to him, for fear that he might try to take over, and he would not mention it to her, for fear that she might turn him down. The impasse continued until one evening, when she arrived home in a rage that, even for her, was formidable.

Elizabeth had always been as casual about her ledgers as she was about her expenditures. She preferred not to look at the books, lest they remind her that some of her extravagances were foolish in light of her capital reserves. She left all the accounts in Irene Delaney's usually capable care. She would simply tell her manageress when she wanted some money, often without telling her the purpose. As far as Miss Arden could see, the system worked perfectly.

That afternoon, the auditor had been in to make an examination of the company's financial condition. After looking at the books, he had the audacity to march into the Pompeian Room and interrupt her in the middle of a treatment. He demanded an audience immediately and led her back into the office. He said, "Miss Delaney must be discharged. The books are in a mess. There are all manner of unaccountable expenditures."

Elizabeth could have accounted for them, but she was not about to tell him that. Instead, she picked up a jar of Cream Amoretta and threw it at him. When she missed, she screamed, "Look what you've done! The wall is ruined!"

She was beginning to find a good temper tantrum the quickest and easiest solution to problems.

Tommy asked, "Did you fire Lanie?"

"Certainly not! I fired the auditor. The nerve of that little man trying to tell me how to run my business."

Actually, the scene had most effectively reduced Miss Delaney to a flood of tears. Elizabeth had put an arm around her and cooed, "Don't you worry, dear. Remember, these men come and go. But you girls are here forever."

Despite Elizabeth's loyalty to her, it was obvious that Lanie could not be trusted to keep the books, because she was too intimidated to ask a question of her employer. It was equally clear that the auditor would not be back and that any subsequent auditor would inevitably meet with the same fate.

Elizabeth timidly asked if Tommy would come in and look after things, until she found somebody else. He reluctantly agreed on a contingency basis. "All expenditures must be checked with me, before you make them."

She sulked. "Well—all right. But, dear, never forget one little point. It's my business. You just work there."

She thought that it would only be for a short time, that it would get him out of the house, and, most important of all, that she would know what he was doing every minute of the day. The strange thing about Elizabeth's feeling for her husband was that she was violently jealous of him. It was a jealousy that stemmed from pride rather than passion. She did not really want him herself, but she did not want anybody else to have him either. That would make her look too ridiculous. Imagine a woman who made a fortune telling other women how to be physically desirable, not being able to hold her man!

Tommy was clever enough to take charge in only those areas of the business where Elizabeth's own interests were not fully developed. He made an office for himself in the wholesale division and rarely set foot in the salon. That was her domain.

Swanson and he hit it off immediately. They both agreed that the markets for the preparations had barely been touched. When Tommy discussed this with Elizabeth, she was astonished. She said, "Gladys feels the same way."

His respect for his sister-in-law was immeasurably increased. They were soon co-conspirators in finding ways to broaden the scope of the wholesale division. When Gladys told him of her desire to go on the road, he thought that it was a great idea, and they descended on Elizabeth together, determined to reopen the discussion. It would be difficult to tell whether they convinced the reluctant Elizabeth or merely wore her down, but she finally agreed to allow Gladys to have her way.

At first, it was not easy for Gladys. There was still a tremendous amount of resistance to cosmetics in small-town America. Every week brought fresh newspaper items about students being expelled, teachers and office workers fired, for wearing makeup. Some small-town shopkeepers did not even know what she was talking about. When she mentioned creams, they replied, "I'm sorry, ma'am. But we don't sell chocolates here."

But Gladys' persistence paid off; she began to win over many stores. What doubts Elizabeth had disappeared with the appearance of new profits. Tommy was ecstatic, and he convinced her to start training new demonstration and sales girls along with the treatment girls. As a result, Arden was among the first companies to send out a trained team of traveling demonstrators and saleswomen. It had nothing to do with feminine emancipation. It had everything to do with good business practices.

To put it mildly, Elizabeth was irritated on the day she discovered that she would have to cancel plans for a new salon, because Tommy had spent most of their money buying materials that would enable Swanson to manufacture enough products to fill the orders that were coming in from Gladys and the other girls. She controlled her anger. She needed Swanson, and she needed Gladys, and, she was beginning to discover, she needed Tommy.

There was no longer any question of Lewis' position at the firm being only a temporary one. Things between them improved so much that they almost convinced themselves, as well as the world, that they were an idyllically happy couple. They even announced plans for a belated honeymoon in Europe. Some might have thought it odd that this couple, married for over five years, should need the chaperonage of the bride's sister, but nobody said anything. Those around her were painfully learning that it was wiser not to question any of Elizabeth's idiosyncrasies. She had honed her temper to a fine edge that cut deeply.

Gladys was actually only accompanying them on the boat. They were disembarking at Southampton, and she was continuing to Cherbourg and, from there, on to Paris. Elizabeth felt that she owed Paris to her sister. She had already been there and had no great desire to return but for Gladys, who had never before been to Europe, it was the dream city of the whole wide world.

In addition to their clothes hampers and trunks, the two women carried identical, large, heavy valises that were crammed full of samples of every preparation in the Arden line. Tommy passed the days of this romantic excursion taking brisk, solitary walks around

At times Elizabeth could put on her own best show, a trait she never lost. Here she was photographed by the famous Arnold Genthe à la Eleonora Duse.

Thomas Jenkins Lewis, Elizabeth's first husband and the man who helped build her empire.

the deck, while his loving wife and sister-in-law remained below giving each other treatment after treatment. The endless applications were not administered in order to make them more lovely for the evenings, but were in the nature of rehearsals of the demonstrations they would be giving upon arrival at their destinations.

Although the Lewises had spread the notion that love and pleasure were the purposes of the trip, it was not the truth. They were only covering themselves in case of failure. The real reason that the trio had set sail was to conquer Europe in the name of Elizabeth Arden.

Rubinstein and Adair were represented in London and Paris, as well as in the United States. Only Arden was strictly local. Elizabeth felt that this was a grievous injustice that could only be redressed by direct attack. The sample cases were her arsenals.

The Lewises settled into a comfortable room at Brown's Hotel. The evenings belonged to Tommy, and he spent them teaching Elizabeth the joys of the high life. They presented the image of a stylish and attractive couple, of uncertain age, unfailingly attired in immaculate white tie and rather fussy but elegant gown, attending theaters and concerts, dining at all the smartest restaurants.

The days were hers. They wore sturdy, conservative clothes and sensible shoes, which, above his protests, she lined each morning with the London *Times*. It did no harm to protect themselves against the evils of the damp London climate. Every moment was precious, and illness did not fit into her schedule.

With Tommy lugging the cumbersome valise, they systematically trudged up Bond Street, over Oxford Street, down Regent Street, and across Piccadilly. They visited store after store, displayed their products to buyer after buyer, and all to no avail. By the end of the first week, they had not taken one single order.

Great Britain had Yardley and Floris and, to a lesser extent, Mary Chess and Rubinstein, as well as numerous French imports. It was the opinion of the important West End merchants that the beauty field was covered more than amply. There was no need for another line, especially one from the United States. Many English ladies still looked down upon their American sisters as rather crude and vulgar.

Tommy was extremely discouraged by the lack of results and was all for chucking the entire project in favor of a leisurely motor trip through the Lake Country. Not Elizabeth. If Central London spelled defeat, she was all set for an assault on the Brompton Road, in Knightsbridge. With fashionable Belgravia and Kensington as neighbors, it had developed into a short but terribly exclusive shopping street, which was distinguished by Harrod's, the finest department store in the city.

In those days, there were no such things as beauty departments, and all cosmetics were to be found under the heading of pharmaceutical goods. Edward Haslam was in charge of them, at Harrod's, and the Lewises made an appointment to see him. A tall, kindly North Country gentleman, he was sympathetic from the outset and offered them some very sound advice. "Find some sales representatives. English. We don't really trust foreigners, you know. Have them take your merchandise around to the provincial cities. Start to build a reputation out there. The landed gentry often purchase your sort of thing locally. If you're any good, they'll bring word of you down to London, and the shops here will be forced to stock Arden."

To show his good faith, Haslam placed a small order for what amounted to $50 worth of their merchandise. Elizabeth was elated, but Tommy grumbled that the profits would not cover their expenses for one day in London.

Elizabeth would not be put down. She cried joyously, "It's a beginning, Tommy, dear. A beginning!"

Gladys was having a sublime love affair. At first sight, she fell in love with Paris, and her passion did not waver for one moment over the next fifty years. Her mission in France was not so difficult as Elizabeth's in England, because the Arden products were not completely unknown. At the request of some of their American tourist customers, they were carried by a few pharmacies in Paris and on the Riviera.

Gladys learned almost immediately that the pharmacy business was a mistake. Beauty-conscious French women bought their cosmetics and preparations in department stores and at parfumeries. Her first job was to redirect the channels of release. In the process, she went to see Raul Mayer, the head of the great French store Galeries Lafayette. M. Mayer was charmed by the little Canadian, who spoke French so prettily, and agreed to let her open a stall in his establishment—at her own expense, naturally—at which she could sell her products.

It went better than Mayer expected, and after a few weeks, she was able to train an assistant to take over, thereby freeing herself to travel all over the country to convince other stores to stock Elizabeth Arden. The orders began to pile up. She kept writing home for more stock and eventually rented a small room to use as her first warehouse.

With business booming, it was natural for Gladys to extend her stay until the weeks turned into months. She had succeeded in separating herself from her husband. As for her son, she would find a way to take care of him later, but she was much too busy to think about it at the moment. It was not that she was lacking in a maternal instinct—she loved her baby—it was only that she was compelled to keep saying, ''Me, too.'' Being Elizabeth's sister was far more challenging than being a mother.

Her first success, the Galeries Lafayette, brought about her first large problem. Some of the merchandise was not moving, and the store returned it for credit. When Gladys saw the stuff, she had a fit worthy of Miss Arden. The Galeries label was firmly pasted on all of the boxes and jars. Obviously, the products could not be sold elsewhere without very costly repackaging that would completely eliminate the profit.

She stormed into M. Mayer's office and insisted he take back the whole shipment, or she would close the account. No matter how hard he tried to dissuade her, she remained adamant, and at length, he was forced to capitulate. The products were proving much too profitable to run the risk of her taking her business over to his largest competitor, Au Printemps.

After the fight was over, M. Mayer began to smile, for he admired the woman's courage. He reached across his desk and patted her hand. "Madame," he said, "you and Elizabeth Arden have a great future in France."

That was exactly what Gladys had been thinking.

CHAPTER SEVEN

Roaring into the Twenties

The war had released the safety valve, and by 1920 all the inhibitions of the Victorian era had whooshed out, collapsing the moral structure that had sustained the previous generation. The new generations was so emancipated that it promptly lost itself. The war to end all wars had brought a frenetic peace that was as edgy as the music that accompanied it. The stock market was bullish and bearish and every other kind of money-producing animal.

There was only one tenet by which behavior was measured. If mommy and daddy didn't do it, we will. If they did, we won't. For anybody with a daring product that had recently been taboo, the new decade was a lush, juicy apple ready for the picking, and the Arden wholesale business began to boom, having doubled and redoubled in the two years since Tommy first entered the firm.

Despite their opposing attitudes toward the sexual side of marriage, Tom Lewis was proving the perfect husband for Elizabeth Arden simply because he had become the perfect business partner, one who increased her profits without demanding any share in her proprietorship. It was in business, not bed, that Elizabeth found fulfillment. Husband or no husband, she remained the virgin goddess of beauty.

That was as it should be, for anybody less innocent might have been disturbed by the fallacy in her vision. Through clever promotion, she was bestowing upon women everywhere, the goal of a perfectly painted face that was actually no more than a childish caricature of sensuality. Somebody more experienced would have known that in moments of real passion, lipstick and rouge are too often smeared, eye makeup runs, and the perfectly painted doll becomes grotesque rather than alluring. Elizabeth was creating an image of beauty that remained framed by the mirror, instead of lit by the eyes of the beholder.

If she was well on her way to becoming the quality cosmetics champion, then Tommy was the promotor and manager who was guiding her to the title. Elizabeth's interests remained firmly fixed upon the salons, while Tommy took over everywhere else. When Gladys and the girls first went on the road, they were instructed to sell to drugstores, specialty shops, department stores, novelty shops, to anybody who would give them an order. As soon as the volume had sufficiently expanded, Lewis put a stop to that policy. The company filled the orders that were already written, but the sales force was told to take no reorders except from stores that he approved.

Tommy and Elizabeth were in total agreement on one overriding principle: Arden must stand for quality. Let the big drug and toiletry firms go after the mass market and make their deals with Kresge and Woolworth, Arden would settle for smaller production and larger profits. They would become a status line by concentrating only on prestigious outlets. It was apparent from the beginning, that Lewis was determined to make the Arden label the same sort of symbol that Elizabeth had made of the Arden salons. He accomplished his goal through advertising and selective marketing.

During the war years, the Arden ads had been larger and more frequent than those of any of her competitors, including Rubinstein. Lewis doubled the volume of advertising. The billing was staggering. So were the profits, as can be seen from an analysis of just one of their products.

Ardena Skin Tonic was a leading seller. A chemical examination would reveal that it was made of water, grain alcohol, boric acid, and perfume. Whatever efficacy it had, was born of the balancing and blending of ingredients. It was an extremely delicate emulsion that was easily thrown off by variations in the temperature and humidity factors. However, the cost of the basic materials was 3 cents, and the retail price was $2.50. Deducting the costs of labor, distribution, expensive packaging, and tremendous advertising, Arden was still able to net a margin of more than 25 percent on each bottle sold at wholesale. The prestige business was, indeed, a good business.

Under Lewis' supervision, the commercial outlets for the Arden line were completely reorganized. At first, it seemed as if he was throwing business away, but his policy soon paid off magnificently.

In New York, he would not sell Arden off Fifth Avenue, which eliminated their first retail customer, Stern Brothers, located a half block off the avenue. One of the first new out-of-town accounts was I. Magnin and Company, the exclusive and expensive West Coast chain of specialty shops. In Chicago, he gave Arden to Marshall Field, and Neiman Marcus handled them exclusively in the Dallas area.

By 1920 the limited laboratory facilities, at 665 Fifth Avenue, were no longer capable of handling the necessary increased volume of production, and the Lewises bought a small warehouse, at 212 East Fifty-second Street, in which they set up the first Elizabeth Arden factory.

On every front, the business was like a healthy child outgrowing its clothes. The salons were proliferating and expanding. Elizabeth leased another floor for the New York salon and was making plans to open new establishments in Philadelphia and Southampton, Long Island. She was also negotiating for space with several hotels in Atlantic City, New Jersey, and finally settled on the Ritz Carlton, which was, at that time, one of the most elegant in the resort town as well as being completely restricted against those "pushy" minority groups.

To stimulate interest in her products, in both the American hinterlands and Europe, Elizabeth initiated a very successful promotional ploy. In essence, it was beauty analysis by long distance. Women were invited to write in, describing their particular skin problems, and Elizabeth responded with solutions to them. With the sure touch of a seeress, she did not have to see the conditions to prescribe the panacea of an Arden preparation. This subsequently developed into the newsletters that have become standard with all of the big cosmetics firms. These are chatty little *billet-doux,* sent out to an enormous mailing list of clients and potential clients, breathlessly describing the particular company's latest little instant beauty miracle.

By the start of the new decade Gladys had decided to remain in France permanently. She had found an ambience there that suited her perfectly and never again wanted to leave it. In her heart and mind, it ranked above husband, child, and past. Distance had erased the past and, along with it, the husband who had been one of its mistakes. She told herself that love was most blind, when it was the only reason for marriage. Fortunately, Elizabeth's success had provided the intoxicating drug that had restored her sight. It was so much stronger than the darkness of love. The most binding pledges were not sealed with the words, "I do," but with, "me, too."

As for the son, if she accomplished her ends, he would be brilliantly looked after and, if she did not, he would be no worse off than he was to start with. The past was over, the present questionable, but the future was something that she could shape.

Gladys' primary objective was to establish distribution of the Arden products throughout France. She journeyed from Brittany to Provence, from Gascony to Alsace, selling, demonstrating, wheedling, begging, charming, until there was not a town of any consequence that did not have a local merchant peddling her wares.

She could not wait for the preparations to arrive from New York and opened her own one-room factory in the Parisian suburb of Neuilly. She hired her own chemists, among them the brilliant Louis Amic, to reproduce the original products and to develop new ones for France and possibly the United States.

Elizabeth kept bombarding her with letters ordering her to open a salon. Like Eleanor Adair and Helena Rubinstein, she wanted the prestige of a European address in her advertisements. But it was more than vanity; it was sound business. In her letters, she gave full credit to the importance of what her husband was doing with the wholesale division, but she also heavily underscored the need for salons. She carefully explained that, in addition to the nice profits they earned, they were the showrooms in which the Arden goods were displayed. She continued to feel this way even after the profits stopped, and the salons began to represent a serious financial drain.

She resolutely believed that the business would not have grown as rapidly without them. One satisfied salon client told ten friends about the wonders of Arden. It started a chain reaction. Each of those ten friends tried the preparations and told ten more, and so on, and on, and on. No matter how Tommy might deprecate them, it was the salons that created the demand.

Gladys trained two French treatment girls and finally opened the first European salon, in Paris, at 255 Rue St.-Honoré, at the start of the summer of 1920. The original clients were almost exclusively Americans who were touring the continent, but word of the marvelous new treatments began to get around, and the establishment caught on with some of the chic Parisiennes. It was not long before it became fashionable to visit Elizabeth Arden. The pattern followed the pattern in American cities. As they were needed, more space was rented, and more girls were trained and hired. Noting the rise in sales after the opening, Gladys was converted to Elizabeth's point of view and started to look around for the right quarters for a second French salon on the Riviera. She found them in Nice, lucratively nestled between aristocratic Monte Carlo and wealthy Cannes.

Edward Haslam's advice, on the English operation, was absolutely sound. Going to the provinces had launched Arden so successfully, that Elizabeth began to think in terms of a London salon, and Tommy, in terms of a factory. He had learned a valuable lesson from what had happened in France. From the time Gladys opened her own factory, shipping costs were eliminated and production costs notably reduced by the factors of modest overhead, cheaper European labor, and access to superior ingredients at a fraction of their domestic price.

He began to envision the establishment of a network of factories all over the world. Not only would they efficiently supply their own environs, but certain items could be manufactured abroad and brought back to America at a savings on what they would cost to make at home. When he told Elizabeth about his plan, she predictably said, "First, there must be salons. And more salons. Everywhere."

Before they could go ahead with the new British venture, they had to find an English manager. Gladys was much too busy in France to take on additional responsibilities. Elizabeth said, "Get Haslam. He believed in me, so I believe in him."

It was a remarkable piece of intuition but, through the years, it was to happen over and over again. She had an uncanny knack for spotting people who could be of use to her. Some of her discoveries observed that they had neither experience nor training, but she was positive that they had something more important—any other qualifications could easily be acquired under her tutelage. She could not identify that special spark she divined in them but, whatever it was, she was certain that it would be useful to her, and she insisted upon having it. She was seldom wrong and, in the case of Teddy Haslam, she was overwhelmingly right.

Haslam was very receptive to her offer, but he would not leave Harrod's without a release from the head of the store, Sir Woodman Burbridge. Elizabeth agreed that this was the thing to do. After all, the gentleman had a title and, more important, he represented several pounds of profit per annum. With a child's vision of courtly behavior, she lisped, "I'm sure a chivalrous knight wouldn't hold you against your will. But it's the polite thing to ask first. Besides, why jeopardize a nice little account by making him angry?"

She exhibited far less politesse when stealing help from the competition. In a terse tone, she would say, "Get him! I don't give a damn what it costs, or what that dreadful woman thinks. I want him. Get him!"

Sir Woodman said that he would release Haslam, as soon as he could find a suitable replacement for himself. At length, the right man was found, and Teddy was free to leave for America, where he was to receive special training in the Arden home office, salon, and factory. The transaction represented the best return, on a fifty-dollar investment, that any buyer ever received.

When Haslam returned to England, he was not alone. Elizabeth left Lanie and Tommy in charge at home and sáiled with him. She adored London and wanted the English salon to be perfection. With this in mind, she decided to supervise the entire operation right down to personally selecting and training the British treatment girls.

She took rooms at 25 Old Bond Street, over the shop of the old and reputable firm of jewelers S. W. Benson. The building had once been the very stylish private residence of the grandfather of Mrs. Montagu-Smith, who, in turn, is the mother-in-law of the American painter who created the legendary *Flair* magazine, Fleur Cowles Mayer.

A handsome Adams mantle and stairway were all that remained of its former grandeur, but they were enough to make Elizabeth decide upon the premises. Despite all that she had accomplished, there was a part of her that was still Florence Graham longing for a past that was not her own, but that would belong to her creation, Elizabeth Arden. She excused the weakness by telling herself that it was sound business to recreate the surroundings to which her clients were accustomed.

The truth was, that each new establishment was the setting she envisioned for her alter ego. When doubting and frightened Florence looked in the gilt-framed mirrors, assured and courageous Elizabeth gazed back from the heart of a magnificently appointed, secure world. That was really why she could never give up the salons. In a sense, they were her proof of existence. When she looked up at the engraved name of Elizabeth Arden, over the red doors, she knew that she was entering a haven in which she would be forever safe and somebody of substance.

Once the salon was successfully launched, Tom Lewis joined Elizabeth in London. He came over to help Haslam start the English factory, which was located in Coach and Horses Yard, directly behind New Bond Street. From the interviews that the Lewises gave to the British press, it would appear that Elizabeth had everything— youth, success, intelligence, money, fame, good looks, a charming husband.

If what she read about Elizabeth Arden was true, why did it all

Miss Arden and henchman
Edward ''Teddy'' Haslam
leaving the church after one
of her nieces' wedding.

Gladys de Maublanc, Miss
Arden's sister, was a complete Francophile and a
perfect head for the Paris
salon. Here she is seen
stepping into the Place
Vendôme from the Arden
salon in pre-World War II
days.

Elizabeth at the peak of her career photographed in England in 1947.

seem a lie, when she was alone in her hotel room; why did she still feel like a lonely, little farm girl? The companionship she should have found in marriage, was not there. There can be no companionship without communication and, aside from business discussions, there was damned little of that between the Lewises. Tommy wanted more than she had to give, and she could accept only the smallest part of what he offered. They settled for the superficial, but affable, facade of the perfect couple. Beneath the exterior appearance, there was a separateness that existed in point of view if not in space. They both plunged into their work, attempting to find a common ground in common endeavor.

The fantastic activity was not only to cure the ills in their private lives. New companies were springing up, and they had to keep outdoing themselves to maintain their lead in the class market. Pond's, Palmolive, Colgate, and the other mass producers were beginning to cast competitive eyes at their special and lucrative province. Pond's must have been especially aggravating, when they came up with a promotional scheme that Elizabeth would have adored to use for her products. In full-page advertisements, in all the leading women's magazines, they featured a series of photographs of, and endorsements by, all the leading social figures of the day. Ironically, most of them were Arden clients, but Elizabeth was so eager to have them accept her as an equal, that she would not have dared to ask their help in her little commercial affairs.

Hinds' Honey and Almond Hand Cream was another inexpensive product that must have deeply impressed the Lewises. In a very rare action for the Arden Company, they duplicated it in a class-market version called, Ardena Milk of Almond Hand Cream. They must also have long retained the memory of a Hinds' advertisement that featured a Charlotte Fairfield photograph of Irene Bordoni, who was then a popular musical comedy star. Miss Bordoni was posed swathed in a medieval, nunlike habit and wearing an expression of virginal purity. A few years later, Baron DeMeyer took a picture of the French model, Cecille Bayliss, that was to serve as the Arden trademark for years. In it, Mlle. Bayliss was swathed in a medieval

:[113]:

nunlike habit and wore an expression of virginal purity. On and off, Elizabeth used it for the next twenty years.

Kathleen Mary Quinlan, Primrose House, Richard Hudnut, and Marie Earle were among the newer firms vying for the expensive-exclusive cosmetics market, but it was the old rivals, Helena Rubinstein and Dorothy Gray, who gave Arden the most trouble.

Mme. Rubinstein and Miss Arden continued to play leap frog in opening salons from coast to coast. Miss Gray persisted in an extremely irritating policy of imitating the Arden products. Miss Arden did not find it the sincerest form of flattery, when Miss Gray came out with a June Geranium Bath Soap a few years after her own June Geranium Bath Salts, or an Orange Flowers Skin Tonic after her Orange Skin Food, and then followed these insults with the injury of a traveling makeup case exactly like the one Arden had been featuring exclusively since 1917.

The Gray establishment featured a line called Russian Products, and Elizabeth cooed witheringly, ''The poor dear must mean pre 1917, because there's nothing revolutionary about what she's done since.''

With Lewis' encouragement, Elizabeth's ideas, and Swanson's resourcefulness, Arden kept bringing out new products almost as quickly as the competitors copied the old ones. Long freed of her pledge to the Ogilvies, that she would not venture into hair preparations, Elizabeth introduced Ardena Shampoo and Hair Tonic in the early twenties. These were accompanied by a complete new line of bath products including Venetian Satin Soap, Velva After-bath, and bath salts in three different perfumes. They substituted in promotions for the eye makeup, which she continued to make but did not advertise. Companies like Bourjois were already flooding the market with cheap editions of the mascara and eye shadows that Arden had made a must for every woman who wanted to look smart.

Intent upon claiming her own place in the product parade, Gladys contributed a toothpaste called Savon Kenott. It was reputedly an old French favorite, and it remained in the Arden line for years. Although Elizabeth was so outspokenly opposed to smoking that she would not permit any of her help to have ashtrays and only reluctantly distributed them to clients, she had no opposition to speaking out, in advertisements, that recommended the Savon Kenott as the one dentifrice made especially for smokers.

When Richard Hudnut expanded from perfumes to cosmetics, Elizabeth Arden did the reverse. She wired Gladys to find her a good line of French perfumes to which Arden could purchase exclusive American rights. Gladys complied with Babani of Paris perfumes.

The house had enough different fragrances for Elizabeth to launch a campaign urging women to match their aromas to their clothes. There was one recommended for the tailored costume, and another for evening wear, and a third for afternoon, and so on, through the entire scented spectrum of wardrobe. If a woman was in doubt about a specific outfit, it was suggested that she write directly to Elizabeth Arden to find out which perfume was the right one to use with it. Until the reply came, which might be a matter of weeks, the woman had two alternatives. Either she did not wear the dress, or she walked around with a bad smell.

The marked delineation of business duties made it almost appear as if Tommy and Elizabeth were running two separate companies under one name. At home, it was as if they were leading two separate lives under one marriage. Elizabeth was spending more time on the road visiting the branch salons, seeing that they were operating smoothly, improving their facilities and appearances. The old fear of loneliness was still with her, and she always took along one of her girls. Even on those occasions when Tommy came along, it became customary to have a member of the staff travel with them, for, even with him there beside her, she was discovering that she was still lonely.

When they were off the road, the Lewises took to surrounding themselves with people. Intimacy was the one thing forbidden in their relationship. They feared the moments alone together, devoid of a third, or fourth, or fifth party to fill the emptiness with audience, for they were performers. And often, it was an extremely amusing show.

They were public people—gay, delightful, charming—he of the dapper worldliness and she so like an enchanted little girl. As the

:[115]:

Arden name became increasingly good copy, publicists found them useful to "dress" the audience at benefits and openings. The silver tray in their living room was piled high with invitations. Like everything else in their lives, these were on display for all to see, proof of their popularity.

Florenz Ziegfeld wanted them for a charity supper on his New Amsterdam Roof. Gatti-Casazza requested the honor of their presence at a benefit at the Metropolitan Opera House. They went to everything, never questioning the fact that most of their invitations were accompanied by requests for donations or subscriptions, that they rarely came from the people Elizabeth most wanted to cultivate, nor were they to those private parties that she only heard about when eavesdropping on a pair of *grandes dames* in the salon.

They were celebrities existing in that ephemeral newsprint world that rated them somewhat above Al Capone and somewhat beneath Anna Gould. Because their energies were seemingly endless, they rapidly became favorites with those who knew no end of night and, by the dawn's early light, oh, say you could see everybody from Fannie Brice to Fanny Ward blinking the new day in at the Lewis apartment.

Elizabeth grew younger with age, the girlish vocal mannerisms more and more pronounced, except when the voice was raised in anger over the often inconsequential mistake of some frightened underling.

"How can you be so *stupid!*" Elizabeth had grasped the girl's shoulders, and was shaking her until the teeth rattled in her head. Tears and terror mingled in the poor thing's eyes. She had only been working in the salon for a few weeks. How was she to know that the client's credit was good, that she was the sort of lady to whom one never personally presented a bill, who would take it as an insult and complain to the manager if one did?

Tommy raced into the Pompeian Room and separated them. He led the hysterical girl out, murmuring the appropriate comforting words. When he returned, Elizabeth was breathlessly seeking control in the meaningless rearrangement of objects on her desk. He said exasperatedly, "What am I going to do about that temper of yours?

Someday one of these girls is going to sue you, and I won't blame her. You've got to apologize.''

"No, no,'' she cried and then continued weakly, "I'll—I'll send flowers.''

In the early days, the fury had been difficult to summon, but as time passed, she found herself able to call it forth with ease. It was a release, something with which to purge herself of all of the choking frustration, and after it passed, it was impossible for her to apologize. She could not understand what had overtaken her, why Elizabeth had felt compelled to wrap the vulnerable Florence in the voluminous cloak of her rage. Like a savage warrior, she could only silently send peace offerings of flowers, or jewelry, or some other lavish gift.

While Elizabeth boiled, Tommy simmered. He was approaching fifty. He looked younger, and he felt younger. Never before had he exercised so much power, and never before had he enjoyed himself so thoroughly. It puzzled him, that there should still be something denied him. Because it was the only thing denied him, it assumed greater importance than all that he already had, and he risked all in its pursuit. He wanted, for one more time in his life, to be as young as he looked and felt. He longed for romantic love and sought it in the most ridiculous and commonplace way. While Elizabeth was occupied elsewhere, he became a philandering man-about-town and, in his escapades, he had a most unlikely companion, his wife's brother.

William Graham had recently come to work for Tommy. The two became fast friends and immediately started to take turns covering for each other with Elizabeth.

Tommy and Willie were actually very much alike. They were roughly the same age, both desirous of something more mettlesome than mere marriage, both vaguely resentful of having had success come their way through the offices of a woman, both mistaking the tinny overture to the *Ziegfeld Follies* for the music upon which love feeds.

Lewis and Graham were not alone in feeling the need for something a little more stimulating, from the opposite sex, than their homes provided. Elizabeth also felt it. She wanted a man with whom she

:[117]:

could be innocently alone, a man who would be flattering, and flirtatious, and chivalrous. She wanted the one thing that a husband could never be, that reminiscence of her girlhood, a casual beau. She began to seek them out among the men they knew in common. Unfortunately, Tommy's reaction was one of relief. There was not a moment when he felt threatened enough to repent, what the Victorian Elizabeth might have called, the error of his ways.

The first of the beaus was Henry Sell. Withstanding periods of mutual rancor, enforced silence, and even relieving separation, he would last for as long as she lived. In the early twenties, Sell was working for *Harper's Bazaar,* and the publisher, Chester Van Tassel, asked his help in handling a difficult but valuable advertiser, a woman who owned several salons and a very good wholesale manufacturing business in cosmetics. Sell met and ''handled'' Elizabeth Arden. Metaphorically speaking, he would go on handling her for forty-five years.

Although they never spoke of it, the Lewises somehow began to feel that they had made the necessary accommodations to a happy life together. Just when Elizabeth was congratulating herself on her invincibility, she was put to bed with a recurrence of the hip injury that she had sustained making the high kick, some thirty years earlier. Apparently, she had never quite recovered from the damage she had done to the sacroiliac joint.

She was laid up for six months, and her doctor kept insisting that only an operation would relieve the pressure on her bones. She was about to agree to it, when she read an article about a group of mystics, who practiced a series of exercises that were allegedly able to cure most of the body's ills.

Instead of going to the hospital, she pulled herself out of bed and over to a drab meeting room in West Forty-seventh Street, where a group of yogis were assembled for meditation. When she got home, she told her husband, ''When I saw those dear little men standing on each other's stomachs, I knew I'd come to the right place.''

She later claimed that she miraculously avoided major surgery only by doing yoga exercises. Never one to shrink from being the

A great believer in daily exercise, Miss Arden took to any new cult with relish. Here she practices her yoga headstand, which she could do with the ease of a sixteen-year-old even in her seventies.

Elizabeth Arden and her longtime friend and adviser Henry Sell. Mrs. Patricia Young, her niece, is at right.

prophetess of miracles, it was only a month after her recovery that she entered a recording studio to make the first records ever produced, giving instructions on how to do exercises. They were an enormous success and, a year later, she opened the first exercise room to be a part of a beauty salon. All the calisthenics, incorporated into the famous Elizabeth Arden system, were originally based on those she had learned from a series of yogis and from a multitude of others. It was another step toward her goal of the salon dedicated to the total treatment concept.

Her miracle cure not withstanding, Elizabeth continued to suffer from pains and weakness in the hip. She went on moving at what often seemed a slightly listing angle to the ground, but it never slackened her pace, as she pursued both business and pleasure at a dizzying speed.

CHAPTER EIGHT

Elizabeth Meets Elisabeth

By 1925 American women were spending an estimated $6,000,000 daily on the purchase of beauty products and on beautifying themselves in salons and hairdressers. From its domestic wholesale division, the Arden Company was grossing over $2,000,000 a year. At first glance, the figure would not seem impressive; they were making less in a year than women were spending in a day. It becomes more impressive with the realization that hers was a very limited class market. She elicited sales from only 3 percent of the female population (the group in the top income bracket) and never made any move to woo the 97 percent bulk, the little women who were spending an average of $150 a year in the beauty market. Moreover, the figure did not include the increasingly impressive Arden foreign sales, nor did it cover the salons, where the majority of her clients were likely to spend $150 a week.

The pious moralists, who had pushed through prohibition, were haranguing about this descent into Vanity Fair. Each week brought fresh stories of schools prohibiting the use of cosmetics among teachers and students, of office workers being fired for wearing lipstick and eye shadow, of irate parents bringing their rouged "flapper" daughters up on charges in juvenile court. It remained a losing battle. The puritans had pushed through the Volstead Act with the help of the adherents of Carry Nation and Susan B. Anthony, but most of those crusading women were on the opposite side in the cosmetics battle. They had joined the throng who painted their faces and called themselves liberated. Those two most prudish of women, Elizabeth Arden and Helena Rubinstein, paradoxically had vanquished all feminine vestiges of a reputedly more prudent age.

There had been an unsuccessful attempt to extend the Pure Foods and Drugs Act of 1906, to include cosmetics. The best the reformers could do was push through a New York State licensing act for cosmeticians. The ladies were asked such pertinent questions as: What are fingernails made of? What causes freckles? What action do the different colored lights have on the skin? What causes dandruff? What is the effect of hair dye on those suffering from eczema? What is electrolysis? Describe the structure of the skin. What is a milium? Name the muscles in the neck.

The licensing act may have restricted the employees in salons, but it did nothing to hamper the actions of the manufacturers of beauty products. The twenties proved the golden age of unrestricted advertising claims for cosmetics. Never again would the companies be so free of government restraint. The promises of a Fountain of Youth that the Indians made to Ponce de León were modest compared to the guarantees, publicly proclaimed by an Arden or Rubinstein, to the users of their preparations.

As a profession, cosmetology was offering unprecedented opportunities to career women. The prospects were so rewarding, that many men—former clerks, salesmen, mechanics, carpenters—were enrolling in beauty culture courses and entering the field. Reporting in the New York *Times,* in November, 1927, Virginia Pope stated the beauty business was a $2,000,000,000 a year business. While the average skilled male laborer was being paid $31.48 a week and the average female, $17.37, a newly graduated beauty operator was taking home between $20 and $30 a week, plus $15 in tips. Within six months, she could be earning $60 plus tips, plus a commission on every product that she sold. Some shops were giving operators as much as 60 percent of what they brought in, and many operators were making between $200 and $400 a week.

Because they consistently paid top wages, the Arden Company had the pick of the most talented people in the field. There were many things wrong with working for Elizabeth—her caprices and temper and huge demands on one's time—but she was never niggardly about salaries. Her girls were the best, and they were paid commensurately with their abilities. Tommy's organizational genius and Elizabeth's financial liberality combined to make theirs the most efficiently run company in what was already being called an industry.

Actresses had a professional need for the best in beauty care, and it was only natural that the Arden clientele included a great many of Broadway's biggest stars. The Lewises adored the theater and openly courted these often lonely ladies, who gratefully accepted and returned their invitations. Elizabeth would have preferred it were this true of her socially prominent patrons, but she took what she could get. She lunched with Helen Hayes, dined with Laurette Taylor and had late supper with Ethel Barrymore.

Along with cosmetics, the theater was becoming respectable, and it was increasingly possible to walk through a dressing room and enter a drawing room. Many of the dashing young members of the upper classes welcomed talented composers and performers with a much greater alacrity than had the *grande dames* of another generation. It had become chic to have George Gershwin or Noel Coward playing the piano at one's party, while Ina Claire or Gertrude Lawrence was elegantly draped over one of the chairs.

If the theater did not bring to Elizabeth the prestige and position for which she longed, it did bring her some people who were to play large roles in her retinue. Genevieve Cliff Daily had started her acting career as an ingenue with Elizabeth's former rival, Lillian Russell, and had gone on to play major roles with many of the large stock companies across the country, but true success and stardom had always escaped her. She was already in her forties, when she first met Elizabeth. With a bluntness that many a hypocrite palms off as honesty, Elizabeth told her to give up the stage. ''Dear, if a woman hasn't made it in her career by the time she's twenty-five, she's not going to make it.'' Coming from a woman who had not even gone into business until she was almost thirty-two, it was a rather odd comment.

Miss Daily protested that she had devoted her life to the theater, and that she loved it. Elizabeth's remarkable intuition was again at work. She said, "Never mind all that nonsense. Come to work for me, dear. I can use you.''

Again, Miss Daily protested. The only thing she knew about makeup was how to apply it in her dressing room. Elizabeth waved the remark aside. "God gave you good hands and a head. I'll give you the rest.''

Against her own better judgment, Genevieve Daily embarked on a training course at Arden. She eventually was manageress of both the Boston and San Francisco salons. When she decided to retire at sixty-five, Elizabeth, who was approaching seventy, shrieked, "Retire! At your age! What will you do with your time? You're much too young, dear. I'll tell you when you can retire.''

It was not until ten years later that Elizabeth reluctantly consented to let her go. She was still convinced that it was a terrible mistake to have all that time on one's hands at a mere seventy-five.

After seeing a show, it was not unusual for the Lewises to go backstage and visit some of their theatrical friends. At *No, No, Nanette,* Tommy was entranced by the show's star, Louise Groody, and some of the other goodies in the chorus. Elizabeth was only interested in a hoofer named Wellington Cross. Duke, as he was called by his friends, had had a successful if unspectacular career in vaudeville and Broadway musicals. On the way home, she said, "Tommy, I think we can use what's-his-name—you know—the dancer.''

A few weeks later, Marilyn Miller was giving a party at the Ambassador Hotel, after the performance of her great hit *Sally* and Elizabeth spotted Cross across the room. She gestured to the actor and told Tommy, "Get him.''

Tommy knew better than to argue. He approached Duke and explained that Miss Arden wanted him to come to work for her. Duke

Wellington "Duke" Cross, the gentleman whom Elizabeth took from the chorus of *No, No, Nanette* and built into one of her top executives.

replied by politely laughing in his face. Tommy said, "Don't laugh. You'll see. If she wants you, she'll get you."

Later in the evening, Elizabeth cornered Duke and repeated the offer, adding, "I'll start you at $150 a week."

Duke responded, "No, thanks. I'm quite happy doing what I'm doing—at $1,000 a week."

Elizabeth snapped, "But it's not steady. I'm offering you a steady job with a future. Stop counting on your toes. Your head is more reliable. And it'll last longer.''

Cross was never sure how she did it, but her powers of persuasion were so hypnotic, that he did join her company as soon as his show closed. He was started in the factory, where he learned all about production. Lewis later brought him into the office and taught him merchandising. A short while later, he was sent to Europe, where he spent two years as sales representative. By the time he retired, he was a vice-president of the company and had rounded out a service of over 40 years.

Duke might not have been one of the ideal beaus but, for years, he was court jester to Elizabeth. It enabled him to walk the precariously thin line between Elizabeth and Tommy, his loyalty unquestioned by either, despite their growing competition for supremacy in the business. One of his greatest assets was his lovely wife, Katie, who had a charm that completely won everybody. She became one of Elizabeth's few real friends and, in a way, also joined the company. She took a job with a former Ziegfeld Girl turned florist, Irene Hayes, where she was put in charge of all flowers ordered for and by Miss Arden. It was a formidable task, but she saw to it that not a bud ever left the Hayes shop, destined for Miss Arden, that was not absolutely perfect.

Flowers were Elizabeth's great passion, and she had masses of them all over her salons and homes. She spoke to each blossom, and fondled it, and never permitted one to be discarded until the last glimmer of life was extinguished. If she saw a maid removing a bouquet simply because it was wilting, she flew into a rage. ''How can you do that to living things? Just cut them back. They'll revive. Cut them back!''

As they were transferred from urn to vase to viol, long-stemmed roses grew shorter daily. Gladioli were a shriveled five inches long before she would admit that they might be ready to be retired. In all things, from women to tiny buds, she had an unwavering respect for life and beauty. But it was always a still life and a distant beauty—cut flowers in a vase, the same perfectly cultivated woman seated in repose across the expanse of a room or restaurant.

Elizabeth Arden first met Elisabeth Marbury, when she was brought to one of Miss Marbury's famous Sunday teas which were frequented by the most celebrated people in New York. There were no social demarcations at these parties. The only quality necessary for an invitation was that the guest had to be *somebody*. The hostess loved to mix the famous from all walks of life and see what happened. It was not unusual to observe Toscanini keeping time to the melodies George Gershwin played on the piano, or Al Smith giving a lesson in American politics to a youthful Prince of Wales, or Groucho Marx flirting outrageously with Peggy Hopkins Joyce.

When Elizabeth and Elisabeth became friendly, people were astonished. They were not at all each other's type. Bessie Marbury was politically a liberal, socially a Brahmin, intellectually a giant,

Miss Elisabeth Marbury, the one time benefactress and mentor for Elizabeth Arden, who brought her to Maine, and Maine Chance.

and physically so repulsively fat that she had to be supported by braces in order to walk. Elizabeth was a conservative, uninformed except about her business, pretty little girl of a woman. Acquaintances wondered what on earth they had in common.

On a superficial level, it was the same things that united Henry Higgins and Eliza Doolittle in Shaw's *Pygmalion*. On a deeper level, each had what the other wanted. Elizabeth was comparatively rich and, except for the Broadway crowd, knew nobody who was anybody. Bessie, though comparatively poor, knew everybody who was anybody. Bessie lived by her wits and was essentially a sophisticated adventuress, while Elizabeth lived by her labors and was essentially a naive provincial. In many ways, it was an even exchange.

Bessie shared a house off Sutton Place with Elsie de Wolfe, later Lady Mendl, who was a prominent interior decorator. Her two closest intimates lived around the corner in de Wolfe-decorated houses. They had both been featured in Pond's ads which would hardly have recommended them to Elizabeth without the larger attraction of their social positions. One was Anne Morgan, the daughter of J. P. Morgan, and the other was the very grand (but soon-to be ex-) Mrs. William K. Vanderbilt.

After their first encounters with the cosmetics lady, Miss de Wolfe pronounced her, ''dreary,'' Miss Morgan, ''dull,'' and Mrs. Vanderbilt, ''tiresome,'' but on Bessie's recommendation, they took her to their collective bosom—and what a bosom it was! In the homosexual underground, Mrs. Vanderbilt and the Misses Marbury, de Wolfe, and Morgan were known as the Four Horsemen of the Apocalypse. This Sapphic circle completely dominated the considerable homosexual stratum of the New York world of arts and society.

It was said that Anne Morgan and Elisabeth Marbury had made lesbianism fashionable. Their positions were so secure that their influence was also felt by an important segment of the upper echelons of the straight world. If anybody could open doors for Elizabeth, it was this unique quartet. Because she was so much in their company, there was much speculation over whether one of those doors might not have led to a bedroom.

Strange as it may seem, it is extremely doubtful that Elizabeth realized that her new friends were lesbians, let alone indulged a similar sexual appetite. Although homosexuals were beginning to appear in great profusion in the beauty-fashion world, Elizabeth always had a difficult time recognizing them. She often refused to believe it of the most flagrantly effeminate of her hairdressers and the most butch of her female employees.

It is possible that her own sexual problems stemmed from the fact that she was latently lesbian and spent a lifetime surpressing these unnatural desires. She adored beautiful women and, except as clients in her salons, would have nothing to do with homely ones. In men, her tastes ran to complaisant beaus who were often, at best, uninterested in sex.

She was always surrounded by pretty women. They were her constant traveling companions, very often sharing the same bedroom, but there was never the slightest indication that these relationships ever got beyond the hand-holding stage. If they had, or if she had ever made a pass at any of her companions, it would certainly have come out. What better excuse could a pretty young woman, who had been fired, have for being discharged than that she had rejected one of Miss Arden's overtures? It would have been far better than having to bear the label of incompetence with which she would stigmatize them. Yet, nobody ever so much as insinuated that there was anything abnormal about her—perverse, yes, but never perverted.

In the early part of the century, Elisabeth Marbury had functioned as American agent for George Bernard Shaw, Oscar Wilde, James M. Barrie, and W. Somerset Maugham. She retained the mentality of an agent for the rest of her life. She enjoyed getting friends to do things for one another and, if an exchange of money was involved, was not above demanding her commission.

In a sense, Bessie became Elizabeth's agent and sponsor. She also functioned as her intimate, mentor and, when the occasion arose, her chastiser. She was one of the few people ever to make Elizabeth bow to any judgment aside from her own. Miss Marbury could, and often did, get away with saying, "No, Miss Arden."

It was at Bessie's instigation that Elizabeth sat for a photographic session with her friend, Cecil Beaton, who was always in great favor in the Sapphic circle. Elizabeth was so displeased with the proofs that she angrily tore them up and threw them in the photographer's face. Bessie calmly commented, "You'll still have to pay for them."

And Elizabeth did. Having paid for them, she used them as picture postcards.

Under Miss Marbury's tutelage, Elizabeth began to acquire an art collection. Not surprisingly, it was dominated by female painters. She bought the works of Georgia O'Keeffe, Marie Laurencin, and Mary Cassatt. She did sit for a portrait by a male painter, Bessie's friend, Augustus John. She wore a gown designed by Charles James, whom she also met through Bessie. After the painting was finished, Elizabeth found the décolletage too daring for her tastes and had it repainted, thereby altering the cut of the frock.

James was one of the first American designers to be considered a serious force in haute couture but, to his dismay, his reputation meant little to Elizabeth Arden. In the future, she would often alter the cut of his clothes—especially after she had him where she wanted him—which was in her employ.

Through Miss Marbury, Elizabeth discovered that it was far more blessed to give than to receive. When she took up charities, she did it with the same thoroughness that she applied to her every other interest. She not only contributed generously to the Opera Guild and the Friends of the Philharmonic, but she also worked with some degree of dedication at every facet of the operation. Part of this diligence was inspired by having learned, from Bessie, an important ploy of society gamesmanship. If you want to meet the "right" people, get on a committee with them. When you're helping them to raise a couple of hundred thousand dollars, they can't very well ignore you.

The house that Arden built into the first of her beauty spas — Maine Chance, Maine — photographed when it was her home and before it was turned into a retreat for the tender loving care of wealthy ladies.

During Elizabeth's education, Bessie played the clever school-marm, careful to maintain a good relationship with the child's family. In the case of Tom Lewis, it was not a difficult chore. He was charming, much more worldly than his wife, and a clever trader. Bessie was Yankee enough to respect a smart shopkeeper.

For his part, Tommy found Bessie every bit as useful as his wife did—and for similar reasons. While she kept Elizabeth busy playing her brand of social games, Tommy was free to play his brand of social games.

Bessie invited both Lewises for a weekend at her summer home in the beautiful Belgrade Lakes country near Mount Vernon, Maine. Elizabeth fell in love with the region on sight. Unlikely as it sounded, Elizabeth exclaimed that she had always wanted a place of her own in the country, a place where she could get away from social and

Elizabeth and the ever-present pet animals at Maine Chance, Maine. Few realized that at one point she was an excellent horsewoman.

Beautiful flowers were always an obsession with Elizabeth. Here she was running true to form back on the early days in the garden of Maine Chance, Maine.

professional cares and be by herself. And this was such a heavenly spot!

Bessie cut right through a sigh on the beauties of it all with a practical comment. Adjoining her own place, a property of 750 acres was available. It was one of the loveliest sites on the lake and had been unoccupied since the main house was destroyed in a fire. If Elizabeth was not simply being polite and was really interested, she would start making arrangements for her to purchase it. Elizabeth looked questioningly at Tommy. Although his actual words were "It's a grand idea," he was just saying, "Yes, Miss Arden."

That was all Bessie had to hear to sweep into action. She supervised the deal with the real estate agent, contracted for the architect, builder, and landscape gardener. When Elsie de Wolfe was unavailable to do the decorating, Bessie contacted another friend, Mrs. John Alden Carpenter III of Chicago.

Elizabeth could not have been more delighted with the arrangement. Rue Carpenter's social credentials were vastly superior to anything that Elsie could offer. It was a contact she wanted to expand, and in addition to paying her handsomely, she wooed her. She opened her Chicago salon for Mrs. Carpenter's convenience and, through her, found her pet charity, The Cradle, a foundling home in that city.

During the construction and decorating of the house, Elizabeth's behavior was completely out of character. Except for giving an occasional suggestion, she let Bessie and her crew take complete charge. It was sufficient for her to be part of the scene as a constant weekend guest in her friend's house.

Tom Lewis was the one who named it, Maine Chance, which it had been for Elisabeth Marbury and was about to be for Tommy, who would find multitudinous reasons for remaining in town while his wife journeyed up to the place, and would eventually be for Elizabeth in the most unexpected way.

CHAPTER NINE

Depression and Divorce

By the beginning of 1929 Elizabeth already had passed her fiftieth birthday. The robust constitution and good looks that God had given to her, combined with the tender loving care that she gave herself, produced a physical appearance that could easily have passed for that of a woman of thirty-eight. As a half century seemed like an awfully long time to have been alive, she blithely dropped twelve years and became a woman of thirty-eight.

Chronologically, this meant that she had arrived in New York City at seventeen instead of almost thirty, which was within the realm of possibility. It meant that she had married at twenty-four instead of verging on thirty-seven, which actually sounded more reasonable than the truth.

A few years later, in a *New Yorker* profile on Elizabeth Arden, Margaret Case Harriman, converted the fable into an approximated editorial truth by stating, "In 1915, when she was about twenty-four, she opened a salon at 673 Fifth Avenue." For the perpetuation of that little conceit, Elizabeth very nearly forgave Mrs. Harriman for the vitriol that flowed freely through the rest of the article. Of course, she did not forgive *The New Yorker*. As a matter of fact, she threatened to cut off all advertising.

The only difficulty in lying about her age was that those around refused to keep abreast of her youth. Tommy was good-looking and energetic, but beginning to look frankly fifty, which was still younger than his years—but not enough younger. Her sister, Lollie, who had arrived in New York several years earlier and occasionally made hats for Elizabeth, created what was more a chronological crown of thorns than a chapeau. She refused to dye her hair or do anything else to care for her appearance. Worse than looking her age, she persisted in telling the world what it was. The same was true of Brother Will. Now, it was acceptable to have an older husband, but it did stretch credulity, somewhat, to have siblings almost old enough to be one's parents. Only Gladys was a saving grace—dear Sister Gladys who dittoed Elizabeth's age, as well as everything else about her. But what good did it do her? Gladys was in Paris.

By the end of the second decade of the twentieth century there were those who thought that Elizabeth really had found the fountain of youth. It seemed to them that cosmetics had been around forever and that Arden had been around as long as they had; therefore, she had to be at least eighty.

To the question of her being an octogenarian, Miss Arden gaily replied, "Let them say I'm over eighty. As long as I look under forty—it's good for business."

She could privately look back on what she had accomplished during her lifetime with some satisfaction. She had been born into the chaos of poverty and had created the order of wealth. Arden salons were opening up all over the world. The American wholesale division was grossing over $4,000,000 a year. Under the astute managements of Gladys in France and Teddy Haslam in England and the rest of the Continent, the European operation was almost as profitable as the domestic one.

Tommy was doing a brilliant job. In policing product distribution, he sometimes simultaneously looked after salon interests. That was the case when he closed out sales to hairdressers in England and France. He had heard that they were using the preparations to give facials and calling them Arden treatments. It was a firm rule that these could only be obtained at Arden salons or in stores licensed, by the company, to give the treatments.

Doing well in Europe and the United States was not enough for Tommy, he wanted to do well everywhere. He personally trained Frank MacMahon and sent him on a trip around the world, putting merchandise in stores in South America, Africa, Australia, and Asia. Wherever the treatment products did particularly well, Elizabeth made plans to open or franchise a salon. Within a year, she could boast, with some degree of truth, "There are only three American names that are known in every corner of the globe. Singer Sewing Machines, Coca-Cola, and Elizabeth Arden."

Her statement was later validated by the writer Heinrich Harrar. In his fascinating account *Seven Years in Tibet,* he commented that it was possible to purchase Arden products in Lhasa.

Everything was going well—too well. Elizabeth was getting restless. There was so little for her to do. She could not afford the luxury of idleness. That was for old people. The secret of her youth was endless activity and, where it did not exist, she had to invent it. She began to meddle in every area of the business. If Tommy complained when she reversed one of his decisions, she would wave her hand imperiously and say, "This is my business. You don't own a share. Nobody does except me." Her head bobbed, as she girlishly catalogued, "I am chairman and president of all the Elizabeth Arden companies in America and the lands across the sea."

Tommy retorted, "President, hell! You think you're the queen of the whole goddamned world."

Elizabeth could not disagree. A queen she was and, as such, she surrounded herself with a court. When her favorite beau, Henry Sell, took over the Blaker Agency, she gave him her advertising account. Henry was clever, and she could trust him both to be diplomatic with Tommy and remain fundamentally *her* man. He was charming and courtly, but it was his patience that enabled him to succeed with Elizabeth. It was often almost as if she was pushing him to see how far she could go. He managed to handle her small cruelties, her capricious whims, her lack of tact with an inexhaustible good humor, excusing all by rationalization. Janet Leckie, author of Sell's biography, *A Talent for Living,* explained, "A sixth sense told

Elizabeth Arden not to push this gentle man too far—not to rough him up, as she often did with her employees, servants, friends.''

Members of the staff at the agency were not recipients of this sixth sense and, consequently, did not share his benevolent attitude. Margaret Thilly, who was account executive, said, ''In reminiscing on the Arden years, they always bring a smile to my lips, but also the same old well-remembered tensions to the pit of my stomach. My vividest impression is of myself taking a quarter-grain Phenobarbital before going up to see Miss Arden. Even then, the proofs palpitated as I handed them to her.''

Leonore Buehler was the chief copywriter on the Arden account. Not only did Miss Arden never remember her name but, from time to time, she insisted on firing her. Miss Leckie described the sequence of events.

''It went like this: Elizabeth would call for Henry Sell and say: 'Hanque, I'm tired of Miss What's-Her-Name's copy. I think you ought to fire her and try somebody else.' Henry Sell, understanding well her capriciousness, would say he had fired Leonore and hired somebody else. When next he presented her with copy (which Leonore continued to write), Arden would say: 'I like these words much better.' Then, sometime later, would come the request . . . 'You know, Hanque, I think I preferred Miss What's-Her-Name's copy. Perhaps, you'd better hire her back.' This ploy went on for years, with Miss Buehler presumably being fired and Miss Smith, Miss Brown, Miss Jones, taking her place until the copy of Miss What's-Her-Name was wanted again.''

In her court, she needed the amusement provided by her wise jester, and so she had Wellington Cross recalled from England to take a position in the New York office. When he returned, he suggested that another ex-vaudevillian, Gus Minton, might make a good replacement for him abroad. She had lunch with the man, and though concerned that he might be a little too American for British tastes, she approved the appointment.

Minton obviously approached the job as if it were an acting assignment. He clipped both his mustache and his consonants and became more English than the English. When he returned, attired in Savile Row clothes with accent to match, Miss Arden ran into him in the corridor and said later to Cross, "What a nice Englishman. He should be working for us instead of You-Know-Who, your vaudeville pal."

Cross responded, "That *is* You-Know-Who, my vaudeville pal."

She never quite accepted that. English was as English sounded. When she needed some bootleg whiskey delivered to Maine Chance for a party, she said, "Get that nice Englishman to drive it up."

During Prohibition, transporting liquor across state lines was a serious offense. Minton was so fearful of the police that he never got out from behind the wheel during the whole trip, which, in those pre-superhighway days, was a long one, made still longer by the slow progress of the driver who was terrified of being stopped for speeding.

When he finally reached Maine Chance, Minton's legs were so stiff that he literally reeled across the lawn. Elizabeth caught sight of him and shouted, "You're drunk! And you're fired!"

Guesthouses and a bathhouse had recently been constructed, and like Topsy, the gracious little hideaway, at Mount Vernon just growed. The solitude that Elizabeth had claimed was her fervent desire must have been the loneliness of monarchs. To the irritation of Bessie Marbury, who had not expected to find an army encamped next door, Elizabeth moved in stately processions.

Merely inviting guests was not enough for Elizabeth. They had to be amused every moment of the day, and Elizabeth was so unnerved by her deteriorating relationship with Tommy, that she did not trust her own charm to be adequate to the job. She brought along hair-dressers and treatment girls to tend to the need of her guests. She also had the head of her exercise salon, Mildred Wedekind, and her girls to lead them in exercises and to perform classical and acrobatic dances. One guest said, "By the end of the weekend I was so exhausted by Elizabeth's treatments, and exercises, and whatnot that I went to bed for four days."

Elizabeth would not have understood this attitude. She reveled in all of the activities. There was nothing that any of the girls did that she did not attempt. One of her favorite escapades was to have Miss Wedekind stand on her head, back to back with her. The droll climax came when the petite Mrs. Lewis wiggled her behind and knocked the tall Miss Wedekind off-balance.

On Sundays in the country, Bessie had her tea parties in a rustic log cabin that she called her music room. As she was pouring, it was not unusual to see Elizabeth, followed by a gaggle of girls, garbed in Grecian tunics, trailing across the fields. Elizabeth would join the tea party and, much to the embarrassment of the other guests, command her employees to perform without so much as a lump of sugar to sustain them.

The horses, for there were horses, fared better. There was plenty of sugar for them, generally proffered by the hand of their cooing mistress. As trainer and riding instructor, she brought along a White Russian named Colonel Prince Kader Guirey. The prince spent his weekdays grinding powder in Elizabeth's factory. A number of noble

Elizabeth in sidesaddle habit, photographed at Maine Chance, Maine, back in the early days before it became a beauty spa.

exiles found employ in her empire, including a Persian prince, a Russian general, and several German grafs, but in those days, it was the White Russians who were definitely all the rage in New York.

Elizabeth was in no position to look too closely into the authenticity of the aristocratic names with which she surrounded herself. After all, she had created a name and rank for herself. With more commercial than regal laissez-faire, she seemed to think there was no reason why they also shouldn't, as long as they were clever enough to get away with it. At one point, she thought that it would give her products a distinguished air if she sent out a troop of dubiously royal émigrés to act as salesmen. It was not until there were massive complaints that buyers could not understand one often bogusly accented word they spoke that Tommy was able to put his foot down and restrict their activities to dancing in attendance on the new Tsarina, Elizabeth.

Despite the fact that most of her girls were supposedly on a holiday instead of a payroll, the costs of the little retreats to the country were astronomical. But 1929 promised to be the best year in Arden's history, and not even Tommy complained about his wife's expensive diversions.

Dorothy Gray was the only thing that disturbed the rosy glow of the first part of that year. Would she never be rid of that awful woman? She had erected her own building just up the street, at 683 Fifth Avenue, and had even had the gall to call it the Dorothy Gray Building. As if that were not bad enough, the little bitch topped it off by winning an architectural award for it.

Elizabeth flew into her husband's office on wings of rage. She cried, "Tommy, I must have my own building."

Before he could answer, he was rudely interrupted by the Depression.

All around them, there was instant mayhem, as hot water was added to economic woes. Firms, that had been in business for generations, suddenly collapsed. Unemployment rose at an alarming rate. Great tycoons were jumping out of windows, under the mistaken apprehension that it was the fastest way to the breadline.

Tommy decreed that there could be no thought of a new building, or of expansion in any direction, until they could judge how the panic was going to affect the industry. By the end of the year, there was devastation everywhere—except in the beauty business.

In 1928, the volume of product trade, for the beauty industry, was $500,000,000. By the end of 1929 the gross had risen to $750,000,000. Elizabeth observed, "The Depression seems to be good for our little business, dear. The more they chew their fingernails, wrinkle their brows, and pull their hair, the more they need us."

Having made that observation, she promptly went out and purchased 691 Fifth Avenue. Tommy was horrified at spending $95,000 for a property that would subsequently be worth several million. She calmed him. "Don't worry, dear. We'll pay ourselves $75,000 a year rent and make a nice little profit."

Rue Carpenter was contacted and told to drop everything to come east and decorate the new salon. Mrs. Carpenter was president of the Chicago Arts Club and a woman of great artistic sensibilities. She was very unhappy with the designer Elizabeth had chosen to work with her and suggested she send for Nicholai Remisoff. Elizabeth cried, "A Russian! Oh, let's get him, dear. I'm mad about Russians— uh—*White* Russians."

Remisoff might not have been White, but he wasn't Red either, and he did have impeccable credentials. He had studied at the Imperial Academy of Fine Arts, in St. Petersburg, and had served an apprenticeship with Diaghilev's great scenic designers, Bakst and Benois. On his own, he had designed *Chauve Souris,* which had been a tremendous hit in both Paris and Moscow. After the opening in New York in 1922, Remisoff had decided to remain in America and settle in Chicago, which was where he met Mrs. Carpenter.

When the artist arrived, Elizabeth showed him around the old salon. At the end of the tour, he said, "It's very rich—and very vulgar."

Tommy and Lanie closed their eyes, awaiting the onslaught but, to their amazement, Elizabeth positively purred. She was delighted with

:[141]:

both the artist and his response. Ever since the idea of a new salon had entered her head, there was nothing about the old one that did not distress her. Across an Aubusson carpet, from a Louis XIV desk, in the Oval Room, she exclaimed, "Tear it down, dear! I never want to see the dump again."

The new salon opened to an ecstatically enthusiastic press. They praised the classical severity of the entrance and reception room, which was permeated with touches of the completely *moderne* in the forms of jade-green glass walls and cut-crystal feathers to shade the wall lights. On the five upper floors, each done in its own striking decor, there were treatment rooms, exercise rooms, massage room, and rooms devoted to teaching tap dancing and fencing.

It was the beginning of her collaboration with Remisoff. From then on, he was to do every new salon and redo most of the old ones. When she purchased a penthouse apartment, at 834 Fifth Avenue, Remisoff did all the decor. She adored everything from the yellow and white drawing room, to the dining room with its Chinese wallpaper and chandelier imported from a Russian palace, to the bar with its prancing pink horses, to the sun-drenched, flower-banked, enclosed terrace. She lived there for the rest of her life, making almost no changes in the gracious clutter that was a part of the artist's original conception.

Remisoff later recalled, "Miss Arden was very intelligent. But she had no creative ability. She understood what I was doing and very seldom interfered. I was the only one she never fired. If we had a dispute, I would say, 'If you want this, hire somebody else.' She would bow. I would bow. And I would leave. The next day, I'd be back on the job and nothing more would be said."

Perhaps she had no artistic creativity, but she did have a sensitivity to color and design. She once halted production of the jars for a new product, because the shade of pink was off by an almost imperceptible degree. The correction cost an additional $100,000, but she considered that a trifle compared to the serious affront to her sense of color.

She had never liked Augustus John's portrait of her, and she made

The first Augustus John portrait of Elizabeth Arden painted in the forties which was superseded by . . .

. . . the famous second Augustus John portrait of Elizabeth Arden to which she had the gloves added at a later date. This one still hangs in the New York salon.

no secret of it. The artist was piqued. In his long career, there must have been many who had not liked his conceptions of them, but his reputation was such that very few had had the temerity to admit it. He offered to do another portrait with no commission or obligation to buy, but she replied that she could not spare the time to sit for him. He persevered, offering to come to her hotel and do a quick sketch which would not interfere with anything else that she had to do, and she agreed.

The second portrait was not as flattering as the first. With a few rapid strokes, the artist had captured an expression that revealed her shrewdness and her sometimes cruel capriciousness. Elizabeth had the perception to see that it was a better picture, and she bought it. Her vanity never permitted her truly to like the portrait, as a representation of herself, but she was proud of it as a representation of Augustus John at his best.

At the beginning of 1929, Elizabeth received an offer of $15,000,000 for her business. Tommy pressed her to accept it. To him, it represented freedom, but she questioned the nature of that freedom. Without the business, would she be able to hold him? Without it, who would she be? Elizabeth Arden would disappear, except as a corporate entity; she would become an anonymous woman named Florence Nightingale Graham Lewis. Rather than face that, she would remain the imperious Miss Arden to whom nobody dared say no. When she rejected the deal, Tommy swore that she would live to regret it, and she could only wonder what he meant by that and what the nature of that remorse might be.

Whatever qualms she might have felt about her decision, at the start of the Depression, disappeared as it deepened, and it became obvious that the industry was going to sail through it brilliantly. By 1935 Mrs. Harriman was able to observe, ''Arden's program of expansion has not abated perceptibly during the Depression. Ever since she found out that the cosmetics business was going to be one of the few industries to weather hard times with any profit (which it has done), she has followed her own inclination to treat the general financial disaster with what amounts to unconcern. 'This

Depression,' she said in its early days, 'is going to make a lot of manufacturers pull in, economize, cut down—and that leaves us a clear field.' Her salons in Los Angeles, Palm Springs, and Miami Beach, and four other salons in department stores have all been opened since 1929; and she has continued to extend her wholesale trade with a zest which causes some conservatives to prophesy gloomily that she will ruin the business by overexpansion. Arden can afford to be indifferent to such predictions. She is the sole stockholder and complete dictator of the business.''

Her unconcern about the Depression was manifest in a short article that she wrote (or had written for her) for the *Ladies' Home Journal*, in 1932. She told her readers that beauty and optimism went hand in hand. She advised them not to hoard new clothes, and that making themselves attractive was their duty to the times. Standards of living should not be lowered. Even rents should not be lowered. ''High ideals and high standards make for endeavor and accomplishment.'' However, if they were feeling the pinch, they could always cut out rich food and concentrate on vegetables and salads. She thought that sort of economy would be good for both beauty and health.

She concluded the piece with a rousing: ''Come on, women of America, let us smile. Let us work! Let us be cheerful—beautiful! Let us spend well and wisely. The crisis has passed. America is improving in health.''

By the time she reached the last line Florence Nightingale had triumphed over Elizabeth Arden. ''It is up to us to do the necessary nursing that means recovery.''

In 1932, Elizabeth was not alone in absurd rhetoric. The Presidential candidates were also indulging in it. Herbert Hoover was saying that, if people voted for Roosevelt, there would be grass growing on the streets. Franklin Delano Roosevelt was replying that, if they voted for Hoover, there would *be* no streets.

The politicians might not have believed what they said, but Elizabeth Arden believed what she said. Ever since Wall Street laid that egg, she had been scrupulously following her own advice and making certain that her personal standard of living was not lowered.

:[145]:

The lavish weekends, at Maine Chance, went on just as before. With new salons opening in Berlin, Cannes, and Rome, the European trips were often business jaunts, but they were conducted on as grandiose a scale as ever, complete with an entourage of favorites.

It was in Vienna, during one of these excursions, that Elizabeth chanced to hear a lecture given by Professor Steinach. The subject was diathermy treatments, the application of heat to tissues in the body by means of an electrical current. For thirty years, physicians had been using it for arthritis, rheumatism, and other inflamatory ailments. During and after World War I, it had proven extremely beneficial in the treatment of soldiers suffering from injured muscles and nerves.

Elizabeth immediately wondered if it could be adapted to serve as a beauty treatment for sagging muscles and deteriorating skin cells in the face. Her inquiries led her to a Dr. Last. She later claimed that she had collaborated with the doctor on the invention of the Vienna Youth Mask. More likely, as had been the case in her dealing with Swanson, she did no more than sketchily tell him what she wanted, and he did the rest.

The Youth Mask was a device made of papier-mâché and insulated with tin foil. It was fitted over the face of the client and attached, by conducting cords, to a diathermy machine. It was Miss Arden's contention that the electricity replenished the cells in a woman's face which she claimed, out of her "vast" experience as a dermatologist, died first under the eyes and then under the chin.

The medical profession would offer no corroboration for Elizabeth's theory. The most it would concede was that diathermy did stimulate circulation, but it added that it definitely could not restore dead cells. This rebuke did not deter the Arden salons from installing Youth Masks, nor did it stop hordes of hopeful clients from paying $200 for a course of thirty-two treatments.

The European tours were often so strenuous, that Elizabeth would stop at one or another of the great spas to take the water and rest but, even in repose, she was still on the lookout for some little novelty to bring back to her salons. At a Bavarian watering place, she found one that was subsequently introduced under the distinctly non-Germanic name of the Ardena Bath.

The bath consisted of applying a thick coating of paraffin from neck to heels. Before it was administered, a physician was called in to examine the potential bather. If a heart condition was discovered, ice packs were placed directly over the heart before the parafin was poured. Upon contact with the skin, the wax created a vacuum which induced perspiration. The loss of moisture was reputed to have two salutary effects: It meant a loss of weight, and it cleansed the pores, purging them of poisons and leaving a fresh glow on the skin. If glow there was, it was most likely the result of a gossamer-thin, glossy film of wax that persisted in clinging to the epidermis, after the bath was over.

The Ardena Bath was but one of the many goodies awaiting the loosely packed clients, who had persisted too long at the dining room table and, consequently, were about to endure too much in the Arden weight-reducing rooms. There were mats for bending and stretching, hardwood floors for tap and rhythmic dancing, boards that reclined the head a good eighteen inches lower than the feet, so that the clients' maltreated and displaced vital organs could slip back to where Elizabeth decreed they ought to be. When Elizabeth happened to be passing through the exercising rooms, she generally paused and ordered the clients to stop what they were doing and stand on their heads. She clapped her hands and gleefully exclaimed to her beef trust, "On your little heads! Come on, come!"

As the tides of fulsome breasts rolled back to meet the dunes of sagging chins, she shouted encouragingly, "We've got to stir up those little organs. Bottoms up!"

For those who wanted to dissolve the adipose in perspiration, without having to assume the rather degrading position of an unlit taper, in addition to Ardena Baths, there were steam cabinets and infrared-light baths. The client who preferred a sensual, rather than athletic or passive, approach to weight reduction, could have a series of massages or a whirl through the giant roller, a contraption of wooden cylinders, designed to "smooth" the pounds away.

Appointments in the exercise rooms were booked weeks in advance. Never before in history had a Shylock exacted a more profitable pound of flesh. As one operator summed it up, "We've got an instrument of torture here to suit the fancy of every fat ass in the world."

Unfortunately, there were no treatments in her salon for a stupid ass, and that was exactly how Elizabeth knew she was behaving toward Tommy, but she could not help herself. Things had really begun to get impossible after he infuriated her by insisting she sell her business, but it would be difficult to say if the actual breakup was brought about by jealousy, resentment of his increasing importance in the business, or hurt pride. Probably, there were elements of all three in it. The split most likely never would have happened had she not for so long acquiesced to the conditions of their marriage, if she had once put her foot down in her private life, as she had done so often in her professional life.

For years, she had tacitly accepted the fact that Tommy had his province in the business and that she had hers, and the two functioned almost independently of each other. Her total acceptance of this can be exemplified by what happened when Gordon Yates first came to work for the company. Yates, who was eventually to replace Haslam as the head of the European operation, was personally selected and trained by Tom Lewis. Weeks passed before he so much as laid eyes on Miss Arden. It was in the employee cafeteria that he recognized the unmistakable little lady standing next to him in the food line. He introduced himself, and she said, "Oh, yes. You're the new boy who's working for Tommy."

Lewis' functions grew larger and more varied, as hers diminished in scope. She could open new salons and busy herself with decorating them, but once they were launched, the running of them became more or less routine. There were long periods when there was nothing for her to do but meddle, and she began to interfere in things that had always been strictly Tommy's business. When this lady, who could easily separate a client from $100 in less than an hour, discovered that her husband was paying some of his salesmen as much as $75 a week, she flew into a fury, screaming, ''Don't you know there's a Depression on?''

The inside fighting abated for a while, when they were forced to join forces against a common enemy. Roosevelt's New Deal government had awakened to the importance of the beauty industry as a potential source of desperately needed revenue. The result was a bill before Congress proposing a 10 percent luxury tax on all cosmetics.

Protests poured into the legislators, from women all over the country, claiming that makeup was essential. In Philadelphia, women marched around federal buildings carrying placards that stated that lipstick was as necessary to them as toothpaste. But the lawmakers remained impervious. None of the gentlemen wore it, and a few even questioned the necessity for a dentifrice. They simply cursed themselves for having created this ruckus, by passing suffrage, and went on to enact the new tax.

Representatives of the leading cosmetics manufacturers met to agree on a common policy toward the new law. Despite their obvious prosperity, they cried poverty and decided to pass the tax on to the public. A woman, trying to look beautiful, was not going to stop trying just because it cost her $1.10 instead of $1.

The industry returned to good business as usual. Except for salesgirls having to say, ''Tsk-tsk,'' and ''Isn't it a pity?'' as they added the tax onto the bill, the new law was causing no greater pain than additional bookkeeping. The manufacturers were convinced all was serene, until they awakened a few weeks later to read an advertisement taken out by the ever-irritating Dorothy Gray. It announced that her prices would not rise, despite the new tax. Her customers would pay exactly what they had always paid.

Elizabeth countered with an ad informing her customers that she was giving them full value for their dollars. They were getting exactly what they paid for—even if it did include the tax.

The industry reconvened and passed a new resolution. They decided that cosmetics lines (lipstick, rouge, powder, mascara) would pass the tax on to the public, while the treatment lines (creams, lotions, tonics) would absorb it. It was a compromise designed to meet the challenge of Gray, whose largest business was in treatment products, and infuriate Arden, who had an equal investment in both.

Tommy raved, "They're cutting the business in half. Do you know what this is going to cost us in time and extra auditing?"

Elizabeth pouted, "It's just too silly for words. What good is a cleanser without some powder to cover what it reveals? One is as necessary as the other. And the public should pay all the taxes. After all, they elected those silly little men who are trying to ruin my business."

She conveniently forgot that because Bessie Marbury was a staunch Democrat, she had cast her first and last Democratic vote for Franklin D. Roosevelt.

With the tax problem resolved, more or less, to nobody's complete satisfaction, Elizabeth and Tommy returned to their private battle stations to resume their private little war that culminated in the strategic battle of the lipsticks. Until 1932, these came in only three shades—dark, medium, and light—designed to be worn by women with the three basic hair and skin tones. Not only lipstick, but all makeup coloration, was reduced to the three-part principle.

Elizabeth wanted to change this policy. She wanted makeup to match clothes. As a first step, she planned to bring out a kit of lipsticks in seven different shades, with fanciful names Charlot, Printemps, Coquette, Red Head, Viola, Victoire, and Carmencita. It would have been more explicit to call them for a green outfit, for a blue outfit, for a red outfit, and so on, but those designations would have had none of the mystery and glamor that Elizabeth well knew were essential ingredients to sales.

It was a revolutionary concept for the cosmetics industry, and Tommy could see no justification for it. He was doing very well with the old system. Elizabeth screamed, "God, you're stupid! Can't you see what it'll do for business? Instead of buying just one set of makeup to match her hair or eyes—each customer will buy several— one for each color she wears."

Tommy stubbornly resisted her arguments, but Elizabeth

prevailed, again reminding him, "It's my business! And I'll run it as I see fit. If you don't like it, you can get out!"

Elizabeth ordered the production of the seven-shade lipstick kit. To introduce it, she personally toured the country with a troupe of seven ballet girls. There were receptions planned in towns from coast to coast, and at each stop, Miss Arden would introduce the girls, individually dressed in costumes matching the different shades of lipstick. The dancers performed to "The Gold and Silver Waltz." The troupe was a spectacular success, making headlines everywhere they went.

While other manufacturers were caught short, scrambling to get multicolored lipsticks into the market, Arden continued to race ahead of them by being first to bring out mascaras, rouges, and powders in ensemble tones. Until Elizabeth took the color situation in hand, two or three "becoming" colors summed up the variety of most women's wardrobes. Redheads generally wore green or brown, blondes blue or pastels, brunettes red or black. Suddenly, Miss Arden told a woman that her face was not an entity, but an essential part of her costume—and she believed. The abolition of slavery to colors was one of her most enduring contributions to the art of cosmetics.

The lipstick victory proved to Elizabeth that she could run Tommy's end of the firm as well as her own, but she still did not make a move. She had years invested in Tommy. Except in business, she was uncertain of her ability to function alone and liked having a man on call, when she needed one.

With all the inadequacies she saw in him, Tommy was her husband, and there was enough Victorian in her to respect the sanctity of matrimony. There were other factors: her pride, she hated to admit failure, and her age—she was in her mid-fifties, no time to start living alone again.

Things came to a head over a treatment girl named Mildred Beam. Elizabeth had fired her for some trifling reason, and Tommy was caught embracing her. She was in tears, and it was generally thought that he was only comforting the poor thing. Duke Cross commented, "There was nothing to it. I'm not saying that Tommy was an innocent. Sure, there were girls. But not Mildred Beam. She wasn't his type. The truth of the matter is—she just wasn't attractive enough.''

Henry Sell agreed with Cross. Everybody agreed, but that did not stop the rumors, and rumors in a beauty salon become distorted and exaggerated with each repetition. By the time they reached Elizabeth it was a long-standing affair. They had been making a fool of her for months.

Elizabeth thought that it must have started the summer before, when Mildred had been included on one of their European trips. With her convenient memory, she completely disregarded the fact that it had been she who had insisted Miss Beam join them and that Tommy had evinced absolutely no interest in her beyond the easy charm he displayed commonly to all the members of their group.

She hired a detective, but it only made matters worse. He turned up all manner of evidence about several other treatment girls, but nothing on Mildred beyond a stale scandal that did not involve Tommy. A man named Clarence Baring had attempted to kill his wife, some ten years before, with arsenic and fever germs. The motive was his passion for Miss Beam, but the girl had been proved innocent of any complicity in the crime.

Elizabeth conceded, ''That's something. But it's not enough.''

The detective told her there was nothing more. She cried, ''Tommy's bribing you. Get me what I want, and I'll pay you more than he can.''

Each time the man returned, it was to tell her about Tommy's infidelity with some other girl in the firm. It was unbearable to think that she had been betrayed by her girls, her ''little dears.'' She shouted that she no longer wanted to hear about any other girls. One was bad enough, but how could she publicly admit that there had been a string of them?

Trouble in the Lewis household soon became common knowledge throughout the company. Bettie Hamilton was the perfect Arden girl. She was hard working and soft-spoken, free to travel wherever the company sent her, resourceful, and pretty, with fair coloring and even features. To Elizabeth's way of thinking, she had only one flaw—she was plump. Elizabeth would look at her and say disgustedly, "God, you're fat!"

Bettie would reply cheerfully, "Isn't it lucky for you that I think with my head and not my rear end?"

They got along. Many of Elizabeth's tantrums were thrown only to see how far she could get with people. If they stood up to her, without standing in her way, she was pleased. If they both stood up and stood in her way, God help them. Bettie stood her ground but was wise enough to stand aside, whenever Elizabeth came plowing through.

In 1933, Bettie was giving demonstrations at the Daniels and Fisher store in Denver, when a wire arrived from Lewis instructing her to direct all correspondence dealing with the firm to him at another address. It puzzled her, and she started to ask around about it. The same wire had gone to all the salespeople, buyers, and salons. The next day there was a contradictory wire from Elizabeth, ordering them to disregard the first message.

Tommy had made his move, and he had blundered badly. He had attempted to cut Elizabeth out of her own business. The wires were a crude, obvious trick, and he should have realized that it would be only a matter of hours before she learned about them.

Lewis did not own one share of Arden stock. He had no claims to her business and, consequently, had committed an act that could be made to look like criminal fraud. When he arrived home that evening, he found his bags neatly packed and waiting in the lobby. The door and elevator men had instructions not to permit him back into the penthouse. He was never to set foot in it again.

This latest incident completed the picture. After leaving Arden, Mildred Beam had set up in business for herself, under the name of Jane Cloud, at 724 Fifth Avenue. Elizabeth had wanted to drive her out of business by telling stores that purchased Cloud products that Arden products would no longer be available to them. Tommy prevented her by pointing out that she could be brought up on charges of restraint of trade. It was clear to 'Elizabeth that the reason he had done this was because he was in partnership with Miss Beam. She had wondered how the girl had raised the money to open a business, and now she thought she knew. Tommy had backed her.

Elizabeth ordered a purge of all those who had been close to Tommy or Mildred Beam. Among the first to be discharged was her own brother, William Graham. Another was a girl named Dorothy Cook, who had spent five years working for Arden as a credit auditor. The result of this dismissal was a $100,000 slander suit.

According to Miss Cook, Elizabeth had descended upon her, exploding right in her face, "You are dishonest! You are a cheat! You are a dirty sneaky liar! You are a traitor!"

Dorothy said that she had gasped, but Elizabeth flared right on, "Every day clients come here with letters from Jane Cloud. You have stolen and given her a complete list of my clients. You are suing my clients to chase them away from me. You should have been fired long ago. Get out of here!"

In reply to Miss Cook's suit, Elizabeth reiterated her charge that Dorothy Cook had supplied her competitor with a list of her clients. And, in a desire to drive some of her best clients over to Jane Cloud, Dorothy had then sued the clients, in Elizabeth's name, for non-payment of small accounts.

The slander suit dragged on for three years and was finally dismissed by Supreme Court Justice O'Brien, who declared that Miss Cook had failed to show that Miss Arden had uttered the alleged slanderous epithets. Nevertheless, the language sounds suspiciously like Elizabeth's when she was on a rampage.

In regard to Tommy being a partner in her business, Miss Beam publicly declared, "It is a vile canard. Mr. Lewis has nothing at all to do with my business, which, incidentally, is prospering nicely, thank you, and he hasn't put one penny of his money into it."

Whether or not Elizabeth inched her out of business, it was not too long before Jane Cloud went up in a cloud of smoke and never again descended to the beauty mart.

As long as Tommy had played it cool, protested his innocence, and remained faithful to the Arden organization, there was little that Elizabeth could do without a sacrifice of her own pride that she was unwilling to make. By sending the wires and encouraging Mildred Beam, he provided her with a spur to action that was irresistible.

A few days later, Elizabeth's attorney contacted him with an offer. In exchange for a cash settlement, he was to permit her to file for an uncontested divorce, in Maine, on the grounds of mental cruelty. Moreover, he was to remain out of the cosmetics business for five years.

He had to accept. At worst, the alternative was criminal charges. At best, it was a protracted lawsuit that he could not afford to wage and, probably, would not win.

After fifteen years, during which he had almost single-handedly built the Arden wholesale division into an enterprise that grossed several million annually, his severance pay was $25,000.

CHAPTER TEN

Maine Chance

Throughout the difficult days with Tom Lewis, Bessie Marbury had been Elizabeth's main support and source of comfort. There had never been another person toward whom she had directed such a depth of feeling. Bessie could be trusted to say whatever was necessary about the iniquities that the male sex inflicted upon the fair flower of femininity, and say it with the good humor of an old campaigner who had a certain grudging respect for the more honorable representatives of the enemy.

Having Bessie close to her provided a large part of the strength that enabled her to go forward with the action against Tommy. With her friend at her side, Elizabeth knew that she need never be lonely again, nor would she ever again be betrayed. She was relieved that there would be no more men in her life, and that she would be able to stay in her garden cultivating bud after bud of beautiful women.

Her attitude toward her business approached the evangelistic. She continually reiterated her own creed of female emancipation. "Every woman has the right to be beautiful. And with my help, they will achieve their rights."

It was her way of proclaiming that she was the power and the glory to all womankind. She would triumphantly survive Tommy. Bessie had opened her eyes to the vision, and she saw herself a goddess on a mountaintop, worshiped by millions of adoring women, all pleading with her to bestow on them the gift and secret of loveliness.

Just when she was feeling most omnipotent, the vision momentarily faded, and she was once more betrayed and alone. Bessie did the one totally unforgivable thing: She died.

Elisabeth Marbury had been a powerful figure in society, the arts, and politics for almost forty years. Her funeral was remarkable for the huge turnout of the celebrated and influential. The police commissioner ordered all traffic on East Fifty-eighth Street halted to allow free access for the cortege.

After Bessie's death, a memorial committee was formed seeking to endow and maintain her Maine home as a shrine to the memory of her life and ideals. The project was to install a library and museum for the use of the people of Maine, and the committee, headed by

Even when sitting on the grass at Maine Chance, Maine, Elizabeth wore her favorite jewels — a string of pearls with a round diamond clasp and an emerald-cut diamond ring.

Cobrina Wright, included Mrs. Franklin D. Roosevelt, Mrs. William K. Vanderbilt, Miss Anne Morgan, Lady Mendl (the former Elsie de Wolfe), and Elizabeth Arden, who was still known as Mrs. Thomas J. Lewis. To carry out the plan, it was estimated that it would be necessary to raise $50,000. The sum was considerably reduced when Mrs. Lewis purchased the Marbury place and presented it to the committee. Mrs. Wright discreetly remarked, "Mrs. Lewis was a close friend of Miss Marbury's."

Things did not quite work out the way the committee planned them. Money was still very tight and, for all the ladies' noble sentiments, Bessie was not a national figure. Except for Elizabeth's generous gift, contributions were almost nonexistent.

Elizabeth grew impatient with the proceedings and retreated to Maine Chance but, naturally, not alone. Weekend after weekend, the house was cluttered with guests, and treatment girls, and exercise girls, and riding masters. It was a deliberate attempt to re-create the happier times she had known there with Tommy and, more important, with Bessie, but there was no longer any joy to be found in them. When they were not dull, they were painful rather than pleasant reminders of better days.

One Saturday afternoon, Henry Sell and she were seated a short distance from the others, watching the gay proceedings. She said disgustedly, "Look at the lot of them. Hanque, this is costing me a fortune—and I'm not getting any fun out of it."

Sell told her about a man, with a place in Lake Placid, who had found himself in a similar predicament. Instead of closing his house and sending his guests away, he turned it into a club and charged them dues. It was the beginning of the very fashionable Lake Placid Club.

"Hanque, what a wonderful idea!" Her eyes roamed, slowly taking in her own property and finally coming to rest on the neighboring Marbury house. She smiled pensively. At the time, Sell could not have known that her vision was of something very different from the resort he had described.

The mountaintop. The Shrine. To Bessie. To beauty. To women.

An elite cult of those who were already rich and also wanted to be beautiful. A place where no male would be permitted, except in the capacity of a servant, and every female would go through the painful, purging ritual of dedicating herself to Aphrodite and to Artemis, the virgin goddess of the moon who once changed the hunter into the hunted stag for doing no more than gazing upon her maidens.

In practical terms, her Maine Chance would combine the elements of a very posh women's club with those of one of the great European health spas. The guests would spend their days in the exhausting pursuit of beauty and their evenings in the display of it for their mutual and private delight.

A full year was devoted to putting Maine Chance in readiness for its new role. Rue Carpenter was called in to make the decor and accommodations still more lavish. Magnificent gardens were planned and planted, after it had been decided that the color scheme would be red, white, and blue for the United States and pink for Ardenaville. A swimming pool was installed, and more than a dozen new buildings for housing guests, treatment rooms, steam rooms, exercise rooms, changing rooms, and recreation rooms. By the time Elizabeth opened the place to its first guests, it represented an investment of $200,000.

At most, there were twenty guests per week who were served by forty servants, including six gardeners, and who paid between $250 and $500, at the nadir of the Depression, for an average weight loss of six pounds a week. Elizabeth had spent months going over the details of how each moment of their day was to be spent. She had commissioned Gaylord Hauser to design a diet that was delicious, nutritional, and phenomenally low in calories. Breakfast was served in bed. Bea Lillie once described the beginning of a Maine Chance day. "You wake up in the morning with someone pushing a rose in your face. And with it comes the day's schedule: rise at 7:30, breakfast at 8, mud packs at 8:15, steam baths at 8:30, exercise at 9—hup, two, three, four."

With all due respect to Miss Lillie's amusing sneer, those breakfast trays were lovingly set with the most delicate pink linen, bone china, and silver. Elizabeth explained, "The poor dears get so little to eat—

:[159]:

the least we can do is make sure they enjoy what they're eating it off.''

The costumes for the day never varied—drab terry-cloth robes, hideous exercise outfits, and shapeless bathing suits. The guests went through a daily routine of weighing, exercises, paraffin baths, massages, facials, and swimming. Hair was set twice a week, but there were scalp treatments and fresh makeups given each afternoon. If they had any free time, they could take advantage of the bowling alleys, tennis courts, six horses, badminton court, or speedboat.

In the evenings, the ladies assembled for vegetable juice cocktails (a bottle of liquor in one's luggage meant immediate expulsion from this paradise) and dinner. Gone were the monotonous clothes of the daylight hours, as they paraded before each other in the most ravishing gowns, expensive furs, and rare jewels.

At first, Maine Chance made little or no profit, but that did not matter to Elizabeth. The place had a special meaning for her. In her advertisements, she proudly boasted of its utter dedication to vanity. ''You experience at once the most rare and wonderful feeling. It springs from the fact that, for the first time since you were a child, you are utterly without responsibility. Everything is planned for you. You don't have to think of anyone but you. You are—and you love it—absorbed in yourself, selfishly and unapologetically. There is only one thing demanded of you. And, again, it is a childlike thing: you have to obey the orders written on your little slip every morning.''

As part of the Maine Chance opening celebrations, in the summer of 1934, Elizabeth hostessed an enormous Democratic rally in honor of the memory of Elisabeth Marbury. Bessie had made it a tradition to give one each summer, but in her wildest dreams, she could not have envisioned the lavishness of this party.

The sumptuous, rich, and magnificently served food, proffered to the invited guests, was a far cry from the meager repasts set before the paying guests. Lest temptation get the better of them, the pampered darlings were quarantined in their quarters across the lawn.

In addition to the local Democrats, thirty-five were invited up from New York, all expenses paid. The private railroad car that took them to Maine was equipped with a special chef, lavishly stocked bar, strolling accordionist, and a hostess to introduce them to each other. Upon arrival, they were requested not to tip the servants. On Monday, those journeying back were given their choice of prepaid transportation by motor, rail, or air.

The celebration was only fitting, for Elisabeth Marbury, at last, had her shrine. When the committee could not raise sufficient funds, Elizabeth withdrew her offer of the Marbury house and added it to the Maine Chance compound, where it remained a favorite retreat for guests for years to come. What more suitable tribute to Bessie could there be than a house filled with maleless women?

On October 5 of that year, Elizabeth Arden paid a visit to Augusta, Maine, where Florence Nightingale Graham Lewis won an uncontested divorce action, on the grounds of mental cruelty. Upon returning to New York, she hired a broken-down actress, named Hedda Hopper, in an amorphous capacity. Mrs. Hopper had an aristocratic bearing and fair Nordic face, which recommended itself to Arden, the business woman. She had appeared fleetingly in a number of films, which recommended her to Arden, the devoted movie fan.

At that point in her life, the actress had failed at everything—stage, screen, marriage, motherhood—she would also fail at Arden, but the story had a happy ending. She was soon to enjoy enormous success as the world's second bitchiest gossip columnist. First position was held by another Arden *aficionada*, Dorothy Kilgallen.

The girls spilled gallons of printer's ink singing Elizabeth's praises in newspapers all over the world. They worked for rival syndicates, which only doubled their worth, for it meant the paeans were in separate sets of dailies. While the columnists were doing their sister act, placing Elizabeth in the company of such immortals as Kay Francis, Lilyan Tashman, and Mona Barrie, *Consumers Report* and *New Republic* were doing exposés on the evils of the cosmetics business. Despite the drubbing at the hands of the intellectuals, Miss Arden grew richer and more celebrated. It only proved that a boost by a bitch was worth more than a pan by a pundit.

Elizabeth took to the road in an effort, as Tennessee Williams once put it, ''to find in motion what was lost in space.'' She toured all the salons in the States, and then she crossed the Atlantic to visit the European establishments, taking along Maud Eily as traveling companion.

In London, they put up at what Elizabeth called, ''that nice little red brick hotel, where everybody is so nice to me.'' She stopped at Claridge's all her life and never once referred to it by name.

In Paris, it was the Ritz. There was a time, when she would have stayed with Gladys in her elegant flat at 4 Rue Fabert, but her sister had barred her after returning home one afternoon to find all her lovely things rearranged, in rooms repainted in colors of her selection. Elizabeth never did understand Gladys' reaction. ''Sister, I don't know why you're so angry. I did it for your own good. I couldn't stand the grubby way you were living.''

When Gladys married the Vicomte Henri de Maublanc, making her the first cosmetics lady to marry into the aristocracy, it was her turn not to understand Elizabeth's anger. Perhaps, she had forgotten that the name of the game was ''me, too'' and not ''me, first.''

The Nazi party had banned the use of makeup at meetings of their women's organization, but that did not prevent the Berlin salon from making a lovely profit on the wives of its leaders, nor did it stop Elizabeth from accepting an invitation to dine at the home of the Hermann Görings. After the meal, she graciously thanked her host by telling him, ''You're too fat.''

Before he knew what was happening, the head of the Gestapo was on his head, shaking up his ''little insides.'' Elizabeth giggled all the way back to the Bristol Hotel. She told Maudie, ''I'd have had him touch his little toes, if I thought he could find them.''

Elizabeth paid for her moment of dictatorial power on the very next day, when Herr Göring requisitioned the salon's bicycle exercising machine, for the further glory of the Third Reich. Very shortly after she returned to New York, mention of the Berlin salon disappeared from her advertisements. She had experienced a bit of Fascism and had decided that it was not good for business.

Although Elizabeth's enmity toward her brother, Willie, continued, it did not prevent her from being extremely fond of his three daughters, Beatrice, Virginia, and Patricia. Beatrice bore a strong resemblance to her and was her favorite, but she became exceedingly close to all three girls during the years following her divorce and Bessie's death. That winter Beatrice had the opportunity to make her debut, at the Ritz Carlton Hotel, together with a school friend who was very much socially registered.

Elizabeth took command. She was determined to make it the most beautiful ball of the season. She wanted the room decorated in multicolored cellophane festoons, with cellophane Prince of Wales feathers in pale pink, and stretching twelve feet high. What she had in mind was a combination of Nicholai Remisoff and the setting for the recent premiere performance of the Gertrude Stein-Virgil Thomson opera *Four Saints in Three Acts.* She hired one of the production's designers, Kate Lawson, to execute the decor. Hedda Hopper was among the guests and commented, "Kate did a grand job—if you like pink cellophane ruffles."

For some time, Elizabeth had been employing wellborn women who found themselves in embarrassed circumstance because of either revolution or depression. They were called into service to provide a guest list that would be as tinseled as the decorations. Grace Blakely Kaiser, whom Miss Arden once had hired only because she wore such lovely lingerie, came through with a cluster of Palm Beachers including Stoatsburys, Munns, Phippses, and Marjorie Merriweather Post. Born a Post Toasties Post, Marjorie always reverted to her maiden name between marriages. It was less confusing that way.

Princess Ketto Mikeladze, an Arden buyer, brought the international set, including Grand Duchess Marie, a cousin to the late czar, Prince Serge Obolensky, Prince Alexis Mdivani, recently separated from Barbara Hutton, and Count Kurt von Haughwitz-Reventlow, waiting to be married to the same Miss Hutton.

Elizabeth looked around at the assemblage and thought that, at last, she had reached the social pinnacle. She was being flattered, pampered, and courted by the people who mattered most in the world. Walter Winchell saluted the party by calling the young debutantes, "the cellophane celebutantes of the year." Elsa Maxwell dubbed it "the best debutante party ever." The year before, she had been similarly effusive about another ball and, in the years to come, the debuts of Gloria Baker, Brenda Frazier, Cobina Wright, Jr., and a parade of others, halted only by war and Miss Maxwell's death, would receive the same accolade. Sic transit Gloria Mundi, Gloria Vanderbilt, and Gloria Jones.

Molly Collum, who would soon play an important part in Miss Arden's life, was among the more attractive and less column-worthy guests. Her escort was Owen Davis, Jr., who managed the Skowhegan Playhouse, which was not too far from Maine Chance. It was the beginning of Beatrice's ambition to be an actress, an aspiration that her aunt felt offered little to a girl who had made her debut at the Ritz, especially a girl with no talent. Pat Young later summed up her sister's career, "I think she was once an understudy in a road company of *I Married an Angel.*

A thirty-five-year staffer in the New York salon recalled, "Bea gave her best performance playing her aunt. She'd come into the salon and order everybody around and throw fits if things weren't done her way. Oh—she was Miss Arden to a T. They were strange girls, all of them.Virginia was supposed to be the great writer. She did some copy for us. Once Miss Arden asked her to write the message for a Christmas card. When she came back with it, Miss Arden went all over the place, showing it to everybody, saying her neice was a genius. None of us had the heart to tell her it was the Twenty-third Psalm. And Pat—we all said, 'Yes, Miss Arden' a lot—that poor girl had to live it."

During the second summer of Maine Chance, Elizabeth again sponsored a Democratic rally in memory of Bessie. In her memoirs, Miss Hopper described the event from the point of view of three celebrated paying guests.

"During the festivities, I heard a hiss from an upstairs window. I risked a peek and there, leaning out, were Constance and Norma

Always with an eye to wooing the press, Miss Arden photographed with the late newspaper columnists Hedda Hopper and Cobina Wright, Sr. At right Ferdinando Sarmi as usual in attendance.

Talmadge, and Constance Carver, ex-wife of Adolphe Menjou. When they got my eye, they jerked their thumbs up, whispering hoarsely, 'Come up! Come up!'"

"I looked around for my hostess. She was nowhere in sight, so I went upstairs to learn that my friends had been there ten days. They were busting to tell me a yarn.

"Having had just enough food during their stay to maintain life, when they smelled turkeys, hams, and chickens roasting, pastry baking—all these delicious smells from the kitchen—they went berserk.

"Waiting till all the help had gone to bed, they sneaked down to the kitchen and stole a whole turkey, took it back to their rooms, and ate it. Now they were trying to figure a way to get rid of the carcass.

"Then someone remembered seeing a shovel leaning against a tool shed in the backyard. So they sneaked downstairs, when everything was quiet, got the shovel, stole into the woods across the highway, dug a hole, buried the evidence, sneaked back, went to bed—and had the first good night's sleep since their crime."

The gathering was the second and last Democratic rally that Elizabeth ever held. From then on, she returned to her basic Republican instincts. "Those terrible little Demmies have no gratitude."

After enjoying her hospitality, the local Democrats had done nothing to prevent the Maine legislature from passing a law making it mandatory for cosmetics manufacturers to pay $1 for each different product sold in the state. Why, it was going to cost Elizabeth Arden $108 a year.

Considering her Maine income, it seems a pittance, but there was that part of her that was and would remain poor, struggling Florence Graham. To it, the hundreds of thousands and millions that Elizabeth spent glibly meant nothing. Those huge sums were unreal, because they were beyond her conception—but $108 was real—it was a bloody fortune.

Suddenly, all sorts of restrictions and regulations were closing in on her. It was a totally new and perplexing experience. From the beginning, it had been she alone who had made the rules by which her companies were run. She had been responsible to nobody in the fulfillment of her personal manifest destiny of spreading the cult of beauty throughout the world. If she had been freewheeling, improvising her creed as she went along, she had done no more than those great pioneers who, in the furtherance of the national manifest destiny, had spread the cult of this nation from coast to coast.

Now, there were fences going up, and the open range was closing. Others were imposing, upon her, higher laws than her own, and she resented it bitterly. It was an infringement upon her rights and privacy, and she retreated into a political conservatism from which she was never again to emerge.

Actually, there was not a new law or proposal that really affected her. Out of a private sense of justice to her employees and clients, she had voluntarily complied with most of them long before anybody thought of making them a part of the law, but their existence, as legislation, threatened her. She was a benevolent despot who, after giving her people everything they needed, found herself threatened by a perplexing revolution that would gain them nothing that she had not already bestowed. It was irrelevant that there might be other companies, less fair and scrupulous, that needed control. She was her own measure of standard and behavior. How dare anybody question her?

Elizabeth resigned from the New York Federation of Women's Clubs, when it started investigating the feasibility of licensing beauty shops. Ultimately their investigation led to a bill being passed, by the New York State legislature, calling for the licensing of salons and cosmetologists. She had nothing to fear from it. Her salons and girls were of such quality, that they could be used as models for the highest possible standards of excellence. Still, she bristled. When a group of clubwomen came to explain the situation, she shouted, "It's the principle! You don't know enough to judge what's right or wrong in my business!"

The NRA set a forty-eight-hour week, eight-hour day, as maximum time, and a $15-a-week minimum wage. It did not affect her help, who earned far more than the minimum wage and were more than adequately compensated for overtime, but she was incensed. She screamed at her manager, "These standards should be set by me and not imposed upon me."

She was a rugged individualist who never got over the resentments which were always based upon a feeling of personal outrage. Years later her San Francisco manager, Lillian Macmillan, telephoned to inform her that a new California law made a five-day week mandatory. Her vituperation was so violent and irrational that it almost seemed to Miss Macmillan that she was personally being held responsible for the actions of the lawmakers. She finally pleaded, "Miss Arden, believe me, it's not my fault."

Miss Arden responded, "God, you're stupid! Where were you when this dreadful thing happened? How could you permit it?"

"I'm not in the legislature."

"I don't care to hear your feeble excuses—"

"If you want my resignation—"

"They can't tell me what to do! I make the decisions around

here!'' The receiver was banged down with such violence that phone wires must have trembled clear across the nation.

A week later, Miss Macmillan received a lovely bracelet and a note which read, ''Keep up the good work. Sincerely, Elizabeth Arden.''

Along with it, she got a formal letter from the home office stating that in the interests of the well-being of her staff, Elizabeth Arden had generously decided to grant them a five-day week. The law was never mentioned in the official announcement. It was Miss Arden's decision and Miss Arden's benevolence. That made all the difference—that, indeed, made it law.

By the mid-thirties there were not yet any outside laws that could govern the vital areas of her business—what she intended to manufacture and how she intended to market it. She was determined to prove, to the beauty world, that she could manage her affairs without the help of Tom Lewis. There was already gossip that she was incapable of doing it. Competitors were gleefully saying that Tommy had made her and that his departure would ruin her.

Although she rarely showed them, there were moments of personal doubt, moments when she longed for his presence in both her private and public lives. Lanie would casually mention having seen Lewis on the street, and Elizabeth would tartly ask what he had to say for himself, to which Lanie would reply, ''He said to give you his love.''

''Did he?'' A half-smile would appear on her face, which she would quickly obscure in a rustle of papers and a rush of orders.

She loudly swore that she would go it alone and never again depend upon anybody. Hers would be the final, the ultimate, the only word—and she would flourish. But the silent doubts remained. She often paused before an important decision and pulled Duke Cross aside, to ask, ''How would Tommy do it?''

Sometimes she heeded his reply, and other times she deliberately disregarded it in an effort to prove her complete mastery of the situation. The radio program was an example. Elizabeth wanted to sponsor Eddy Duchin and his orchestra on the air in a program also

Elizabeth when she had her radio program on NBC in the thirties.

featuring the dramatization of a "beautiful" wedding and the latest gossip of a society columnist.

Both Henry Sell and Duke pleaded with her not to do it. Radio advertising was for mass markets. Her specialized trade would not benefit from it. Duke said, "Tommy always turned down radio proposals."

"Did he, really? Well, he wasn't always right, dear. I think I know my business. I'm signing the contract."

From the first show, Elizabeth realized that she had acted hastily, and trouble developed almost instantly. Each week, she would find an objection to an item from the gossip columnist. "She's my client. He can't say things like that about her."

To a song, "That number's soupy. Change it."

To a marriage. "Are they kidding? Next week, we can have them back with the story of a beautiful divorce."

Her summation of the dress rehearsal was always the same. The minute the closing theme was over, she was on the phone, from the sponsor's booth, shouting, "It's terrible! It can't go on the air! I won't pay for it."

"Oh, yes, you will. We've got a contract." The station official would gently hang up on her, while the whole company watched the dumb show of her continued assault. Those who could read lips blushed.

She viewed the network with what they called "typical Arden suspicion." She began to suspect that they were cheating her on the time, and she became determined to get every second due her. She hired a man who timed horses at the racetrack to sit in the corner, stopwatch in hand, and time the broadcast. He inevitably told her that the time was accurate to the fraction of a second, and she invariably replied, "No wonder you haven't picked a winner in years."

At the end of the first period, the radio show was not renewed. The mistake had cost her $200,000, but she persisted in not taking the advice of those she paid to give advice. It was the beginning of the

Arden revolving door. Managers came and went; agencies came and went; people, on every level of employment, came and went. There was only one criterion. If they agreed with her, they remained, and if they disagreed, they were out.

The policy did not prove sound business. In the two years following her separation from Lewis, she lost $500,000 and had to draw on the European company to keep going. After the fifth manager had left in a period of three years, she meekly said to Duke Cross, "You pick one this time."

Duke said hesitantly, "There is one great guy. Harry Johnson."

"Get him for me."

"The trouble is—he works for Helena Rubinstein." Elizabeth's eyes began to sparkle, and she showed real enthusiasm. She would give anything in the world to steal somebody from "that dreadful woman."

"Get him for me, Dukie. Oh, do get him! I don't care what it costs."

Johnson had heard of Miss Arden's record with managers. It cost a five-year contract at $50,000 a year. Although she generally avoided contracts as if they were some highly contagious disease, she gleefully signed this one and momentarily considered mailing a copy to Rubinstein.

After Johnson examined her books, he said, "I'm going to need a first-rate comptroller to straighten out this mess."

She shrugged. "Hire one."

"The best in the business is over at Madame Rubinstein."

She happily clapped her hands and exclaimed, "Get him! Get anybody you need."

By the time Johnson was finished eleven people had crossed the line from Rubinstein to Arden. Madame bellowed, "'That woman' is stealing my people! I will get even!"

It was the start of a policy that was to cause pain to several of the people involved and great amusement to the rest of the cosmetics industry. "That dreadful woman" raided Arden, and "that woman'' counterraided Rubinstein, until a metaphorical rut was worn in Fifth Avenue, as help continually tramped back and forth between Rubinstein, at 715, and Arden, at 693.

Toward the end of the year in which Johnson went to work for Elizabeth, Madame Rubinstein was lunching with a *Harper's Bazaar* editor, named Elinor McVickar. She asked, ''What do you think of that woman's husband?''

''Tom Lewis? A very bright man.''

''Good. He comes to work for me. But you mustn't tell a soul. I leave for Australia tomorrow.''

The day of the expiration of Lewis' agreement not to work in the cosmetics industry, he went to work for Helena Rubinstein. That ''dreadful woman'' had scored a decisive but slightly Pyrrhic victory. As he had never been great before he worked with Elizabeth, so was he never great after he left her.

CHAPTER ELEVEN

Early Starts

In the summer of 1931, just as her marriage was beginning to falter seriously, Elizabeth discovered a new love. It was to sustain her through all of the difficulties that she would have to face in the years ahead. So strong was this attachment that there were times when she considered giving up her business for it. No man or woman ever laid a claim on Elizabeth's heart to compare with what she could feel for a frisky, prancing, doe-eyed yearling.

During the Saratoga racing season, the Lewises accepted an invitation from an old friend, Fred Johnson, to spend a long weekend at his cottage in the famous old spa. Johnson was a prominent horseman, and they were invited to the many parties that were almost as vital to the great stable owners as the horses they bred.

The couple presented their usual winning public facade. Elizabeth was particularly charming and charmed, for these simple animal lovers bore names like Whitney, Vanderbilt, Payson, and Belmont. It was almost as if the doors of those great Fifth Avenue mansions, that had so thrilled her when she first arrived in New York had at last opened to allow her a peek inside.

The decade-long winter of the Depression had descended upon the rest of the nation, but in Saratoga, the summer was as brilliant as ever. The beautiful ballroom of the old Grand Union Hotel glowed with a *fin-de-siècle* magnificence, and those who could still smile in the face of the death of a world as they knew it kept time to a funeral march that sounded to them exactly like a waltz.

At nineteen, Alfred Gwynne Vanderbilt was already possessed of the dark good looks and sophisticated air that were soon to make him society's candidate for the kind of worship usually inspired only by film stars. When he asked her to dance, he thought it no more than a polite gesture to a rather pretty, older woman, but to Elizabeth, it was dreamtime. She closed her eyes, allowing the years to slip from her in a five-minute whirl around the floor.

Cinderella was in the arms of Prince Charming, and she had better not lose her dainty glass slipper. It would be too mortifying to have him discover that it was lined with old newspapers.

Sam Riddle watched the graceful couple and said, "You know, I like that woman." His companion raised a jeweled finger and smoothed an immaculate eyebrow that had all but been removed by one of Elizabeth's operators. Sam laughed. "She's a doer. You wouldn't understand about that, my dear."

Of the people who accepted Elizabeth during that first Saratoga season, Samuel D. Riddle was destined to be the most important to her. He owned a lovely old house on Union Avenue that has since become a part of Skidmore College. He was distinguished, socially eminent, and not at all interested in her sexually. In short, he had all the attributes she found most attractive in a man. He also happened to be the owner of a darling little horse named Man o' War.

At the track, one afternoon, Sam listened patiently to one of Elizabeth's monologues devoted to the glories of her business. At length, he interrupted her by saying, "You know, you ought to get yourself a hobby."

After the races, she requested that he take her down to the paddocks for a closer look at the thoroughbreds. She fell hard for one of the stallions and made straight for his stall. A stableboy called out, "You better keep out of there, ma'am."

She gave him a supercilious look. "Don't worry, I know all about horses. I was raised with them."

"You don't know about that one. He's in a dangerous mood."

Sam Riddle, the owner of the famous horse Man o' War, and Elizabeth back in the days when he helped her start her racing stable.

Elizabeth at her farm in Lexington, Kentucky, photographed with two of the ''darlings''—Blue Fantasy and her colt by Bemborough.

She lifted the latch and entered, calling gaily over her shoulder, "Nonsense. That sweet little baby wouldn't harm a hair on my head."

That "sweet little baby" was a snorting nine hundred pounds of nervous horseflesh with an ornery gleam in his eyes. For a few seconds, all breaths were caught as she walked straight up to the animal and started to caress him. "That's my little darling," she cooed. "That's my sweet little love."

Breathing was resumed when, to everybody's astonishment, the horse started to nuzzle her and behave as docilely as a newborn colt with his dam. When she came back out, the stableboy muttered grudgingly, "Lady, you've got more guts than sense."

Elizabeth laughed. "I've been told that before."

Sam Riddle shouted, "That's it, Elizabeth! Your hobby. Horses!"

"Hobby-horses?" She laughed still harder. As they were returning to their box, she commented thoughtfully, "You know, Sam. You might have something there. I've always had a way with horses. Ever since I was a little girl."

In the beginning, she thought that she had neither the time nor the facilities to do anything but raise a few show horses. Her first acquisition was a half Arabian, named Leading Lady. It was not long before she purchased three more, Lady in Black, Old Gold, and Cherry Red. With the latter two, she won blue ribbons at horse shows all over the East.

After Elizabeth's horse took first place at one of the important shows, Riddle congratulated her, and she said, "Thanks. But it doesn't have the same thrill as the turf. As a matter of fact, it's beginning to bore me."

"Naturally," he replied. "The only excitement is in the races. That's where you belong."

"I don't know enough about it."

"That's easy. I'll teach you." She quickly accepted his offer. Again, the Arden luck was riding high, for she could not have found a more knowing or patient instructor.

Leslie Combs was another man who entered Elizabeth's life very

Elizabeth and her neighbor from Kentucky, Leslie Combs 2nd, at the Belmont Ball in 1953. Although not so friendly in later years, Elizabeth can take credit for helping him achieve success in horses and breeding.

Miss Arden at Monmouth racetrack with two of her nearest and dearest—Katie Cross, the wife of Duke Cross, and Sam Riddle of racing fame.

early in her racing career. Combs was eventually to become one of the greatest horse raisers in the world, but at the time he met Miss Arden, he was most famous for his talent for finding moneyed track novices who would employ his talent for breeding and boarding their fledgling stables. As Elizabeth's adviser and manager of her horses, he was able to grow with her, so that, by the time she was the most successful woman in racing, his Spendthrift Farm had become one of the best breeding establishments in the United States.

The year that Bessie Marbury died, Elizabeth took time away from Maine Chance to rent a cottage at Saratoga for the racing season. Lewis, who was still trying to patch their threadbare marriage, came along, but she had little time to devote to any groom but the one who was attending to her horses.

She had recently acquired a little horse named How High, with which she had already won a $1,440 purse at Aqueduct. Despite the fact that it was a pittance compared to what the upkeep of her horses cost, it was a figure that she could understand and sold her on the idea that racing was not only fun, but could be made to pay. She began to tell interviewers, ''If I ever sell my business, I'll devote my time to horses.''

This must have been particularly aggravating to Lewis, since she had refused to sell her business to devote her time to him.

Elizabeth was in the market for horses, a good trainer, and the best jockeys. A pair of brothers, Sammy and Joe Renick, were among the best riders in the business, and she was determined to have Sammy work for her.

Duke Cross was her house guest on the weekend that she finally got Renick to agree to come around and see her. They made a date to meet at her cottage late one evening. Extremely nervous, she needed something to take her mind off the impending interview and dragged Duke off to the local movie theater, promising, ''It's a marvelous picture. I've been dying to see it.''

''What about dinner?''

She disposed of food with a fluttery wave of the hand. ''People eat too much.''

The ''marvelous picture'' turned out to be a maudlin little number, called *Smilin' Through,* and Elizabeth wept copiously through it all. At its conclusion, Duke got up and prepared to leave. She pulled him back down into his seat and, wiping a last little tear away, sighed, ''Wasn't it thrilling? We've got lots of time. Let's see it again.''

''But dinner—''

''Get a candy bar,'' she snapped crossly.

He shrugged. ''I'm not hungry anymore.''

''You see? The less you eat, the less appetite you have. It's good for you.''

Duke was doubly bored through the second showing, but Elizabeth cried just as heartbrokenly as she had the first time around. In place of the dinner they craved, she would often submit her escorts to a double helping of the most lachrymose fare in town. A tasteful cinematic fadeout was far more satisfying to her than anything that happened on the other side of the bedroom door.

Renick and Elizabeth sat downstairs, drinking and talking enthusiastically about horses and races. Tommy had already gone to bed, and Duke sat on the sidelines listening quietly, as the conversation grew louder and more animated.

A sleepy and disgruntled Tom Lewis appeared at the top of the stairs and asked angrily, ''Do you know what time it is?''

Elizabeth cocked an eye at his pajamas and replied calmly, ''Time you were in bed.''

With that, she sweetly returned to Renick and inquired, with a flirtatious smile, ''You were saying—before we were interrupted?''

She did not address another word to her husband, who had no recourse but to withdraw, muttering imprecations under his breath. It was, indeed, the end of a love story.

Renick came to work for her. Having watched her help come and go, he said, ''She was a liberal woman, but one who registered her prerogative as a woman and wasn't loath to change trainers at a whim.''

As he later learned, she did unto jockeys as she had unto trainers.

By 1935 the business began to gain the ground it had lost when Tommy left, and Elizabeth was deeply committed to her stable, spending money to build it up as quickly as the company could earn it, sometimes, more quickly, causing one of the most profitable enterprises in the cosmetics industry occasionally to totter on the brink of ruin. She belonged to both the Belmont and Saratoga Racing Associations and rented horse barns at both tracks. She also took a cottage, year round, at Belmont and another, for the season, at Saratoga. She linked her two major interests in aphorisms that were beginning to be widely quoted.

"Treat a horse like a woman, and a woman like a horse. And they'll both win for you."

"I judge a woman and a horse by the same standards. Legs, head, and backside."

Both Gladys and Swanson made discoveries that contributed to the profits with which Elizabeth supported her expensive new hobby. Swanson came up with the formula for what has been called Elizabeth's most successful preparation, Eight Hour Cream. It actually did contain medical properties and worked so well on skin eruptions, abrasions, and burns that children's hospitals used it for treating these afflictions in the young.

Elizabeth would personally offer it to clients with her own special endorsement. "You must try this. I use it on my horses."

At the same time that Swanson was developing the new cream, Gladys was discovering a wonderful new perfume that had been concocted by a chemist in Grasse, in the south of France. She leased it in the name of the Arden Company and dispatched a flagon to Elizabeth, along with a list of possible romantic-sounding French names for the fragrance. Elizabeth took one whiff and said it would be called Blue Grass, in honor of her horses. One of her managers complained, "You'll never sell it with that name. It'll remind people of manure."

He was wrong. Blue Grass was a winner, the largest-selling perfume she ever manufactured.

By the time her sixtieth year arrived Elizabeth Arden had succeeded, in business, beyond any dream that Florence Graham had ever had. Reviewing her career, *Fortune* magazine wrote:

"She has probably *earned* more money than any other woman in U.S. history, and she has done it by commanding the sun to stand still until she got the right shade of pink in a bottle, the right texture of cream in a jar, and a ribbon tied *just* so around a hundred-thousand soapboxes.

"It is not for volume of sales that Arden is noted, nor for number of accounts, nor for eveness of distribution. Arden is noted for being tops—in the "treatment" cosmetics business. In this chancy field of enterprise, ruled by high price, high style, and high tension, Arden was first to arrive, and she has been the Tiffany of her trade for all the years since then. Other lines, other salons, most notably those of Helena Rubinstein, may grow and prosper, but none have yet been able to achieve the size or, more important, the prestige of Elizabeth Arden's own particular business."

It would probably have been enough for any other woman of her age, but Elizabeth was not any other woman, or it would never have come about. And she was certainly not her age—by physical looks, mental outlook, or verbal admission.

There were great areas of her that remained untouched, unrealized, unfulfilled. She could not afford to remain idle, or the ever-pursuing specter of Florence Graham would overtake her and lay claim to the inner emptiness. Elizabeth had to remain in control of every area of her being to make certain that she would not be possessed by Florence. To win the race with herself, she needed her swift and beautiful horses.

She could love these sensual creatures without being threatened by them. They were the children who could absorb the ferocious maternal instinct that had once been sublimated into the creation of an industry. They were the incentive demanded by the compulsive need to win, a need that still remained unsated for all that she had already conquered.

On a different level, the horses provided access to the world of high society to which she so desperately desired to belong. Her critics said that she had a servant's respect for the rich. It went much deeper than that. They represented property to a tenant farmer's daughter. Those, who would laugh at her foibles, might take a closer look. In a way, her social climbing started another fashion; today it is society that is courting its hairdressers, cosmeticians, and dress designers. Poor Elizabeth was simply again ahead of her time. In the contemporary world, those she once courted would be scrambling to climb to her level.

Miss Arden's approach to owning a stable was exactly the same as her approach to her other great love, the cosmetics business. The quintessence of this philosophy was that she had to be in complete charge.

This brought about inevitable conflicts with trainers, jockeys, and stablehands. When they disagreed with her, they were out. The same revolving door that stood in front of her executive offices was swiftly erected at the entrance to her stables. But she did hire the best people in racing, and they came to work for her because, even if they were fired within the first week, she guaranteed them a full year's wages.

In the first five years of the operation of her stable, she gradually increased the scale of her operation but, in the process, bought more than her share of disappointing yearlings. The stable ran in the red for seven years, causing a drain on the business, but she did not cut back on any front. She went on paying herself a salary of $75,000 a year, while her living expenses (and this was a low tax period, during a great Depression) mounted to $200,000 a year. The Arden Company had to make up the difference and completely maintain the upkeep of her stable. When she bought seven yearlings for $54,000 during a single week in the late thirties, she telephoned her manager and told him to pay for them—and he did.

Loss and costs were irrelevant, for she was convinced that she would eventually win, and was only doing what she had always done, spending money to make money. Working on her private equation of horses to cosmetics, she startled the racing world by decorating her Belmont horse barn as tastefully as she did her salons.

The barn was painted in her racing colors, cherry-pink, white, and blue. Plants were hung over the stalls, and soothing music was piped in; they were even sprayed with Blue Grass perfume. Blue and pink cashmere blankets protected her little darlings from draughts, and the jockey's silks, custom-made of the finest taffeta available, were sent to the best dry cleaner in the city, a man who ordinarily handled only Paris originals and charged prices very nearly as exorbitant as the original cost of the garments.

After accustoming themselves to the garish extravagance of the boudoir decor, the trainers daily had to adjust to the sound of Elizabeth cooing baby talk to the horses. They were even more unsettled by her fretting that ''this little darling's ankles are hot'' or by being ordered to drape a blanket over that ''poor perspiring baby.'' One trainer commented, ''When I was a kid, my mother used to say—only horses sweat. People perspire. That's not true in Mrs. Lewis' stable. Over there, the horses perspire. It's the trainers who sweat.''

There was no king, in the sport of kings, who lived more royally than an Arden horse. They were fed only the finest blue clover, so as not to ''upset their little tummies.'' When one of them became ill, Elizabeth called the Mayo Clinic. The indignant specialist refused to diagnose for a horse, and she said, ''What would you do if he were a baby?''

''I wouldn't enter him in the Santa Anita handicap,'' the doctor tartly replied and hung up.

In place of twenty-five-cent petroleum jelly, the horses' bruises were treated with $10-a-jar Eight Hour Cream. Twenty-dollar-a-gallon lotions were used in place of the more than adequate $2-a-gallon fly spray, because Miss Arden objected to the odor of the spray. Her olfactory nerves were again offended by horse liniment. ''That smelly stuff can't be good for the little darlings.'' From then on, they were rubbed down with Ardena Skin Lotion, which began to arrive in enormous demijohns, just as it had in the early days of the salon.

After a while, the preparations mysteriously disappeared almost as soon as they arrived. Some of the stableboys had started a nice business of selling her goods at half their normal retail prices. When Elizabeth learned about it, she did not know if she was more shocked by the undercutting of her business or by the stealing from her little darlings. She put a stop to it by having the factory make up the stable orders in scent-free lots.

As outlandish as some of her ideas were, she did institute a few innovations that became standard practices. She insisted that her horses' legs be massaged for twenty minutes before and one hour after races. The Eight Hour Cream proved as good for horses as it was for women and began to appear in stables all over the world.

As she had in the early part of her career, Elizabeth played a name game in the racing world. The original name of her stable was Mr. Nightingale, taken from her own middle name. She had often changed her marital status, but this was the first time that she changed her gender.

Within a few years, she changed the stable's name to Maine Chance. She saw no difference between putting a horse in shape and putting a woman in shape, and there was no reason why her separate establishments, devoted to these two different activities, should not share the same name. As she said, "Thoroughbreds are like women. They must be petted and cared for in the same way."

Her own track name was never Elizabeth Arden, nor was it Florence Nightingale. For racing, she had other identities. At first, she was known as Mrs. E. Graham Lewis and, subsequently, reviving the marital misnomer with which she had started in business, she was Mrs. Elizabeth N. Graham.

No matter what name she dreamed up for herself, Elizabeth Arden was the only identity that interested the world. Chanel was right, when she said, "There is only one Mademoiselle in the world, and that is I; one Madame, and that is Rubinstein; and one Miss, and that is Arden. Why should any of us give up these titles, that we have earned and made famous, merely to assume some man's name?"

Even to the social types that she so assiduously cultivated in the horsey set, the thing that weighed most heavily in her favor was their desire to know Elizabeth Arden. Jock Whitney responded to her overtures, because there was a favor he wanted from Miss Arden that had nothing to do with horses.

Whitney and David O. Selznick had formed a company to produce films in Technicolor. As their first production, they had scheduled the original version of *A Star Is Born*, which was to star Janet Gaynor and Fredric March. Before they could start, they had to solve the problem of makeup. Ordinary picture makeup looked artificial and was too heavy to wear comfortably under the very hot lights necessary for color.

Whitney asked his new track colleague if she would go to the Coast and try to come up with a cosmetic that would work for the new process. A Whitney request was the same thing as a command to Elizabeth, and she was off to Hollywood with one of her best chemists in tow.

After a few weeks of experimentation, she came up with a line of preparations that worked perfectly for color filming, and she started a firm called Stage and Screen to manufacture it. However, there was not enough profit in it, and she soon got out of it. Elizabeth was not sufficiently interested in film society to waste time and money on it. After all, those people had backgrounds that were even more obscure than her own.

While she was on the Coast, she was invited to visit the set of the movie version of Clare Boothe Luce's play *The Women*, which had an important sequence that took place in what was obviously supposed to be the Arden New York salon. She was shown the Metro-Goldwyn-Mayer duplication of her premises and became enraged. ''Those walls! They're only paper *trompe l'oeil*. In my salon, we use real marble.''

The set designer reassured her, ''On screen, it will look real.''

''It's phony. They always told me Hollywood was a phony town. Now I know what they mean.'' She marched up to the director, George Cukor, and screamed, ''It's a fake! Take my name off, or I'll sue.''

Mr. Cukor replied, ''Your name doesn't appear.''

''I'll still sue. Everybody will know it's me.'' Mr. Cukor was famous for his talent for handling difficult women and had directed such temperamental creatures as Greta Garbo, Joan Crawford, and Katharine Hepburn. In *The Women* alone, in addition to Miss Crawford, he had Norma Shearer, Rosalind Russell, Joan Fontaine, and Paulette Goddard. But nothing had prepared him for Miss Arden on a rampage. It was only after screening the completed film for her that she calmed down. After it was over, she said, ''Why, that's a very nice little picture. You only made one big mistake. You should've used my name.''

Her first horse trainer was Clarence Buxton, but she did not hit her stride until after she had fired him and his five successors. Lucky number seven was Louis Fuestal, who had been recommended by Sam Riddle, for whom he had developed Man o' War. But luck played no part in Fuestal's first year with Arden, for it was the year of her first big fire.

In March, 1937, Leading Lady, Lady in Black, and Old Gold all were destroyed in a blaze in her barn at Belmont Park. To help replenish the lost stock, she purchased a yearling, Great Union, for $9,200. The grandson of Man o' War, the horse showed great promise immediately, and some even spoke of him in terms of a good Kentucky Derby entry. But it was at Saratoga, not Churchill Downs, that Great Union really came through for Elizabeth. As a three-year old, in 1939, he won her first major stakes victory, the Merchant and Citizens Handicap. After the race, she was able to tell an interviewer, for the Saratoga paper, that her stable was in the black, at last.

Eight was Elizabeth's favorite number, and she always bet it, when one of her own horses was not running. It was eight years after she bought her first horse that she won her first big race. She had arrived in New York in 1908 and had been born in 1878. She had opened her first salon at 503 (totaling eight) Fifth Avenue, and it was eight years later, after the end of World War I, that she was at the post ready to start the big race for dominance in the cosmetics business.

CHAPTER TWELVE

That Dreadful Old New Deal

By 1936 American women were spending $4,000,000 a year at the hairdresser's, and Elizabeth Arden realized that it was the propitious moment to open hairdressing departments in her salons. Although it was not generally known, she was already in the hair business, as owner of a small establishment, Au Printemps, at 3 East Fifty-third Street. It was run as a completely separate unit from the salon, and only good customers knew that they could finish off their Arden treatments by having their hair done just down the street.

The time had come to amalgamate. Most of the salons were in financial trouble, and there were tidy profits to be made in hair and nails. Elizabeth was ever the good theatrical manager and wanted to launch the new venture with a suitable amount of newsworthy publicity. She had to find a gimmick, for there was nothing very dramatic about another hairdresser in a town filled with them, and she settled upon her favorite device—snob appeal.

The French were considered the greatest coiffure experts. Their American counterparts were forever seeking an identification with them. Every little Jake with a permanent wave machine advertised himself as Jacques, and every little Gertie with a hair dryer was automatically Giselle. Elizabeth decided to import the genuine French article. She dashed off a note to Gladys telling her to find a good hairdresser and send him over as quickly as possible.

Guillaume started in the New York salon with a tremendous

fanfare of advertising and press interviews. Once the Frenchman's name was established in the fashion magazines, she intended to take him, and a group of his assistants, on a national tour that would inaugurate hair departments in all the salons. Along the way, assistants would be dropped off to take charge in key locations, and others taken on and personally trained by Guillaume, until there was somebody schooled in his methods at every one of her establishments.

Elizabeth adored going on tours and swooping down unexpectedly on one of her salons. She would say gleefully, "It keeps everybody on their toes, dear."

Almost as much as touring, she loved moving her personnel around. "A little new blood perks up the old arteries." The most trusted girls constantly had to be ready to pick up and move to another city and salon. Whether because of or despite her temperamental outbursts, they usually went where they were told to go without a murmur of complaint. She had the most remarkable gift for instilling loyalty. No matter how taxing her demands became, her girls thought of her as kind, considerate, and generous. Indeed, most of them had a still deeper feeling. Elizabeth was family, and you didn't stop loving a sister or mother simply because she was a little short with you.

Although Elizabeth professed a reciprocation of this familial attitude—"my little London family," and "my little Chicago family," and "my little Los Angeles family"—her real attitude toward them was that of a master chess player's toward the pieces on the board. If necessary to win the game, they were abruptly shifted at her discretion and with no thought to the disorientation that it might cause in their private lives.

One of the earliest girls, Sally Bulkeley, moved from New York, to Washington, to Palm Beach, with side excursions to Europe. Rose Mornay annually shifted from New York, to Palm Beach, to Southampton, to New York, and back to Palm Beach. Genevieve Cliff Daily jumped from Boston, on the Atlantic, to San Francisco, on the Pacific. At a moment's notice, the demonstrators were pulled off the road and placed in a particular salon for months at a time and then, just as suddenly, put back on the road. And everybody from everywhere had to be ready to travel with Miss Arden, whenever she felt the need for a change in companions.

To many, these moves appeared to be another example of Elizabeth's capriciousness, but they were not. She knew exactly what she was doing, and they were part of a grand design for the successful operation of her business. There was only a limited number of trustworthy girls who were free to move, and there was a constant supply of salons in need of bolstering. The next best thing to straightening them out herself was to send a representative who had been trained to do it her way.

As for those singled out to be her traveling companions, they filled her lonely need and, at the same time, bound the girls to her. They went first class all the way. They got to see and do things that were very different from their ordinary lot in life. And they got to know a very different Miss Arden, a gay and elfin creature who was more like a cozy school chum than a tyrannical employer. Connecting doors between adjoining hotel rooms would be left ajar; two train compartments would be converted into one large bedroom. Sometimes they would give each other facials and exercise before retiring, and other times Miss Arden would run a pink ribbon through her hair and giggle. "Let's go to bed without taking off our makeup. But you mustn't tell a soul. It'll be our little secret." Then the stories and reminiscences would begin, the confidences be exchanged, and they would talk, in tittering whispers, until the early hours of the morning and, occasionally, fall asleep chastely holding hands. Although few realized it, the girls had spent the night sharing dreams with little Flo Graham, still on the verge of her great adventure.

After they returned, many lived in hope of another invitation. It served Elizabeth's purposes very well. It made them work harder, while also giving evidence to their less fortunate colleagues of what could be theirs, if they earned it.

The addition of hair, manicures, and pedicures very nearly completed Elizabeth's plan for the establishment of one place where a woman could satisfy all of her cravings for beauty—an elegant and expensive supermarket of feminine vanity. She was already carrying exclusively designed handbags and negligees, scarves, and a limited amount of ready-to-wear clothes. It was just the *haute couture* that was missing—apparel designed especially for Arden, made to order for her clients, and available only at her salons. She started hiring people like Terry Quinby and Helen Cornelius, women who had fashion rather than beauty background, but she was not ready to go all the way. The time was not yet right. In a few years, it would be, and Elizabeth would be prepared to face ''the new and glorious challenge.'' At an age when most of her contemporaries were looking forward to enjoying the benefits of the new Social Security laws, she was still looking forward to enjoying glorious new adventures.

There was nothing extraordinary about that. Elizabeth had never behaved like most of her contemporaries or like most of anybody else. While they had all been worrying about whether or not they would survive the Depression, she had survived it largely by ignoring it. When the stock market crashed, she bought a building on Fifth Avenue, as well as a lavish penthouse on the same street. She never halted her plans to open new salons and the early thirties witnessed Arden debuts all over the Western Hemisphere—Rio de Janiero, Buenos Aires, even her hometown of Toronto. One wonders if she was ever tempted to call that one, the Florence Nightingale Graham Memorial Salon.

While other prices declined, hers rose, as she introduced one lavish item after another. At one of the lowest points in the financial disaster, she brought out $20 fitted handbags and relied on her special little girls to put them across. Her trust was not misplaced.

Bettie Hamilton was working as a demonstrator, in the Arden section, at Daniels and Fisher, in Denver. When the handbags arrived, she called Miss Arden and told her that there were complaints from the regular salespeople. Although it was the pre-Christmas season, the best for sales of the year, they claimed that they would not be able to push such an expensive novelty. Miss Arden replied sweetly, ''You take over, dear, and see what you can do about it. If you do it yourself, dear, I'm so sure it will work out very nicely, that I'm shipping you another batch.''

When the multimillionaire theatrical producer Helen Bonfils entered the shop, Bettie pounced on her, announcing that she had just the right present for Miss Bonfils' mother. Miss Bonfils looked at them and said happily, ''Not only Mother. Everybody on my list. It makes life so easy. I'll take them all—and as many more as you can get.''

Bettie smiled, thanked God and Miss Arden (not necessarily in that order), and said, ''A new shipment will be in before Christmas.''

By the mid-thirties, there were twenty-nine Elizabeth Arden salons, nineteen in the United States, and the rest scattered all over the globe. She was the sole proprietor of all except the two in France. To avoid confiscatory French taxes on foreign-owned firms, she had given them to Gladys, along with the entire French business. The gift was subject to her control and would revert to her, should anything happen to her sister. Aside from anything else, she did not trust Henri de Maublanc, who consistently made the mistake of condescending to her.

Elizabeth was the complete and only owner of all of the rest of her companies and persistently never saw any reason to go to the trouble of separating her personal finances from those of her business. This attitude led to her first battle with the government.

The Democratic administration was becoming difficult about separating income taxes from corporate taxes. When the Internal Revenue auditors came to examine her books, they were stunned by the complete jumble of firm and personal expenses. they demanded an explanation, and she responded, ''It's my money. I can spend it as I choose, can't I?''

''No, Miss Arden.'' The statement was followed by the most ghastly silence. Bessie Marbury had been completely wrong. That horrible little man in the White House could not be good for the country. Why, he was trying to ruin her with that dreadful old New Deal of his, and what was bad for Elizabeth Arden was assuredly bad for the nation. His minions had dared to say the unspeakable to her. They had said *NO!*

It took the government men and her own accountants weeks to arrive at her tax base. It was finally accomplished by a juggling act that would have been more at home in Barnum and Bailey than in the realms of mathematical calculation.

Were it not for her compulsive expansionist tendencies and her zeal for perfection (coupled with her expensive love of horses), she would never have suffered a losing year. She felt that every Arden customer should be able to find precisely the product she needed. During a decade when everybody else was concentrating on a few large-volume items, she was manufacturing 108 different products and stocking them in 595 separate shapes and sizes. A great many of these were what are called boarders. They either just about made back their cost or were losers, eating into the profits of those items that showed large and healthy returns. The big money came from creams, tonics, and face powders, while eye shadows, lipsticks, fitted bags, mascara, and a slow moving army of fluff all fell into the boarder category.

It did not matter. She persisted in a policy that no other head of a large corporate body would have permitted. If there was no more than one customer, who wanted a specific product, it had to be available for her.

A woman, in Bangor, Maine, loved one of the first lipstick shades that Elizabeth Arden ever produced. It had been long out of the line; but the woman persisted in ordering it, and Miss Arden decreed that she should have it. The royal order meant that manufacturing devices had to be cleansed of current dyes, the old lipstick shade remixed, and the machine reset for it. Each of these lipsticks cost about $300 to make, but nobody could dissuade Elizabeth from filling the order. That woman was being loyal to one of her products, and she would return that loyalty by providing her with what she wanted.

The great source of the company's new financial troubles was the wholesale division, where it had traditionally both made its expenses and its large profits. It was not that Elizabeth had changed any of Tommy's methods—she actually held them as sacred as the Scriptures—but between the horses and salons she did not have the time or patience to run the wholesale with his combination of tact and rigid control. The operation became sloppy and unprofitable. This was a delicate business that took everlasting attention to details. During the years of managerial insecurity that followed Tommy's departure, it seriously faltered. It was not until the advent of Harry Johnson that things began to pick up.

Johnson did for Arden what Tommy was unable to do for Rubinstein when he went to work for her. He galvanized Lewis' system by adding twenty-five years of experience, during which he had traveled around the country for various cosmetics manufacturers and built up an amazing following of buyers. Where Johnson went, they went.

There were other factors, not strictly connected with business, that counted strongly in his favor. Working with Madame Rubinstein had taught him how to handle an extremely volatile iron butterfly. The education stood him in good stead during his years with Miss Arden. Another great asset was that he loved the races. He knew about horses and was an extremely adroit handicapper. This enabled him to do what nobody else had been able to do with Elizabeth— change the subject. When the lipstick war threatened to turn bloody red, he had reserves from a more peaceful common sphere of interest to bring up.

The Lewis system, perpetuated by Johnson, was based on an elastic but interlocking sales force. At the top were ten high-powered salesmen, earning between $7,000 and $17,000 per year, with commissions and expenses added to that. After the debacle of the White Russians, the only outside qualification that Elizabeth demanded of her salesmen was that they be over six feet tall. Caesar may have wanted to be surrounded by fat men, but Miss Arden preferred tall ones. They gave her the pleasurable delusion that she was dainty and helpless.

Bert Chose was the best and highest paid of this impeccably groomed corps. He was the Pacific coast representative, and one of Elizabeth's particular favorites. Like Miss Arden, he had originally worked for Squibb. They first met in Los Angeles, where he was introducing the newly acquired Squibb Lentheric line. For its debut, he arranged an extremely imaginative, large display of flowers. The moment she saw it she knew that she wanted the man responsible and took a special pleasure in hiring him away from her former employers. Elizabeth never thought twice about stealing the competition's help, but when they did it to her, she screamed, "It's outrageous! Foul play! It must be against the law!"

In addition to the salesmen, fifteen "Arden women" worked under Harry Johnson's jurisdiction. These personal representatives floated around the country in a perfumed cloud of pink powder, through which could be glimpsed the loveliest complexions imaginable, and from which sounded carefully modulated debutante drawls. In the thirties they were paid an average of $7,000 per year, plus expenses.

It was the expenses that rankled Elizabeth, and she was continually trying to find ways to cut them down. At one point, she bought a building on East Fifty-second Street in which she wanted to house and feed the demonstrators, when they were in New York for meetings or training. They rebelled. Beneath the gentle aura of refinement, these were tough ladies of the road, and they refused to be kept in a dormitory like schoolgirls. In due course, the boardinghouse was converted into a warehouse.

She was quickly discouraged from trying another of her money-saving ideas. She wanted to buy a company plane that would be used to pick up the Arden women at the end of day and either transport them to their homes, to sleep in their own beds, at their own expense, or to their next stops, in which case, they could sleep on the plane and save hotel bills.

It was pointed out, that the distances between representatives was so great that it would take several planes, and even so, the weather might not permit them to land. She replied, "That's the beauty of it. Commercial airlines might be frightened by a little snow or rain. Not me. With my own planes and my own girls, I can do whatever I like."

Miss Arden in front of the Fifth Avenue salon complete with two standbys—the famous red door and its doorman, ''Fred.'' A friend's poodle leads the way.

Elizabeth Arden in front of her shop on Worth Avenue, Palm Beach. The red door was the trademark to the entrance of her salons throughout the world.

Miss Elizabeth Arden with some of her guests from New York who came to Chicago for the opening of "The Elizabeth Arden Building" on fashionable Michigan Avenue. Left to right: Mrs. Patricia Young (Miss Arden's niece); Mr. Earl Blackwell; Colonel Serge Obolensky; Miss Arden; and in the background, Mr. Joseph Kingsbury-Smith.

"A lot of the towns we visit have no airports."

"They will. Soon, every fair-sized town will have an airport—just like they have train depots." She threw up her hands and grumbled, "The trouble is—nobody around here has any vision except me."

The plane went the route of the boardinghouse, and she continued to pay expenses. But the ladies produced wonderful results, and they were worth it. When one of these magnificently groomed ladies arrived in some small city, the department store had already paved her way with large announcements in the local papers. As "Miss Arden's personal representative," she was given possession of the most prominent cosmetics counter, and the customers crowded in for consultations. It was a great show, produced by a glamorous combination of subtle salesmanship and an ineffable evocation of intimate urgency. When the representative departed for her next stop, she left behind a quickened demand for Arden products and an increase of sales, during her week's stay, that was usually equal to more than a month's normal business.

Keeping these ladies in her employ presented a constant challenge to Elizabeth to which she responded with gifts, trips, and bonuses. She knew how attractive and efficient they were. When they were not marrying, they were being wooed away by one of her competitors. After a special favorite moved over to Dorothy Gray, she said disgustedly, "How generous can I get? I'm spending a fortune training girls that end up selling the glop that little woman originally stole from me."

Elizabeth thought it was better to train her own girls, because she trusted neither the department store sales forces nor their managers. "PM" (or push money) was one of the larger reasons for Elizabeth's mistrust. She would not pay it, nor would any of her girls last long, if she discovered that they took it. The practice was unfair, illegal, and insidious.

If a company or store demonstrator thought that she might not make her minimum sales and was thus in danger of losing her commission, she was often susceptible to the offer of push money by some rival company. By pushing his line, at the expense of the one she was hired to represent, she earned a bonus from him on each jar she sold. Under the Robinson-Patman Act, this was an unfair trade practice, because the customer was being pressured into buying a product without the salesgirl identifying herself as its representative and, worse than that, often while reputedly representing another product.

That was the kind of cutthroat business that cosmetics was—and still is. The profits were high enough to absorb all manner of hidden costs. The manufacturers were united on only one point—whatever the price, the customer would be the one who ultimately paid it.

In Harry Johnson, Elizabeth had found a man who was well schooled in all the facets of her business—including the iniquitous ones. She was free to travel, enjoy her new social position, and spoil her horses into winning for her.

"That dreadful man in the White House has put me in a *tem-*

porary business!'' Miss Arden screamed, as assistants scurried in all directions, rather than serve as substitute for Roosevelt and recipient of her wrath. This baleful reaction was to the announcement of new investigations into cosmetics advertising by the Federal Trade Commission. It was beginning to insist that all medicinal claims for products had to be substantiated. A manufacturer would not be able to claim a permanent cure for a skin condition without proving that it was true. The most he could say was that a condition might be temporarily improved.

It was the start of an era of increased government control over all facets of industry. As it had been completely without controls, since its inception as an industry, the beauty business felt the restrictions more severely than many of the others. At first, Miss Arden had been all for the limitations. Twisting her favorite necklace of enormous pearls, so that the diamond clasp lay just above the cleavage of her breasts, she said to a reporter interviewing her, ''It's good. It'll drive the fakes out of the business. Besides, it doesn't touch me. I made stricter rules for my products at a time when the government still thought that face cream was something you got from the wrong end of a cow.''

She also applauded the FTC plan to overcome the push money system. It decreed that henceforth demonstrators and special salespeople would have to be identified with the product they were selling. Her competitors might scream, but it suited Elizabeth perfectly, because it was already true of her representatives.

The FTC claims actions had emanated from the American Medical Association, which had already set up a Board of Standards for cosmetics advertising. Among other things, the board insisted that no allergy-free claims could be made in advertising; skin fresheners and tissue creams should be discontinued, because there was no evidence that tissues could be replenished by cosmetics; hair products could not make therapeutic claims; and a list of all ingredients in cosmetics should appear on the package or be available upon request.

Unless these requirements were met, the products could not be advertised in the AMA magazine, *Hygeia,* nor could they use the advertising line ''Accepted for advertising in the publication of the American Medical Association.''

Elizabeth's reaction was, ''Who'd want to use that line? It'd make Ardena sound like a first cousin of Lysol. I never did like doctors. They're the reason I'm not a nurse today (which was not quite true—patients were the reason she was not a nurse). They're not in Congress, so what difference do they make to me?''

She was soon to learn the answer to her query—a big difference. What Elizabeth had not taken into consideration was that, though the AMA had no authority to make laws, it did have a powerful Congressional lobby. The principal purpose of this group was to prevent Roosevelt from pushing through any legislation that even remotely smacked of socialized medicine or control over the medical profession. To do this, it was necessary to do some minor things to help prove that the doctors were dedicated and altruistic servants of the people.

The beauty business was a large and cheap target. The truth was that though cosmetics rarely did anybody lasting good, it rarely did them lasting harm, and that was more than could be said of some practitioners of medicine. It was a case of the sizzling pot calling the whistling kettle a big mouth.

The one good result of the AMA campaign was the passage of the Wheeler-Lea Amendment extending the authority of the Food and Drug Administration to cosmetics, and that was where it found a large target in Elizabeth Arden. In essence, it meant that she would have to substantiate any claims she made for her products.

When the government informed her that she would have to change the name of Orange Skin Food to Orange Skin Cream, because it was not a nutrient, she cried, ''That's not true!'' and produced a letter from a client stating that the woman's cook had mistaken a jar of Orange Skin Food, which, for some reason, was in the refrigerator, for icing. She had covered a cake with it, and it was eaten at a family party with tremendous gusto and no bad aftereffects.

''All of my products are nutritious. Why, a very good client, Mrs. Robert Warwick, always feeds Velva Cream to her dog, while she's

:[199]:

having treatments, and it's the healthiest little thing anybody could ever hope to see.''

The Food and Drug Administration ruled that this evidence only proved that her products were made of pure fats and harmless when taken internally in small quantities. Miss Arden retorted, ''They might, at least, have said they were also delicious.''

It might have been with reluctance, that Miss Arden complied with the regulations of the FTC and FDA, but comply she did. This was more than could be said of many of her competitors, who squirmed and turned, trying to find ways of circumventing the law. The result was that, in 1937, the FTC brought suits for malpractices against Helena Rubinstein, Chanel, Woodbury, Richard Hudnut, Yardley, Primrose House, Bourjois, and Bristol-Myers. Elizabeth Arden was one of the few giants to escape federal action.

This was largely due to Harry Johnson's adroit handling of both his boss and her business. One morning, after a particularly encouraging sales report, she bustled into his office waving a list of yearlings that she had recently purchased. She tossed it on his desk thrilled, ''Pick one.''

He was bewildered. ''Go on. Pick one.'' Johnson twirled a pencil in the air, closed his eyes, and let the pencil dart randomly onto the list. ''This one.''

''He's yours.'' She quickly turned to leave. She looked back at the door. ''I'm so very pleased with you.'' And she was gone before he could say another word.

Johnson was astounded. He had heard of her spurts of extravagant generosity, but this gesture was truly fantastic. He had always wanted a horse of his own, and now he had one, which he appropriately named General Manager.

From the beginning, General Manager showed great promise, and when the Belmont silks became available, Johnson bought them. He was slightly precipitous.

At about the time he bought the silks, the FTC informed the Arden Company that it would have to discontinue any advertising for Velva Cream Mask, Eight Hour Cream, and Ardena Orange Skin

Cream that claimed muscles would be lifted, contours of the face changed, pores refined, or skin nourished.

Elizabeth sailed into Johnson's office in an absolute fury. She shouted, ''They're out to destroy me! Now, the only thing I can say about my products is—this is a cream!''

Johnson tried to calm her down, but it was to no avail. She was twisting the large diamond ring on her finger, as if to make certain that the government had not already confiscated it. She noticed the jockey's silks that were draped over the back of a chair. ''What are they?''

''The Belmont silks. I bought them for the horse you gave me. I'm making arrangements to have him stabled, and I'm going to start racing him.''

Her eyes narrowed. ''I never gave you any horse.''

''Yes, you did. Don't you remember—'' Her expression told him that she did not, and he did not pursue the subject. That was the last reference he ever made to General Manager, which remained with the other horses in the Maine Chance stable.

In 1939, Elizabeth went to Paris for the opening of her new salon at 7 Place Vendôme. She gazed from her doorway, across the magnificent expanse, to the corner where she had paused to look back

Elizabeth in full regalia, photographed at her sister's home in Paris.

exactly twenty-five years. All the dreams, and some she had not dared to dream, of that gentle late summer evening had come true.

For all the changes that a quarter of a century had brought about, the times were not so very different. War was again in the summer-softened air. A militant Germany was once more threatening its complacent, worldly neighbor. And although Elizabeth had come in triumph and was surrounded by a throng of employees and well-wishers, she was still as alone as she had been on that long-ago first visit. She wondered if a leisurely stroll around the square would turn this bright sunlight into the earlier tremulous twilight and bring her back to the start of her long journey, washing years away to re-create her in the image of that younger woman seeking escape, in a fierce ambition, from the emptiness of her life. The refuge was gone in ambition fulfilled, but the emptiness lingered on in the quiet moments away from the crowd.

After the tumultuously successful reception, the de Maublancs and Elizabeth journeyed down to Gladys' lovely country home, in Jouy-en-Josas, just three miles south of Versailles. It was not the most comfortable of weekends, for Elizabeth still disliked Henri de Maublanc intensely. She had heard that he often boasted, ''The Graham women know nothing about love—except for Gladys. And she only knows, because I taught her.''

Aware of the antagonism between her husband and her sister, Gladys contrived to keep them apart as much as possible. One afternoon, while the two sisters were strolling in the garden, Elizabeth said, ''It's very beautiful here. How can you be happy with that awful little man?''

Gladys laughed. ''It is beautiful. And I am happy.''

''He's driven your son away.'' John Baraba had always disliked his stepfather, and as soon as he was old enough, had run off to join his real father in America.

''I'm not happy about that. Let's forget about my private life. We've got to have a serious talk about the business.''

''It's fine. You're doing a great job. I adore the new salon.''

Gladys pulled her sister down onto a garden bench. ''There's a war coming. We all know it. And France is totally unprepared.''

"A fine time to open a new salon," Elizabeth commented sarcastically, and then she took Gladys' hand. "When the war starts, you must come back to America."

"I'm not leaving. This is my home. I've a better idea. I want to turn the business over to Henri."

"Never!"

"Elizabeth, listen to me—"

"He doesn't know enough about running it."

"Henri has certain friends. They're very unpopular now. But if the worst happens, they'll be running things."

"You mean he's a Fascist."

"I didn't say that. He admires the order that Hitler has brought to Germany and loathes the disorder that exists in France."

"Do you approve?"

"No. I violently disapprove."

"How can you go on living with a man you don't approve of?"

Gladys shook her head sadly. "Flo, Flo. Little Flo. You still don't know a damned thing about what happens between a man and woman."

Elizabeth did not want to continue the discussion, but Gladys was relentless. She explained that the only way to make sure that the business went on running smoothly, no matter what happened, was to make Henri its titular head. If the French won, his noble lineage would ensure continued operation and, if the Germans invaded and conquered, his powerful friends would do as much.

Elizabeth shook her head violently. "I don't want a Nazi running my business."

"Why not? You've had them running things in Berlin."

"That's different."

"Would you rather close down in France?"

The queen was in check. Elizabeth was silent for a few minutes. She got up and strolled away. Without turning to face Gladys, she said, "It's your business. I suppose you must run it as you see fit."

Henry Sell could scarcely believe the deal. He knew that the Arden business was a great one, but he had had no idea of the enormousness attributed to it by the industrial community, until the offer was made.

United States Steel had asked him to act as intermediary in a proposal to buy Elizabeth Arden. It was willing to pay $25,000,000, tax free. He called her for an appointment, stressing the urgency of his need to see her as quickly as possible. She told him that she had a cold, but that he could come up to the apartment that evening for dinner.

When he started to explain the proposition over dinner, she held him at bay, insisting that they gossip about mutual friends. After dinner, she was still evasive and had him wait, while she had a massage and went through her nightly beauty ritual. At last, he was summoned to her bedroom. She lay propped up by some pillows, looking exceedingly kittenish in a frilly pink bedjacket and nightgown. She giggled and said coyly, "Here we are, Hanque, alone, at last. Now tell me what's on your mind."

They discussed the pros and cons of the deal until two in the morning. He explained that she could have an income of over $1,000,000 a year without ever having to touch capital. She would be free to spend as much as she liked on the horses, play Lady Bountiful, travel, do anything her heart desired. She was fascinated and finally said, "You know, Hanque, it might be a very good thing to do."

"I think it would," he replied.

"We'll discuss it in the morning. You go now. I'm very tired." He said good-night and started out of the room. When he reached the door, she called, "Just a minute."

He turned. For the moment, she looked like a very little girl lost in a big bed. She asked in a curiously plaintive and childlike tone, "But if I sell, what would Elizabeth Arden think of it?"

He sighed, "I don't think she'd approve."

She nodded her head with a child's solemnity. "I don't think so either."

That was the last that anybody heard of the offer.

CHAPTER THIRTEEN

Second Marriage and Second War

"Is it mine? Is it all mine?" she asked, as she gazed at the new Elizabeth Arden factory in Long Island City. After the tour was over, she laughed girlishly, and twisting her impressive diamond ring, she cried, "Isn't it remarkable what a woman can do with a little ambition!"

It was an exclamation rather than a question. The reply was an overt affirmative that echoed through the extensive new facilities. The world was going to hell, but 1939 was a heavenly year for Elizabeth Arden. Totalitarian states were aggressively expanding everywhere, and she was no exception. She had just returned from Europe where, in addition to the new salon in Paris, she had opened a new factory in North Acton, England. She had experienced many lonely failures as a woman, but as a corporate entity Elizabeth Arden had become an institution, a household word throughout the world.

Her exploitational expertise was legendary, and she was asked to deliver an address before the Advertising Federation of America. Capsuling her entire approach to promotion, she said, "It is my firm belief that the chief essential in selling beauty, as in selling anything else, is the repetition of certain essentials. Repetition makes reputations, and reputations make customers."

Her demonstrators and salesmen were treated to another choice bit of Arden advice. "Get your facts right. Keep it short, keep it sweet, and keep it to the point. You can write a book about what you don't know. But you've really got to know your subject to put it in one sentence.''

Elizabeth's grasp on her empire was never firmer. Her employees whispered that she knew every girl, on every floor, in every salon, and, what was more frightening to them, she had each rated in her mind. The treatment girls suffered the most, for Elizabeth had started as one and still held up her own healing hands as the ideal toward which they must all strive.

She was forever tiptoeing around the treatment floors and peeking into the tiny rooms. If she was unhappy with what she saw, she entered and, pushing the girl aside, took over the ministrations. This usually elicited a loud ouch from the client. With the growth of her stable, Elizabeth had forgotten that a woman's face took a lighter touch than a horse's hindquarters.

She never hired anybody to do anything that she was not willing to do and was not convinced that she could do more efficiently than anybody else in her domain. She promoted a bit of corporate uneasiness, and that suited Elizabeth to perfection. She confided to Bettie Hamilton, ''I don't want them to love me. I want them to fear me.''

Love was something she always mistrusted, while fear was a constant upon which she could rely. She could see it; she could even touch it. It was tangible in eyes that sought escape from her scrutiny, in tiny beads of perspiration, in trembling hands.

She adored her little tours of inspection and was not at all deluded by the sudden flurries of activity they engendered. She knew that the switchboard operator had alerted all departments that she was on her way. With a malicious chuckle, she told Rose Mornay, ''They think I don't know—they all run like flies, when they hear I'm coming.''

With the outbreak of World War II, the leaders of the American cosmetics industry went into a state of shock similar to the one experienced by the rest of the economy just ten years earlier, at the start of the Depression. They realized that the better part of their foreign trade would be completely eliminated. This meant retrenchment in every area of production and a new emphasis on the often neglected Latin American market.

Elizabeth Arden was one of the few who were not too concerned. In a sense, she was already mobilized for war. Like Gaul, the Arden empire was divided in three. North and South America were managed out of New York. France and the French colonies were under Gladys' supervision in Paris. The rest of Europe, Asia, and Africa fell to Teddy Haslam in London.

As Latin America had always been Elizabeth's, it had not been neglected. She was too competitive, even with those in her employ, not to want to prove that she could surpass them. There were salons in most of the major American capitals and excellent distribution throughout the continent. While her rivals feverishly scurried around trying to open this new market, she calmly expanded the excellent organization that already existed.

With capital shortening, as a result of a restricted market, most of the beauty tycoons were afraid to stock up on raw materials. Miss Arden's attitude was buy, buy, buy. She foresaw that before long, war industries would be given government priorities on things like oils and alcohol, and many of her essential ingredients would become scarce. Some of her advisers were alarmed at the extent of her purchases, but recalling World War I shortages, she would not be deterred. Besides, Elizabeth had always enjoyed buying more than selling. She explained to Pat Young, ''When things get tough, that's the time to stick your little chin out.''

The result was that with her head held high and her little chin stuck out, Elizabeth could afford to face the war with her customary courage and no surcease in her traditional pursuits. Christmas was one of those traditions, and it went on as usual during the first year of the war and through all the years that followed.

Miss Arden's season to be joyous began in the middle of the summer and, by the time December arrived, it had turned her staff into a nest of Scrooges who wanted, but did not dare, to shout at her, ''Bah, humbug!''

There were literally thousands of gifts that had to be assigned and ordered. The list was divided into groupings labeled A, B, C, and D. The A list was composed of important editors, society friends whom she wanted to impress, top executives, and leading buyers. The women usually got things like expensive alligator bags or negligees from the salon collection. Woe unto the female who wanted to exchange her present for a comparable amount of treatments. Elizabeth threw a fit. She had paid the wholesale price for the bag or negligee, and in return, the ungrateful wretch wanted to extract the retail price in labor.

Wrapping began right after Thanksgiving. Night after night, the staff stayed late and, under Elizabeth's scrupulous supervision, packaged the gifts, tying them in little pink bows and florettes. Should the result not come up to her standards, Elizabeth's reaction was quite the opposite of the Yuletide spirit of peace on earth and goodwill toward men. Over a misplaced ribbon, she would roar at an aide, in whom she had invested enormous authority in a crucial area of her business, "Get that bow straight, or I swear I'm going to bounce you!"

Presents went out as soon as they were ready and were sometimes forwarded as early as the first day in December. Given Elizabeth's quixotic disposition, it often happened that she had stopped speaking to somebody between the date the gift was delivered and Christmas Eve. She once wrote to a recent former friend, "As we are no longer speaking, I think it's only fair that you return my present. It's quite expensive and, under the circumstances, much more than you deserve."

In addition to regular presents, Elizabeth liked to send little "fun" extras to particular favorites. It might be a pincushion, or a monogram pin, or a package of gold-foil-covered chocolate bees or coins. One year her secretary worked well into Christmas Eve dispatching the little extras. Elizabeth kept her on after they were finished, while she double-checked her entire list.

She suddenly looked up and shrieked, "My God! I've forgotten somebody!" She pointed an accusing finger at the girl. "You! You are stupid! Why didn't you remind me?"

She went on muttering, as if her helper were not present. "What'll I do? It's unforgivable. Oh! I know!" She tossed a bag of candy coins across her desk. "Merry Christmas, dear."

When the girl returned from her holiday, there was a note instructing her to go to the fashion floor and pick out a suit (these sold for as high as $500) as her real gift.

Elizabeth was meticulous about everything that went out under her name. The D list was the largest and least expensive group, but she still wanted it to be something that the receiver would enjoy and started shopping for it as early as June. One year she discovered a leatherette case that could hold small sample vials of three of her perfumes. It retailed for $5, but her cost was $2.50, and she was convinced that she had made a real find.

She was with one of her publicity men, Emmett Davis, account executive for Lanfranco Rasponi's public relations firm, when a sample arrived for her inspection a few weeks later. The company had not yet had time to make it up in the color she had selected, and the one before her was in a perfectly hideous shade. She screamed, "They're mad! I can't send this. It's terrible."

Davis tried to calm her down, explaining that it would look much better in the right color, rationalizing that it was a real bargain at the price.

She shook the case at him and retorted witheringly, "How would you feel waking up Christmas morning and finding this piece of crap under your tree?"

The pains of preparing for Christmas were often forgotten by the time the holiday arrived. Her generosity awed most of her staff into forgiving her. In addition to bonuses and special remembrances for her pets, everybody from ladies' room attendant on up received baskets of preparations, some valued at as much as $30, even in 1939.

The first Christmas of World War II was a very special one. To celebrate the opening of the new factory, she had Duke Cross put on a special show using amateur performers, among her employees, as his cast. Chartered buses transported the entire Manhattan staff to Long Island City, and by the time they were all assembled there were between 1,500 and 2,000 guests. These parties became annual events, until the year when the factory was organized by a labor union. She never forgave them for that and never gave them another party.

Just as her office door was always open to her help, so was the door

:[209]:

to her penthouse apartment. When the mother of one of her favorites arrived for the holiday, Elizabeth invited the pair home for tea.

Elizabeth at home was very different from Elizabeth at work. Seated beneath the Augustus John portrait, her eyes catching the glow from the great crystal chandelier, she radiated charm, and the only lumps her guests received were made of sugar.

The tea party was an enormous success, and it gave her a lovely idea. On Christmas Day, she would have open house for all of her employees and let each bring a mother, or father, or wife, or sweetheart.

By that time in her life Elizabeth had become a brilliant and famous hostess. She went about ordering this party with the same care she would have shown had the guest list included the king of England. She called upon Henry Sell to help with the arrangements. They spent hours going over details with her butler, Frederic, who would have been considered perfect Hollywood casting for the role of the typical English servant. He was told to spare no expense. She wanted the house filled with flowers, the food and drinks to be divine and plentiful.

As the party progressed, everything was perfection—except the guests. The parents, wives, husbands, what-alls were not uniformly elegant or even uniformly clean. Some were downright seedy-looking. The apartment reeked of tobacco and cheap perfumes. Elizabeth muttered, ''They might, at least, wear Blue Grass. After all, they get it wholesale.''

Somebody, who had been using a priceless Meissen vase for an ashtray, knocked it over. Elizabeth smiled graciously. ''It's nothing, dear. Nothing at all. Just a little knickknack. German, don't you know.''

Bestowing bloodcurdling coos and ahs to left and right, she gradually inched her way toward the stairs, slipped up them, and was not seen again. The next day Sell was summoned to the penthouse by a seething Miss Arden. She shouted, ''The idea of those dreadful people in my house! Whose idea was it?''

''Yours.''

Miss Arden's Fifth Avenue apartment — a mélange of Art Deco, smoked mirrors, satin-upholstered furniture, and a terrace with a smashing Central Park view.

"Not mine! Never mine!" She sent for Frederic and waved a sheaf of party bills under his nose. "How could you have ordered all those expensive things? How could you be so stupid as to spend all that money on that sort of trash? God, how could you be so stupid!"

She paused for breath, and Frederic said politely, "If you will pardon me, madame. Nuts, madame!"

He wheeled around and left the room. For a moment, she was flabbergasted, and then she began to laugh uproariously. "Hanque, wasn't that funny?"

She rang for Frederic again. When he returned, fully expecting to be fired, she said jovially, "You're a very funny fellow. I haven't laughed that much since I can't remember when."

He bowed. "Thank you, madame," he said and quietly exited. A few minutes later, her dog bounded in with a Christmas gift, from Frederic, neatly tied around his neck.

Frederic was given a raise.

On New Year's Eve, Elizabeth managed to get a telephone call through to Gladys in Paris. She begged her to come home. Gladys replied, "I am home. This is my country, and I won't desert it now. There is one thing you can do for me. Find my son. See that he's all right. Send him my love."

The word went out to all of the Arden people across the country. They were to start searching for John Baraba. Bert Chose wired from the West Coast that John was in California serving as a pilot in the United States Air Force, and a family truce was arranged.

Elizabeth had maintained her friendship with Charles James ever since he designed the dress she wore in the first John portrait. He was the perfect escort—amusing, talented, and very social. Not only was he society's pet dressmaker, but his family was one of the best in Chicago, which, in turn, was one of Elizabeth's pet cities.

One evening James took her to dinner at the home of the great art collector and philanthropist Mrs. William H. Moore. The house was filled with porcelains of museum quality, and Elizabeth picked up an exquisite eighteenth-century covered pot. She exclaimed, "It's so beautiful!"

Surprised to hear her volunteer an artistic judgment, James asked what it was she liked about the piece. Elizabeth replied, "It would make a lovely little jar for Joie de Vivre."

Mrs. Moore was taken aback and asked why that was so. Her guest explained in a fey tone, intended to soften the harsh edge of her shrewd business observation. "It's elegant, and it has rounded corners. Jars with rounded corners are best for packaging, because it takes less cream to fill them."

For Elizabeth, the only enduring esthetics were those that applied to horses and cosmetics. But the days of the lovely and economical little pots with rounded corners came to an end in 1940, with the passage of the Food, Drugs, and Cosmetics Act. One of its provisions was that the amount contained, as well as the composition and purpose of a product, had to be clearly indicated on the package. There could be no more deceptive packaging or ingredients deemed harmful to the users.

Although it was not the case with Arden, it meant recomposition of formulas, eliminating the offending substances, for many manufacturers. It universally meant redesigning labels and containers. Given Elizabeth's acute sensitivity to the looks of her products, this was a more onerous chore than the reformularization was to her rivals. It took months of living at the top of her lungs before she was finally satisfied with the work of her designers.

With the closing of European markets, Elizabeth decided it was time to broaden her domestic outlets. Her products began to find their way into chain drugstores, like Liggett's, Whelan's, and Walgreen's, as well as pharmacies all over the country. The new stores were like new playthings for Elizabeth, and she took to swooping down on them in the same unexpected way she did on the salons. She adored driving down from Maine Chance, stopping at all the drugstores along the way. She would sweep in and say to the manager, "How do you do? I'm Elizabeth Arden."

As the poor man came out of shock, she would add, "How's business?'

If it was not good, she would step behind the counter and start demonstrating how to sell her preparations. She would later march into her office and announce to her staff, "I made quite a few nice little sales today. What's new around here?"

She once dropped in on the St. Regis pharmacy and asked to see her display. She took one look and began to scream in a tone that must have stopped the music downstairs at the Maisonette. "Wrong! Wrong!! They're so naked! Where are my pretty little ribbons?"

She grabbed a bottle and shook it menacingly at the manager. She pointed at its unadorned neck. "There should be a ribbon right here." She slammed it down with a shattering force. "I'll pay for it! You'll pay for it! Somebody will pay for it!" She tore out of the store, shouting into the faces of passersby, "Somebody will pay for it!

Within a half hour, a stony-faced girl appeared in the shop, carrying a pair of scissors and yards of pink ribbon. She spent the rest of the afternoon silently cutting small lengths of ribbon and methodically tying them around the necks of the bottles.

As conditions worsened abroad, Elizabeth's concern for Gladys intensified, but there was nothing she could do about it, for Sister still insisted upon remaining in France. She was also worried about her many friends and employees who were still over there, and there were things she could do about them.

Mrs. Wonnacott was a special favorite in the London salon. When the blitz began, Elizabeth became extremely agitated over the danger to the woman and her young son and sent for both of them. She wired, "Wonnie, come to New York immediately. Lanie needs your help."

She also tried to send for the manager of the London salon, Diana Wall, but like Gladys, she refused to leave Europe. She was later killed in the bombing of the Guards' Chapel, and Elizabeth never forgave herself for not having been more insistent.

When her famous Maine Chance chef, Maurice Cordonnier,

resigned to join the French Army, she brought his wife, Josie, to New York to act as her housekeeper.

She never spoke of the things she did, and very few of her friends were aware of the number of Europeans she helped and supported throughout the war. Maria Hugo, the Duchesse de Gramont, and her six-year-old son were destitute when they arrived from France. Elizabeth found a place for her in the business and a school for the boy.

She was actually criticized for helping Madame Hugo. It was said that it was only done for self-aggrandizement and that she had reduced the aristocrat to the level of a slave by demanding that she be on call at all hours of the day and night. Actually, this had nothing to do with the lady's title. It was something demanded of many Arden employees. Elizabeth paid well, and she expected total devotion in return.

In the case of Maria Hugo, the fact remains that the pragmatic Elizabeth did support and give a job to a woman who was of very little practical use to her. The social prestige was negligible. During World War II, the one thing that New York society did not need was another impoverished aristocrat.

France fell in June, 1940, and Paris was occupied by the Germans. There was no longer any chance of getting Gladys out. She was the wife of a Frenchman, and had been born in a country officially at war with the conquerors.

America was not yet in the war, and Elizabeth could still send and receive letters from Gladys, but there was nothing she could do to help her. In a material way, there was nothing that had to be done, for, ironically, the French profits continued to mount. Under the occupation and the collaborationist De Maublanc's management, the company continued to prosper. Losing a war had obviously done nothing to lessen the Frenchwoman's drive for chic, and neither patronage of the Arden salon nor purchase of its products fell off to any marked degree.

Elizabeth continued to worry, but she told herself that, with the help of De Maublanc's protection and influence, Gladys would remain relatively safe. She reckoned without the streak of courage shared by all of the Graham girls. It went deeper than Gladys' safe, habitual me-tooism. She could not help resisting, nor could she help being outspoken in her antagonism toward the Nazis. Henri, who genuinely loved her, could not shield or gag her for very long.

There was a great stillness in the apartment. Neither thoughts of her beloved horses nor her cherished business could get through to Elizabeth during that seemingly endless, time-suspended moment. Embraced by the warm light of the sun-drenched terrace, she stared blankly across the open expanse of park and wondered how there could be so much freedom left in the world. Gladys had been interned in the infamous North German concentration camp Ravensbruck.

In the days that followed, the story was pieced together. She had been part of a group that had been secretly helping Allied pilots, shot down over occupied France, to escape. Had it not been for Sid Jones, Henri's influence might have shielded her for a much longer time.

Jones was bilingual and had worked for the company before the war. The RAF parachuted him into France on a special mission. When the Germans began to close in on him, he contacted his wife who was still living in Paris. In turn, she got in touch with Gladys for help and money. Mrs. Jones was being watched by the Gestapo, and the two women, along with another confederate, Solange de Luze, were caught and sentenced to Ravensbruck.

For the first time in her life, Elizabeth was totally helpless. She reached for the only panacea that had ever proved effective—her work.

If she had been difficult before, she was now impossible. Her slight tolerance for inefficiency lowered to the zero point. The revolving door operated with such dizzying speed that even trusted friends and associates, like Henry Sell, were caught in it. By December, 1940, Sell's Blaker Agency was out, and Pettingel and Fenton (Fleur Fenton became Fleur Cowles and, subsequently, Fleur Mayer) were handling her advertising account. Within five months they resigned, giving as their only excuse—"circumstances."

It was a dreadful world, and she loathed it; but it was a new world, a war world, and as ever, she moved with the times. In a sense, she became an activist, but only because it was good business. Her traditionalist, ultrafeminine approach was redesigned to fit the new role that women were playing.

America was on the verge of entering the war, and Selective Service was removing men from every sphere of the economy. Women were taking over as they never had before. During World War I, they had been used as common laborers or in very subordinate white-collar capacities. The new war placed them in positions of control. Under Oveta Culp Hobby's command, there was even soon to be an enlisted Women's Army Corps.

Elizabeth introduced an Arden career course geared to fit women for their new roles. For $40, a client was entitled to ten two-hour sessions given, after business hours, two evenings a week. There were courses in clothes selection, and career orientation, as well as the usual Arden specialties of exercise, diet, complexion care, makeup, and hair and hand grooming.

Arden, the recharged feminist, made a speech before the New York League of Business and Professional Women in which she derided "the all too prevalent assumption that women are handicapped by sex and temperament to assume managerial and executive duties. *It never handicapped me!* Women invented management, and we originated group control. Government itself is simply a magnified copy of household law and order, for which our great grandmothers furnished the pattern. The word 'economics' means home regulation."

With Maria Hugo, Wonnie, or her New York assistant manager, Florence Owens, as companion, she was constantly on the move, back and forth to Maine Chance Farm, descending on stores and salons all over the country, appearing at all of the major horse sales and track events.

Under Leslie Combs, her stable was continuing to grow and prosper. Its colors were becoming a prominent and important factor in buying, breeding, and racing. Elizabeth's infatuation with her horses was active to the point of being rampant.

Paris *haute couture* was out for the duration, and she decided that the time had come for her to enter the custom-made clothes field and to add the final item to her total woman salon concept. Her first step was to hire an expert copyist and start doing, with small changes, adaptations of the work of all the prominent designers. This led to a lawsuit, brought by Charles James, who claimed that she had stolen the design for a skating skirt from him. Amazingly enough, there was very little rancor on both sides, and they continued to see each other socially. In a style not unlike the Mafia, they did not allow business difficulties to impinge on social relationships. After all, business was one thing and dinner at the Colony was quite another.

Hattie Carnegie, an American designer who ran a women's specialty shop, quickened Arden's entry into the rag trade. When Elizabeth heard that Miss Carnegie was beginning to manufacture cosmetics under her own label, she said, "If she can make lipstick, I can make dresses."

Miss Carnegie joined the ranks of Helena Rubinstein and Dorothy Gray on Elizabeth's list of dreadful little women. When she heard that the designer was in her salon, she sent word to the treatment girl, who was about to work on her, "Blast her out of her chair!"

The more Elizabeth did, the more she had to do, for the loneliness of Florence and the loss of Gladys continued to haunt her. She entered politics for the first time since the Democratic rallies after Bessie Marbury's death. This time, she was where she belonged, on the side of the angels—a true, almost blue-blooded, Republican.

She became part of a group of professional women who advocated the election of Wendell L. Willkie in his 1940 campaign, opposing Franklin Delano Roosevelt, for the presidency. Edna Woolman Chase, editor-in-chief of *Vogue,* Mary Vail Andress, a former officer of the Chase Manhattan Bank, fashion consultant Mary Lewis, and Hortense Odlum, who had been president of Bonwit Teller and was the wife of Atlas Corporation's Floyd Odlum, were the other women involved.

In her speeches, Elizabeth rallied the already converted with stirring sentiments like, "They say the moment breeds the man. How thankful we Americans should be to have this great man, Wendell L. Willkie, appear in this critical hour of our history."

She was publicly on record as being one of "we Americans." The true depth of her commitment to American citizenship can best be measured by a statement she later made to Douglas J. Roche, of the Canadian magazine *MacLean's*. "I'd become a citizen of anywhere I was making a living."

Despite Elizabeth's campaigning, Mr. Willkie lost the election, and within a month, Mr. Roosevelt's government showed Miss Arden what it thought of her. The FTC summoned her controller, Joseph Danilek, to give testimony on her use of demonstrators in alleged violation of the Robinson-Patman Act. It was said that the act required sales services, such as demonstrators, to be given on a proportionally equal basis to all retail outlets, and not simply to those buyers who guaranteed the purchase of a large enough quantity of her products to make it worth Miss Arden's while.

In response, Mr. Danilek emphasized that the demonstrators were intended to educate the public to the newest in fashion trends, not primarily to make sales. He asserted that the minimum of $10,000 a year in purchased product, was not the first factor considered by Arden in making one of her women available. If $10,000 annually was not the primary motive, he failed to identify what else it might be.

Those nasty Demmies were at it again, and Elizabeth was not about to let them get away with it. She continued to appeal the FTC decisions right up to the Supreme Court and, after years of fighting, actually won a practical, if not legal, victory. By the time she was finished the strength of the Robinson-Patman Act had been diminished to the point of repeal, and demonstrators, the heart of her approach to sales, were permitted to operate almost as freely as they had before.

It would have been truly incredible, if all of this aggravation had not taken its toll on the looks of a woman close to sixty-three years of age, and it did radically alter Elizabeth's appearance. As Oscar Wilde put it of another woman, "Overnight, her hair turned gold with grief."

It was more than grief and more than the artistry of her hair colorists that wrought the deep change in Elizabeth. It was love. For the first time in her life, Elizabeth was romantically in love and experiencing a pubescent physical passion. The object of these disturbing stirrings was Tom White.

White was an extremely powerful executive in the Hearst newspaper and magazine empire. At various times, he had served as general manager of all the papers and specific manager of the New York *Journal-American* and the Detroit and Chicago dailies. Though nepotism was strongly denied, his sister, Carmel Snow, was then editor-in-chief of Hearst's *Harper's Bazaar* magazine, and she was later succeeded in that job by his daughter, Nancy White.

White was the first man with whom she had ever become intimate who combined the courtliness of a beau with the magnetic virility of an extremely masculine animal. They shared common interests in politics and horses, and he could talk to her, man to man, without once making her feel like less than an extremely desirable woman. Perhaps he understood her so well because he had spent most of his life dealing with a very similar despotic empire builder in the person of William Randolph Hearst.

Whether or not the affair was ever physically consummated, it was an extraordinarily intimate and complex relationship restrained by several insurmountable obstacles. White was a Catholic, and he was married. A divorce was out of the question and, even if it had been possible, it is doubtful that Elizabeth could ever have sufficiently overcome her religious prejudices to permit a marriage.

Except for large gatherings, their meetings were, perforce, rather clandestine—long drives in her car, dinners for two in out-of-the-way places, or in the privacy of her home. It all added to the atmosphere of old-fashioned romance that Elizabeth found so thrilling.

:[220]:

A favorite beau of Elizabeth's, the famous Tom White (T.G.) of the
Hearst Corporation whose sister was Carmel Snow. His daughter Nancy
White took over the reins of *Harper's Bazaar* as editor in chief when her
aunt Carmel retired.

The leisurely pace of their involvement was disrupted when America was forced into the war by the attack on Pearl Harbor. The country was suddenly suffused with an aura of urgency. A sense of uncertainty and of too few remaining hours lowered the old standards as surely as the dimout did the lights of New York City. The war and the accumulated years of her life combined to impress the abridgment of time upon Elizabeth. It did not make her impetuous but, perversely, enforced an uncharacteristic embrace of caution. When her feeling for White threatened to become too consuming, she abruptly broke with him.

Work again provided the sanctuary to which she returned with an astonishing vigor, shutting out the rest of the world, locking herself in the closed corporation of her business. Nothing was right. Her staff would never learn to do things her way which was the *only* permissible way.

The few who knew about her attachment to Tom White said that the prince caught her on the rebound. Others claimed that he was no more than a great convenience to her. The war was putting men at a premium. The younger ones were in the armed forces, and the older ones were booked weeks in advance. When her White Russian chums offered attractive Prince Michael Evlanoff, Elizabeth was definitely interested, despite the fact that he was seventeen years younger than she was. As far as the public was concerned, she too was often seventeen years younger than she was.

Evlanoff was not actually a White Russian—he was a Tartar—but his title was reputedly a better one than that of Helena Rubinstein's Prince Gourielli. That in itself would have been sufficient recommendation for Elizabeth, but he was also reportedly financially solvent, which was almost unheard of among the exiles.

It was said that the prince was the beneficiary of a private trust fund set up in Sweden by the late Dr. Nobel supposedly in gratitude to Evlanoff, who was briefly his secretary, for helping him to escape from Russia during the Revolution. The prince was able to draw on this fund by special dispensation from King Gustav, who had relaxed wartime restrictions on exchange, so that Evlanoff could hold his head up in this country, as a self-supporting man, and occasionally reach for a check with his own money in hand.

Elizabeth's head was turned by this titled gentleman, who behaved like her concept of the beau ideal. She had never had such an attentive and amusing escort, a man who danced divinely on the dance floor and in attendance off it. He took her out beautifully to the Stork Club, and El Morocco, and Twenty One, and the Monte Carlo and never asked for anything in return—not professionally, or financially, or emotionally. He was charming, and gay, and agreeable. When they entered a club, the headwaiter bowed low, and it was "this way, your Highness," and "may I be of service, your Highness," and "anything you wish, your Highness."

They always had the best tables, and the Café Society types, whose names appeared daily in Cholly Knickerbocker's column (written by a Russian with a name as Italianate as St. Petersburg—Igor Cassini), stopped by to greet them and exchange the latest gossip. It never occurred to that naive farm girl, who had built her own empire, that this deference was being accorded more to her than to him. She simply saw it as a marvelous whirl.

When she entered the hospital for an operation to remove fluid from her lungs, the prince visited every day, bringing each time fresh bouquets of exotic and expensive flowers. She loathed hospitals, and he was a great comfort to her. He flirted and said the sweetest things, making her feel beautiful and desirable without once presenting a sexual threat to her. She thought that this was as it should be at their age—love without passion, warmth without fire.

She came home, where Josie faithfully nursed her back to health. Flowers and Evlanoff continued to arrive daily. She began to think that it would be very pleasant to have this great comfort always by her side, and when he proposed, the little girl giggled, and cooed, "Yes, my darling prince."

During the weeks before the wedding, Elizabeth was kept busy preparing for her ascension to the aristocracy. She later claimed that their calling cards were engraved, Mr. and Mrs. Michael Evlanoff, but her own bath, bed, and dining room were emblazoned with symbols of royalty. All of the linens—sheets, towels, pillow slips, napkins, tablecloths—were of the finest quality, often handmade of linens and laces imported from Europe. She had laid in an enormous stock to tide her over the war years and every piece was sent out to be especially embroidered with the Evlanoff crest.

Orders were given to convert her upstairs library into a bedroom for the prince while they were on their honeymoon trip. As much as she hated to sleep alone, she was obviously not prepared to share a room with a man, even if he was her husband. She had done that once, and to her way of thinking, that was one time too many.

Charles James made a smashing trousseau for her, including the dress in which she was married at Maine Chance. After the ceremony, the happy couple departed for a trip to Nassau and then to Phoenix, Arizona. Elizabeth wept a little. It was really rather like her favorite kind of movie—lots of suffering with a happy ending.

The first indication of trouble in paradise was a wire sent to Miss Delaney. "Stop all alterations on my apartment immediately." It was signed "Miss Arden."

The honeymooners returned in a state of armed truce that, given Elizabeth's disposition, would inevitably have to become open hostilities. It was clear that something had gone awfully wrong during the trip. Florence Owens and Pat Young, who were in positions to have had Elizabeth's confidence, always refused to discuss it.

Serge Obolensky said, "I got a call from her. She was in tears. She said that she'd married Evlanoff and loved him, but that he had done awful things to her. Later I found out from him that the awful things consisted of asserting his male rights and thinking that he could be boss. He started issuing orders. That was not very bright, you know. One thing you could not do with the cosmetics girl was to try to give her orders."

The honeymoon was shrouded in mystery on the East Coast, but the people in the West Coast salon knew what had happened. By the time they got to Phoenix the prince had grown bored with paying court to the old lady who insisted upon being treated like a little girl. The marriage had never progressed beyond a very chaste courtship. She was not eagar, and he was, at the very least, reluctant.

Evlanoff sent for a very close male friend, and his boredom immediately evaporated. Elizabeth flew into a rage. Having her husband wander off with his boyfriend was not her idea of a romantic honeymoon. The fact that she had sent for Burt Chose was no justification for his behavior. That was different. She wanted his advice on a business matter, and what was a mere honeymoon compared to business? After the war, she was planning on opening a winter branch of Maine Chance in Arizona.

And so it came to pass that the fairy-tale prince and princess spent their honeymoon closeted with different men.

Evlanoff obviously thought that this was not grounds for divorce. He persisted in claiming that all would have been well were it not for the people in Elizabeth's business. He said that they were the ones who wanted him out and exerted great pressure to get rid of him.

True to the perversity in her nature, Elizabeth decided to give the marriage another chance and permitted Evlanoff to take up residence in her library. It was a repetition of what had happened with her first husband, just after the first World War. She was enraged to find Evlanoff still in a dressing gown when she was dressed to leave for her office in the morning. As she had not offered him the alternative of a position in the business, it was a slightly irrational anger.

Bills began to arrive, including some for expenses incurred in the process of courting her, like the flowers that arrived daily during her illness. Of the alleged Swedish income, she later said, ''That is not true, and I have documents to prove it! He never had a penny in Sweden. And as for King Gustav's ever giving his permission to export capital, that is pure fantasy.''

Her respect for royalty still intact in spite of the episode with the prince, she added, ''The king's name should never have been mentioned.''

Her marital difficulties did not prevent Elizabeth from insisting on her royal prerogatives. After all, they were the only pleasant things to have come out of the alliance. When the Marquise de la Chapelle refused to call her Princess, she pouted, ''Where's your damned *noblesse oblige?* For years, I've called you Marquise.''

She told Evlanoff to get out, but he would not leave. Elizabeth decided that siege was her only alternative. She would starve him out. She put locks on the refrigerator and bar and instructed Josie not to give him anything to eat. The prince furtively nipped out and back for his meals. During one of these short expeditions, she was ready for him and had him barred from the apartment.

The prince's story of what happened was: ''I left with only the clothes on my back.''

Elizabeth's version was: ''He came with two suits and left with twenty-two.''

As soon as he was gone, she spent a small fortune having the crests, stitch by stitch, removed from her linen. From then on, the only crest she used was one she had designed for the house of Arden. A nightingale was woven into it. It might have been to punish herself, but she would never again forget that a part of her was still Florence N. Graham.

Whether or not she ultimately made a settlement on the prince is in doubt to this day. Some say yes, and some say no. She repeated the Lewis pattern and again sued, in Maine, on the grounds of mental cruelty. She insisted that she wanted the divorce to be conducted in as dignified and quiet a fashion as possible. ''I am naturally disillusioned, but I bear no malice. I've worked hard all my life. I've kept my own records straight. I want the record to be straight on this, too.''

Her desire for dignity did not prevent the New York *Daily News* from running the story of the divorce under the headline: PRINCE ROYAL 4-FLUSH, SAYS MISS ARDEN.

''Look out for Miss Arden. She's on the warpath.'' The word

swept through the salon. Her enmity was directed particularly toward those performing personal services for her. Her hair had always been thin and difficult to set. It suddenly seemed as if this were the hair-dresser's fault. The dye was never right, and she took to blending her own colors, muttering to the abashed young man, "I don't know what I pay you for. You wouldn't know a blonde from a Ubangi."

She grabbed her treatment girl's hands and thrust them aside. "Your fingers have all the sensitivity of an amputee."

In the middle of one of her nightly massages, she screamed at the woman who had been doing her for years, "You've got the touch of a herd of wild elephants. Get out of here!"

Things reached a point where the help would rather have resigned than work on the boss. Manicuring her was an almost impossible task. Her hands were constantly in motion doing a dozen things at one time. Once Rose Mornay had just finished applying the polish when Miss Arden grabbed a phone to make a call and smeared it. She blasted, "God, you're stupid! Why didn't you hold my hand?"

"I'm not here to hold your hand." Miss Mornay gathered her things together and made an angry departure. She had taken enough abuse and had decided to leave the salon for good. The following day Miss Arden personally called, as if nothing had happened, to ask how her little headache was, and when she was returning to work.

The next time Rose manicured her, Miss Arden confided, "You don't know how tired I am of these yes people."

What she refused to admit was how deeply Evlanoff had wounded her vanity; she preferred creating a scene to asking for sympathy or help. One afternoon three recipients of her rages, Elinor Mc-Vickar, Carmel Snow, and Henry Sell, were commiserating over lunch. One of them commented, "The trouble with Elizabeth Arden is that she's having a lesbian affair with Florence Nightingale Graham."

Soon after the divorce became final, Tom White telephoned to ask her to dinner, and she happily accepted. She took out the photograph of him that she had hidden away when she got married and stared at it for a long time. She was grateful to have him back in her life but she knew that from then on, he would be no more than another beau. Their brief moment was over, and perhaps it was just as well.

She carefully set the picture down on top of a chest and seated herself at the dressing table, banked with hundreds of little vials that she had collected all over the world. The golden-haired queen could not bring herself to look into the mirror, for she knew what was waiting for her there, what was always waiting when she was alone— the icy blue eyes of that forlorn wraith she had tried to bury long years gone.

CHAPTER FOURTEEN

Rags and Nags

The fall of France marked the end of the Paris domination of the American high-fashion market. The Parisians would never again fully recover their prewar monopoly on style. Throughout the early forties, New York designers were rising to positions formerly held by Chanel, Schiaparelli, Patou, Lanvin, and Molyneaux. The fashionable American women were becoming conscious of names like Claire McCardell, Valentina, Mainbocher, Traina-Norell, Adrian, and Charles James.

In 1943, Elizabeth felt that the time had arrived for her to have her own designer and clothes exclusively available at the Arden salons: Charles James was the one who suited her best. He was flattered but wary. He told her that there was more to it than merely having a collection. She needed a showroom, fitting rooms, cutting rooms, sewing rooms.

She nodded to each and said, "Perfect. You design them and supervise their construction. You can have the entire second floor at 691." She smiled encouragingly and patted his hand. "Charlie, it's your baby. You're in complete charge. I won't interfere."

For James, it was a dream come true. For both of them, it would soon be a nightmare. They were two extremely positive people, accustomed to having their own way in their work. He took her at her word and believed that he would be in complete charge. Unfortunately, it was a promise that she was constitutionally unable to

:[229]:

Elizabeth Arden with two *grandes dames* of fashion. The late Carmel Snow, who was for many years the editor in chief of *Harper's Bazaar* (on the right), and Marie Louis Bousquet, former Paris editor for *Harper's Bazaar*.

keep. Elizabeth was a compulsive meddler, especially in things that were in any way connected with her salon.

At first—all was serene. His plans for reconstruction were excellent; his collection was all that she had ever desired. It was true that they were both a little puzzled at the lack of overwhelming newspaper interest in their project for, like all dreamers, they believed that their plans were earth-shattering news even in time of war. She advised him, ''Dear, if you want to get into the papers, take the pictures and stories to the newspapers, yourself—and sit there, until they have to see you if only to get rid of you. It works. I know. I've done it myself.''

One of the first big clashes came after she asked for James' help in doing something original in one of her Fifth Avenue windows. He bought an exquisite and expensive ruby glass vase. He set a little spotlight behind it that gleamed through, making it a shimmering scarlet beacon.

One afternoon Sam Riddle came to pick her up for lunch. As he entered her office, he was laughing so hard that for a moment he could not speak. She asked what was so funny, and after gaining control of himself, he replied, ''Your window. My dear, I didn't know you were running a red-light house.''

She stormed downstairs, snatched the vase out of the window, stormed back up to the second floor, and shoved it into James' hands. ''Take it. I never want to see it. It's yours. And don't think I'm going to pay for it either.''

While James was recovering from the shock, she looked around at

Charles James, the brilliant fashion designer whose on-again-off-again association with Miss Arden started in 1929 through an introduction from Elisabeth Marbury.

the incomplete construction and added for good measure, "When are you going to do something about cleaning up this mess?"

From then on, there was no satisfying her. Progress on the new rooms was too slow, and the bills were too high. He tried to explain that because of the war, materials were both scarce and expensive, good workers were almost impossible to find and demanded astronomical wages. She would listen to none of it. It was all his fault. She should never have started with him. She screamed, "You're too temperamental."

Nothing will make a temperamental man more temperamental than being told that he is temperamental. James became edgy and started to have fights with almost everybody. He angered the building manager to such a degree that the man leaped on him and tried to strangle him. If they had not been separated, he might have seriously injured James. When Miss Arden heard about it, she commented, "Too bad he didn't try again."

The collection was finished before the showroom was ready, and they decided to introduce it in Chicago. It seemed like the perfect plan. Elizabeth had always loved the city, and James came of a socially prominent local family. They made arrangements with her special charity, The Cradle, to sponsor the show.

There was only one flaw in the scheme. At the last minute, Elizabeth refused to allow James to come west with her. She claimed that he had too much work to do in New York. He claimed that she was afraid that he would get most of the press coverage. If this were true, her fears would seem to have been realized. He recalled, "Even without being there, I got all the credit for the success. She was barely mentioned. She got so furious she wanted to take my name out of the clothes and use only her label."

Success breeds forgiveness, and the collection was truly dazzling. A truce was negotiated, and Elizabeth's peace offering was to introduce Charles James' first Arden collection to New York, at a Red Cross benefit party at the Ritz Carlton. An unknown pianist, named Leonard Bernstein, who often played at her private parties, provided the music for the fashion show. In honor of the designer, she called the evening "One Touch of Genius."

It may have been because Miss Arden's genius refused to acknowledge publicly that she was his muse but, after the show, the relationship again started to deteriorate. The big blowup came when the drapes were hung in the new showroom. Elizabeth did not like them and decided that they had to go. James had finally reached the breaking point. "The drapes remain!" he cried. "You have no taste—except what little I've managed to teach you."

"I've got enough taste to know that these stink!" She grabbed at the heavy curtains and started to pull them down. "They go! And you go!" She whirled around, the fabric still clenched in her fist. "Now, you get the hell out of here! Out!"

James was almost relieved, for he knew that he would never be able to create another collection under the conditions imposed by Miss Arden. She later asked him to return, but he had had enough of her. All of the aggravation and loss of self-esteem—all of the time and talent and labor—that went into setting up *haute couture* in her establishment and designing her first and, many fashion experts still claim, greatest collection represented a financial return of only $6,000 for the inordinately gifted man. When the fashion floor actually did open at Arden, the name of the designer of the first collection was withheld from the press.

James later became very philosophical about the whole adventure. He and Miss Arden were eventually reconciled, although he continued to refuse to work for her, and she became godmother to his son. He said, "It wasn't her fault. At least, not all of her. Only her bust."

It was James' theory that her great power of command came from the depth of her diaphragm. "You could stick a hat pin into her cleavage and never scratch the skin."

Although Elizabeth was not a great reader of anything aside from advertising copy and the racing form, she was deeply hurt by a novel that appeared in 1943. Despite the writer's demurrals, Ilka Chase's *In Bed We Cry* was something of a *roman à clef* with the central character a thinly veiled portrait of Elizabeth Arden. The one flattering aspect was that the heroine was a good many years younger than Elizabeth. The one completely false note was that she was a creature with very healthy sexual drives. It was gossiped that the book was about the famous cosmetics queen, and it became a best seller.

The heroine was a cosmetics tycoon with a salon that was famous for its little green door. The first husband was in business with her. The potential second husband was an aristocratic European exile. In the book, he was far more like Otto Preminger, with whom Miss Chase was rather well acquainted, than Michael Evlanoff, but it was that sort of thing that made the guessing game all the more exciting for the titillated readers.

Elizabeth felt that it was a special betrayal. Miss Chase was the daughter of Edna Woolman Chase, the editor of *Vogue,* and thus in a position to gather all the backstairs dirt about the beauty business.

The actress-turned-writer summed up her own point of view when she said, "I don't know why Elizabeth Arden was so angry. I didn't know her very well." She paused and added, "Helena Rubinstein was very helpful."

"I hadn't realized it. It's extraordinary." Wonnie was speaking. Elizabeth looked up from her desk somewhat perplexedly. What was she going on about? The Englishwoman smiled. "It'll be thirty-two years, this month, that Lanie's been with the company.

Elizabeth lifted her eyebrows quizzically. Company? It had been no company, when Irene Delaney first came to work for her—a couple of overworked girls in a couple of two-by-nothing rooms, that she had grandly christened a salon.

Thirty-two years. Well, that should be worth something, Elizabeth thought. Who else had ever stuck with her that long? She was a fine girl, that Lanie. She knew everything, and she held her tongue. Interviewers crawling around, trying to find out all about Elizabeth

Arden, she really knew, and she never said a word. It should be worth something.

She sent for her controller, Maurice Goldstone. "I want you to buy $32,000 worth of Series G war bonds, in the name of Irene Delaney. That's one-thousand dollars for each year Lanie's been with me." She laughed. "What about you, Goldstone? Do you think you'll make it to thirty-two months?"

The controller apparently knew figures better than he knew the alphabet. Instead of Series G bonds, he bought Series F bonds. A Series F bond cost $750 per $1,000 and had to be held for twelve years before it matured to full value. A series G bond initially cost the full $1,000, but it accrued interest during the period that it was held. The difference was $8,320 which Mr. Goldstone placed in his own pocket. No, it did not seem as if he would last those thirty-two months.

Lanie might not have known how to keep the Arden books as well as Goldstone could—it once had been suggested that she be fired for her ineptitude in that department—but she did know the difference between a Series F and a Series G bond. When she explained that difference, Elizabeth could hardly contain herself. She sent for one of her vice-presidents, Charles Mooney, and instituted a thorough investigation.

The result was that Mr. Goldstone was taken to court on charges of war bond fraud. Elizabeth was so used to court actions that it was only a minor irritation. The really disturbing thing was that the incident somehow had tainted her lovely gesture. She had wanted it to be a gracious and sentimental occasion, and it was spoiled for her.

For all her authority and success, she could not control the unpredictable behavior of others. It was as if they were in rebellion, as if they had to see how far they could push her, as if her rigid rule presented a challenge to them. She could not understand them. All she wanted was what was best for Elizabeth Arden, and that was surely also best for all those dependent on her.

The years of having been proven right were meaningless. They still

:[235]:

would not accede without a battle. Her lawyers had been against the fashion floor. They had argued that it could only lose money in America. She had been adamant about getting her own way and, in the end, had won her point. The clients came to see the unprofitable couture, and remained to buy the very profitable *prêt-à-porter*.

It was getting too easy in the business. A good shout, and she had her way. It was enervating and just a little boring. There was no rejuvenating challenge. Fortunately, there was another sphere of interest in her life and, in it, there were new battles, new contests, new laurels to be won.

In the late thirties and early forties, the installation of parimutuel machines at the tracks turned racing into a big business. Until their appearance, bets had been taken by bookmakers, and the tracks had been supported by entrance fees, tickets, rentals, and racing associations. Many of the most important were in debt; Belmont, which is still the largest as well as one of the most beautiful in the country, ran in the red for forty-eight years. Prizes were slight, and the cost of raising thoroughbreds so high that only the rich could afford to keep large racing stables.

The betting machines changed the entire picture. The tracks were able to keep a large part of the proceeds from gambling, and they became profitable enterprises. The individual racing associations wanted to attract the best horses for important events, and the winner's money rose to five and six figures. As a result, owning a stable became big business, rather than only the pastime of the privileged.

Elizabeth's phenomenal luck and sense of timing had worked again. She was in at the beginning of another industry, for, whether or not it was admitted by the haughty monarchs of the turf, the breeding and racing of horses had become an industry.

It was no wonder that she often confused her two businesses and treated them interchangeably. The parallels were striking. As it had been at the beginning of her cosmetics empire, the first big growth of the Maine Chance stable took place during a great war with all of its incumbent priorities and restrictions.

Gas rationing ruled out horse trailers. For the duration, no special trains would be run to the tracks. The carefully bred horses had to be shipped to the nearest regular train station and then walked from there across lawns to their destination.

Elizabeth thrived on the obstacles. Through the years, she had grown expert at finding ways of circumventing prohibitions, and it was not surprising that her stable managed to travel in great comfort—and so did she, for wherever her darlings ran, Elizabeth appeared. She said, ''The babies do better, when they know I'm there.''

Astonishingly enough, she was right.

Increased air service made it easier for her to be omnipresent and, between tracks and salons, she began to clock hundreds of thousands of miles of travel each year. With her tight schedule, it was never certain which plane she could make, and reservations in different names were held on all flights through the day. Managing this in wartime was extraordinary. There were twenty servicemen for each available seat, but that did not daunt Elizabeth. Her hogging of space might mean that an officer was late in rejoining his command, but that was inconsequential when compared to the possibility of Mrs. Graham's not being on hand to give her little pets a pre-race pep talk.

After lovingly whispering in the horse's ear, she would take the jockey aside and, shaking a menacing fist at him, shout, ''Get out in front and go, go, go!''

The jocks often responded with the same dispatch as her sales force when, pounding that fist against her desk, she cried, ''To get along in this world, you've got to fight, fight, fight!''

It was never the animal's fault, when her exhortations did not work, and the race was lost. She would tear into the jockey, shrieking, ''I told you not to use your crop! It's no wonder the poor darling couldn't run. You scared him half to death.''

After that, the trainer would get his share of her wrath and then, turning fondly to the poor loser, she would massage his legs and coo

:[237   ]:

lovingly, "There, there. Don't be ashamed. Mama will take good care of her darling baby."

In her dealings with trainers, she had a mother's skepticism toward a schoolmaster who has reprimanded her child. She much preferred to listen to the advice of stableboys, for she felt that they really loved her babies. She did not know that, behind her back, the boys called her "Mrs. Mudpack."

It was almost a rule that anything a trainer did was open to suspicion. One of them went to a great deal of trouble to get her Colonel Bradley's barn at Saratoga. It was considered the best on the premises, because it was separated from the other barns and away from the noise and the often overstimulating atmosphere of the track area. When she saw it, she lashed out at the poor man. "God, you're stupid! I ought to bounce you! How dare you house my horses this far from the track? By the time the darlings have walked the distance, they'll be too tired to run."

With Leslie Combs remaining in fixed position as her adviser and horse manager, the trainers came and went with such dizzying speed that it became a standard racetrack game to try to name all of the men and women who had ever worked for Mrs. Graham. Most of them echoed the sentiments of her first trainer, Clarence Buxton. When asked why he had left, he replied, "I insisted on treating a horse like a horse. She couldn't understand that."

Louis Fuestal established something of a record by remaining with her for two years, but he was already an old man and only biding time until his retirement. After he left, the revolving door was spinning so swiftly that it all but disappeared.

One trainer was fired, because he had the audacity to tell her that her preparations were bad for the animals and, what was more insulting, they smelled worse than horse liniment. Another, Guy Bedell, told her off before she got a chance to tell him off. A third departed in disgust over her interior decoration of the barns. He said, "Seems like we spend more money for paint than anything else.

And then, in 1944, along came the third important Tom in her life, "Silent" Tom Smith. He was almost seventy and had learned a good deal of tolerance during his early years. He had spent twenty-five years knocking around, trying his hand at everything from being a sheepherder, to blacksmith, to cowhand, to trainer of second-rate horses on a cheap Western rodeo circuit. The big chance in his life came late, when he took a $7,500 claim horse and trained him into the mighty Seabiscuit. By the time he started at the Maine Chance stable he was one of the best trainers in the country.

Elizabeth was soon convinced that he would not hurt her darlings and that he really knew about horses. She said, "He spends a lot of time just staring at the horses and, when he's through, they know they've had the third degree." She paused thoughtfully and then added with some surprise in her voice, "Come to think of it, he does the same thing to me."

She was also convinced that he would play it straight with her, and when he suggested that she spend $287,000 for twenty babies during his first year with her, she did it without a murmur. Her confidence paid off, for among them, she acquired the following year's colt and filly champions, Star Pilot and Beaugay.

Her stable earnings, for 1943, were a niggardly $6,865. By the end of '44, under Smith's guidance, the figure rose to $79,235. He was spending money, but he was getting results, and that was all that mattered to Elizabeth. She was determined to be a winner, even if she went broke in the process.

True to his nickname, Smith silently put up with all of her idiosyncrasies. He let her talk all the baby talk that she wanted, on the theory that the horses did not understand what she was saying. He permitted them to be rubbed down with all her preparations, explaining laconically, "They don't do them any harm." When she wanted one groom fired, because he had a mean face and another because he had unruly hair, he did as he was told.

He followed any orders that would make her happy, so long as they did not hurt the animals. He said, "I try not to hurt her feelings, and yet do it my way."

For Elizabeth, 1944 was a very good year. She had her two Toms,

Smith and White, business was excellent, and her stable was developing very nicely. By summer it appeared that the war in Europe was entering its final stage, and on August 25, Paris was liberated.

The Arden Place Vendôme salon had been closed during the week of street fighting that had preceded the German withdrawal. On August 29, an International News Service correspondent, Lee Carson, filed a story about its reopening that was picked up in newspapers clear across America. Miss Carson had an appointment to get the works. The Parisiennes incredibly had retained all their chic, and the American reporter wanted to face them with a face as well cosmeticized as their own.

Elizabeth might have been pleased to read that Paris was once again ripe for the profit picking were Gladys not still in an internment camp. She pulled every string she could to get a phone call through to Henri de Maublanc and listened patiently while he boasted of having kept the salon open all through the occupation.

He assured that she would be happy with the figures. He even had managed to get raw materials and had continued to manufacture the products. Jars had been the only problem, but the dear clients had been so brave. They had dutifully washed out their old jars and brought them back for refilling. There would be some resentment for their having remained open, but it would not amount to much. All the big fashion and beauty establishments had done the same except Molyneaux, who was British, and Chanel, who had been closed but had offered very little resistance to the highly placed German who had kept her very comfortable at the Ritz.

Elizabeth screamed, "Never mind all that crap. Tell me about Gladys."

"Gladys has been remarkable. Not only did she survive Ravensbrück, but she helped many others to survive, too."

"Did you get her released?"

"That was impossible. She had done a terrible thing."

"You could get materials to manufacture creams, but you could not get your wife out of a concentration camp?"

"I did get her transferred to Vittel, here in France. It's a much better place. Only English and American women are interned there. Soon it will be captured by the Allies, and we will be together again.''

"Henri, get the hell out of my salon. And stay out! You're bounced! I don't ever want to see you again.''

She slammed down the phone and buried her face in her hands. The sobbing began, and it was uncontrollable. She had been able to live with what had happened to Gladys, so long as her freedom had remained a distant hope but now that it was so close, the waiting period would be a long and unbearable anguish.

By late autumn it was over. She could take down the map that she had hung on her wall. The pins that had marked the Army's interminably slow progress to Vittel had reached the Rhine.

Again influence was exerted, and she got through to Gladys on the phone. Sister bubbled about saving herself and the others at Ravensbrück. "We did exercises every single day and drank as much water as we could hold. The good old Arden theory of flushing out the poisons.''

Beneath the surface ebullience, her speech was slow and betrayed a

Elizabeth congratulating Antonio Castillo after the opening showing of a fall collection.

great fatigue. Elizabeth said, "I'm going to get you over here as soon as I can."

"Not too soon. I've so much to do in Paris. The business and—" Her voice broke.

"What's wrong? Darling, are you crying?"

"I've got to sell the house St. Jouy-en-Joses."

"But you love it so much."

"If Henri ever shows his face there, the peasants threaten to hang him."

"That dreadful man!"

"You mustn't say anything against him. He saved my life. I wouldn't have lived through it if he hadn't got me to Vittel."

"You must come here."

"I know. Soon, dear, soon."

By the beginning of 1945 the sixty-five year-old Gladys had recovered her strength sufficiently for the sisters to resume their old business association. Elizabeth had an idea, and Gladys attended to its execution.

Miss Arden wrote, "Find a good young French designer who wants to come to America when the war is over. I want Elizabeth Arden to be the first in New York to carry French *haute couture* again."

Antonio Castillo was not French, he had been born in Madrid, but he had worked for Chanel, Paquin, and Piquet, and he was considered one of the most promising of the new generation of designers that would emerge with the end of hostilities. Contracts were signed for him to come to New York as soon as it was possible.

In the meantime, Elizabeth Arden presented a new spring collection with no designer given credit. Miss Arden's personal touch was evident in the many ruffles and the demure conservatism of the cuts. It was all prettiness and innocence—clothes for a middle-aged and over-aged maiden to wear at the dawn of a new world.

Peace was coming, and Elizabeth was rushing out to meet it, as if its trailing glories were all for her. On the track, they were. "Silent" Tom's astute handling was paying off, and it was win, win, win. He

Miss Arden at Saratoga racetrack with Jack Treat, gentleman-in-waiting and vice-president of Arden Sales Corporation, the wholesale side of the Arden empire.

observed, "Once this war is over, good blood's gonna come high. Now's the time to buy."

Elizabeth was as silent as her trainer. She merely nodded and spent $321,700 for seventeen yearlings. Tom was beginning to have a grudging admiration for the little lady. Beneath the frills and tantrums, she was quite a sport, and some of those crazy theories of hers were proving not so crazy after all. The filly might even have a little horse sense.

There was the time the swelling wouldn't leave War Date's sore knee. Brave as they come, she just climbed under that big, cranky animal and started to massage him just like she was giving the business to the puss of some la-de-da dame. Damned if the swelling didn't disappear.

A woman who lined her own shoes with newspapers would naturally consider herself an expert on knowing when they were too tight. One of the colts was limping, and she decided that it was because one of his shoes did not fit properly. She ordered it yanked off, and she was right. In language that would make a blacksmith blush, she fired the one who had been responsible and then sweetly hired another, twittering, "Baby needs a new pair of shoes."

It was when "Silent" Tom got into personal trouble, that the lady's class really showed. On November 8, Smith was handed a one-year suspension by the Jockey Club for allegedly administering a mild stimulant, ephedrine, to a Maine Chance horse, Magnific Duel, before he won a race at Jamaica with an insignificant purse of $1,900. Elizabeth stood by him all the way. She even hired his defense attorney. When he lost, she kept him on as unofficial trainer and hired his son, Jimmy, to act in the official capacity until the sentence was over. Aside from personal loyalty, Mrs. Graham had an excellent reason for retaining him. Smith's guidance had led Maine Chance to an annual take of $589,170, making it the highest winning stable of 1945.

At sixty-seven, she had reached the pinnacle of a new career. Everything had worked out beautifully during that very sweet year. The world was at peace. Sister was safe and would soon be with her. She had even found a very suitable new beau. For some time, she had been thinking that life was too short for a girl to waste time sitting around all alone at the telephone, and she arranged for this one to be on tap when she did the calling.

Jack Treat came to work for the Arden Company in the middle of that year and, no mistake about it, Jack was a treat to his employer. He was very competent at his job, or he would never have been hired, but he was also handsome, charming, amusing, and available. With no wife to encumber him, he was free to play Essex to this particular Elizabeth. The fact that he was almost half her age did not unduly disturb her when they were out together, for she rarely thought of age.

Her private life was in order, and she was free to look forward to what she hoped would be the best year of her life. She had two great horses, Lord Boswell and Star Pilot, and had her heart set on winning the great racing triple crown, the Kentucky Derby, the Preakness, and the Belmont Stakes.

She was also preparing for the February opening of the first Castillo collection. Word was filtering back from France that three newcomers, Balmain, Balenciaga, and Dior, would be the sensations of the season, but she was not disturbed. Elizabeth Arden was offering her fashion-hungry clients the best of Paris right in New York, while restrictions were still making transatlantic travel almost

Miss Elizabeth Arden Graham, as she preferred to be known in racing circles, shakes hand of jockey Bobby Permane after he won the race aboard her thoroughbred Knockdown at Belmont.

impossible, and others were not yet ready to go into full-scale operations.

Castillo's elegant clothes opened to rave notices, and overnight the unknown Spaniard was the darling of the fashion press. Elizabeth was well pleased, mostly, because all the reviews had given as much credit and attention to her as they had to him. Her publicity department had discreetly seen to that; Elizabeth Arden was determined never again to place second to a Charles James' first.

Once the show was out of the way, she turned her attention back to readying her stable for the big races. Among the horses purchased during the previous year, Leslie Combs had bought one at the Alfred Vanderbilt sale, on personal instructions from Mrs. Graham. This order had nothing to do with racing. Her eyes were still firmly set upon a position among the social stars, and none shone more brightly than the dapper Mr. Vanderbilt. She had sent word to Combs, "Buy one horse out of courtesy."

He had paid only $2,000 for Knockdown, and for Elizabeth, it was hate at first sight. The animal was everything that she could not tolerate. His groom called him Big Foot Hoss, and he was ugly. She would not have an unattractive woman working in her salon, and she would not have an unattractive horse working in her stable. He also had a wicked disposition and would not permit her to fondle or baby talk him. She instructed Smith, "Find a buyer and get rid of him."

Smith took a long and appraising look at the critter and allowed as he would—someday. Before that day came, Knockdown was entered in the $100,000 Santa Anita Derby, along with Mrs. Graham's little darling, Star Pilot, who had already won purses totaling $187,385. His owner had visions of making him the biggest winner in racing history. Unfortunately, those visions were not communicated to Knockdown, who got out in front and refused to give way.

After the race, she went down to see her winner. She told Smith, "I do believe that horse is beginning to like me."

She made a flirtatious pass at the animal and started to move in on him. Knockdown pinned back his ears and let out a bloodcurdling whinny. His groom shouted, ''You get one step closer, lady, and he'll knock your brains out.''

When Knockdown again beat her darling in a nine-furlong workout, Elizabeth reluctantly scratched Star Pilot's name as a Derby entry and penciled in the ugly duckling.

She had three horses entered in the Churchill Downs classic, Lord Boswell, Knockdown and, to set the pace, Perfect Bahram. The week before the big race, they were ensconced in Lexington, while the rest of the Maine Chance stable—twenty-eight extremely valuable thoroughbreds—was in her barn at Arlington Park, for the Chicago racing season.

Shortly after midnight, a flash blaze broke out in one of the unoccupied Arlington Park box stalls. Mrs. Graham's night-watchman, Gilbert Jones, smelled smoke. He opened the door, and the flames shot out at him.

After sounding the alarm, he roused eighteen stablehands to help him remove the terrified horses. ''I rushed straight off to Beaugay, because she's my favorite, and somehow I got her out of there, rearing and kicking. Someone held her outside. I don't know who.''

Before the night was over, it had developed into the costliest fire in racing history. Twenty-two of Elizabeth's prize horses and two lead ponies perished. The six that were saved besides Beaugay included War Date, Blue Fantasy, and Jet Pilot.

An investigation was instituted by morning. Track director Ben Lindheimer issued a statement to the press. ''Special fire and police protection are an important part of our operations, but it was impossible to check the flames, because of the explosive nature of the fire.''

The special investigators were ordered to report directly to the Illinois racing commissioner, Major Ednyfred Williams. It was learned that two grooms had been assigned to the room in which the flames were discovered, but one had been out of town and the other away from the barn. The major commented, ''How long either was gone before the fire, we don't know.''

A preliminary investigation proved that faulty wiring was not responsible. During the early stages, the electric lights had remained on. The commissioner said, ''I can't help but feel that this sad thing happened because of the carelessness of some individual.

Although the mystery was never cleared up to anybody's complete satisfaction, Jones was eventually held responsible for the blaze. He was fined $50. The value of the lost stock was placed at a good deal more than the $500,000 for which the horses had been insured.

When Elizabeth received the news, the breath drained from her body, leaving behind an ashen and deflated old woman. Tom White was on the phone comforting her most of the night. At one point, she whispered, ''If I were superstitious—you know—it's my second fire. Things happen in threes.''

She flew directly to Louisville, and Leslie Combs whisked her off to his Spendthrift Farm, in Lexington, where her horses were boarded. She was much too upset to make any comment to the throng of newsmen awaiting her arrival. In her name, Combs assured them that the disaster would have no effect upon her plans to enter her horses in the Derby on the following Saturday. Lord Boswell, Knockdown, and Perfect Bahram would run as scheduled.

''She'll stay in racing,'' he prophesied. ''She's enjoyed it too much to quit now. Her horses are her only recreation.''

A makeup artist and a hairdresser were flown down from the New York salon. On the morning of the big race, they set to work on a strangely serene Miss Arden. She slipped into a chic new Castillo suit and set a pert hat at a jaunty angle. Looking extremely pretty, she took Combs' arm, winked, and said, ''I'm ready. Shall we go?''

The big crowd of over 100,000 was concentrating on the odds board, but the inner racing circle, seated in boxes close to Elizabeth's, kept stealing glances at her. If they expected to see any signs of defeat, they were disappointed. She rarely seemed less untroubled, as she nodded, and smiled, and waved. One old Kentucky gentleman studied her appreciatively. He tipped his hat and bowed, commenting, ''The winner of this race isn't going to be the only great champion around here.''

The odds came down. Both Lord Boswell and Knockdown were two-to-one favorites. The big event began, and Elizabeth clutched Combs' arm, muttering incantations meant exclusively for her unheeding horses. At the finish, her smile broadened, and blinking back tears, she said, "Well—that was a bit of a kick in the pants, wasn't it?"

Assault, an eight-to-one underdog, had beaten the two favorites and won the day. Elizabeth was asked about her racing plans. She responded, "I think I'd better buy some new horses."

Soon after, she spent $229,500 for seven carefully selected youngsters. Her losses from the fire represented over a half million. Her stable earnings had slipped over $100,000 from the previous year's high—but she was still in there riding to win.

Derby Day had not been a total disaster for Maine Chance, but the many gloating over the proud lady's defeat did not recall that until much later. The first race of the day had marked the debut of the two-year-old Jet Pilot, one of the horses rescued from the fire. He galloped home nine lengths in front of the nearest contender. One onlooker observed "There's the next Derby winner."

CHAPTER FIFTEEN

Second Chance

Jet Pilot had always been a mischievous little darling. Suddenly, he broke free of his box. Given the chance, it was exactly the sort of thing the little rascal would do. How often she had told them to keep an extra watch on him, but nobody ever paid any attention to her. She was only the foolish woman who happened to own him.

He was running, bolting—his halter flying wild and free. The apple tree—"Watch out!" She tried to scream, but her voice was strangled in her throat. The loose halter became enmeshed in one of the low branches. Jet Pilot was yanking furiously, trying to pull himself free. "Stop," she tried to shout. "Don't! Easy, baby, easy."

But there was still no voice. There was nothing she could do but look on in mute horror. The poor baby was terrified. He thrashed around, but that only made things worse, as the halter shortened and tightened around his neck. Then, it was over. There was a great stillness. The magnificent beast had strangled himself, and all her hopes were dead with him.

"God," she cried. "God, don't let this happen to me. Not to me! Not me!"

The room was dark and silent except for the hum of traffic from the avenue far below. She could feel the tears, irritating, cold streams running down her cheeks. Her neck was sore, the muscles overextended and tense, her throat constricted, as if she had been shrieking for hours. A dream, it had all been a dream. She began to laugh hysterically, but the laughter died as quickly as it had started. Not a dream—a premonition—the Ides of March and all that. They had to be warned before it was too late. She put on the light and reached for her bedside phone.

The ringing awakened ''Silent'' Tom. Cussing under his breath, he answered it. ''Tom, it's Mrs. Graham. I've something to tell you. Something—'' The voice was shrill and often incoherent, as she described her dream. ''You've got to do something about it. Go and see that Jet Pilot is all right. Make sure of it.''

Tom stifled a yawn. ''Now, Mrs. Graham, you just take it easy and go back to sleep. There ain't a tree within a hundred yards of the stable.''

''That was the last time you looked,'' she screeched. ''You lazy old man! Get up and take another look. That's an order. Do it now or, I swear, I'll bounce you!''

The phone was slammed down in his ear. One of these days, he thought calmly, one of these days, Mrs. Graham—

Her jockey, Eric Guerin, and his agent were on the plane to Louisville with her. Guerin had been her second choice, and Elizabeth did not quite trust the capabilities of the twenty-two-year-old, who was about to ride in the Derby for the first time. She decided to add a little incentive.

In addition to his regular fee, if he won, Guerin was in for 10 percent of the $91,160 purse. She promised to double that for a win.

The weatherman's prediction for the 1947 Derby Day was fair and warmer, but after a night of light but steady rain, the morning was gray, damp, and trifle chilly. The threatening sky did not stop the first fans from arriving, at Churchill Downs, as early as 7 A.M. By the time the horses started exercising at 11:30 most of the record crowd of 115,000 had found their places.

The track was described as ''muddy'' for the first four races and ''slow'' for the rest of the day. During the early part of the afternoon, the sun made a few feeble attempts to break through the heavy clouds.

The *Time* cover of Elizabeth Arden, May 6,
1946, when she was at the height of her
racing success.
Cover portrait courtesy Time *Magazine.*
Copyright © Time, Inc. 1946.

As the start of the main event approached, the board gave two-to-one odds to the favorite, Phalanx, while Jet Pilot was listed at better than six to one. The Pilot had already racked up more than $100,000 in winnings, but the Louisville sages held out little hope for him in the most important race of his life. Their opinion was that he was a speed horse and would not be able to go the mile and one-quarter distance. "Silent" Tom remained silent, just as he had when Mrs. Graham had called to inform him that it was going to be a wet track, which he already knew.

Jet Pilot started from the outside post position and, after a few yards, streaked into the lead, but early leads did not portend anything in this race. Many jockeys reined in at the beginning, conserving their mounts' strength for the telling final quarter of a mile.

He was still in the lead at the end of the first quarter. By the three-quarter mark he was a length ahead of the closest horse and a length and a half at the mile. This did not disturb the experts. As they'd already said, he was a speed horse. Now wait. Watch. See what happens. The big timers, Faultless and Phalanx, started to make their bid. The distance shortened, and into the homestretch, it looked as if they might outdistance the leader at any moment.

It had been a hand race all along, but with Phalanx at the Pilot's neck, Guerin decided to use the crop. His hand stopped in midair, as he recalled, just in time, that the sensitive animal had swerved the one time he had hit him in a trial run. Instead, the jockey only waved the stick before the horse's eyes. Jet Pilot got the message. With a last surge of speed, he crossed the finish line a head in front of Phalanx and two beyond Faultless.

Elizabeth set some kind of Derby record for smiles as she entered the winner's circle. There were loving pats on the Pilot's nose and handshakes for Smith and Guerin. The trainer opened his mouth for the first time that day and told her, "After it rained, I was pretty sure we'd win."

"It's on to the Preakness," Elizabeth cried delightedly. Tom held his counsel. The champion had been suffering from a break in his hoof and had been forced to wear a special shoe to hold it together

:[253]:

against the threat of a crack. It was heavier and more cumbersome than a racing plate and had been removed for the Derby with no apparent ill effects. The trainer wondered how long their luck would hold.

From the beginning of the Preakness, the experts could see that the Pilot was having foot trouble, and he finished fourth to Calumet's Faultless. They withdrew him from the Belmont to be "freshened up." He was never again entered in a major race and was put out to stud in 1949. None of his descendants amounted to much, but the gallant Jet Pilot had entered racing history by winning the big one, and had brought Elizabeth back from utter defeat to the crowning achievement of turfdom.

By the middle of the Derby summer "Silent" Tom had just about had enough of the tantrums, and the follies, and the unpredictable nature of the lady, and he resigned. Elizabeth was never to find another trainer she trusted so well. In the nineteen years that followed, she went through over fifty of them, finally concluding, "I think in all truth, I am a better trainer, myself, than most of those whose profession it is. I at least take the trouble and have the heart to be close to the horses and give them personal attention."

She caused a desert to bloom—with the help of an excellent Swedish gardener. She found a barren wilderness and created a paradise—with the help of several hundred thousand dollars. And, lo, the faithful did come. The fatties to slim, and the drunkards to dry, and the skeletons to put on flesh. In the shadow of Camelback Mountain, many miracles came to pass. And Elizabeth was many times enriched.

The second Maine Chance spa, just outside Phoenix, Arizona, was more opulent than the first because, from the very beginning, it had been designed to Elizabeth's specifications for grandeur. She once ordered a new cottage built at a cost of $100,000. The construction took place, while she was in the hospital having a gallbladder operation. By the time she first saw it the building was completed. She shouted, "Where's my view? What have you done with my view?"

The house was facing in the wrong direction and did not get her favorite vista of Camelback. She shook her fist at the contractor. "It's all wrong! You must turn it around immediately."

"But Miss Arden, it'll cost a fortune."

"Turn it around!"

"Yes, Miss Arden."

Elizabeth ruled Maine Chance like an empress. It did not matter that her court was composed of paying guests, they still had to give homage. As the head of Saks Fifth Avenue, Adam Gimbel was one of Arden's more important customers. His wife, Sophie, was a famous dress designer with her own custom department within the store. Mrs. Gimbel was a very elegant lady who, in her own way, was every bit as imperious as Elizabeth.

Sophie arrived for a stay at Maine Chance very late in the afternoon. It had been a very fatiguing journey, and she decided to have dinner in her own room. Word came from Elizabeth that she was expected to dine at her table. Sophie replied that she was extremely flattered by the invitation but, regretfully, was too tired to take advantage of it.

Word came back that nobody was permitted to eat in her own room and that Elizabeth still expected her downstairs. Mrs. Gimbel became extremely irritated and again declined. She was going to have her meal where she damned well pleased.

Another message. There could be no infraction of the rules. If Mrs. Gimbel could not come downstairs like everybody else, Mrs. Gimbel would go without food. Her irritation turned to fury. To hell with the rules! She was hungry, and she wanted a tray sent up immediately.

The tray arrived, but the only thing on it was an official looking letter. It stated that as she was unable to obey the rules of the establishment, she would be expected to leave the premises by seven thirty the next morning. Sophie looked at the empty tray and then at the letter. She was not the sort of woman to eat her words, and so she departed before the hour designated.

The exchange obviously did not make Mr. Gimbel very happy, and what did not make him very happy did not make Saks very happy. At his next birthday, a messenger waited patiently outside his office. He carried an enormous bouquet of flowers from Elizabeth Arden that were to be delivered personally to Adam Gimbel and to nobody else.

To many, the two Maine Chances would have seemed hopelessly extravagant enterprises, but they suited Elizabeth's theory of economy by providing a much tidier operation than had been possible with only one. Each was opened for four months at opposite ends of the calendar. She could keep the same staff for both, shipping them back and forth with a one-month holiday between the start and finish of the respective seasons. At first, she also shipped the linens and china up and down between Maine and Arizona. Her manager convinced her that it was more economical to have two sets of everything. It lessened the wear and tear, saved the cost of packing and shipping, and reduced the chances of breakage.

Elizabeth took a real pride in what the two Maine Chances accomplished for women. She often watched them leaving at the end of their stays and said, "They do look much better than they did when they arrived."

Many agreed with her, but the writer Jessica Mitford was not among them. Perhaps it was because the plump, vaguely leftish, and snobbishly aristocratic Britisher was fresh from writing *The American Way of Death* and could see no justification for wealthy and indolent American women to put themselves through tortures worse than death for the sake of their vanities. In a *McCall's* piece, in which she treated Maine Chance in much the same way that she had previously treated Forest Lawn, she wrote skeptically of the results. "It's like taking old Tray to the vet for a clip and bath. He quickly reverts to his usual state."

She also observed that she had been treated "ever so gently and kindly by everyone. Like a half-witted child aged seven." Nevertheless, she lost five pounds in one week, and most women would gladly suffer some immature coddling to do the same.

By the time she reached seventy, Elizabeth was beginning to think of herself as possessing something of the infallibility of a god. She told a *Saturday Evening Post* interviewer, in 1948, "If one of my

Elizabeth Arden with her favorite niece, Mrs. Patricia Young, entering the Metropolitan Opera House on opening night.

products fails, there's something impure in the user's system. She should try a little enema—and if that doesn't help—a high colonic will.''

Charles Revson was a new and rather formidable competitor. His Revlon matching nail polish and lipstick created one of the biggest sensations in postwar cosmetics. She might have been thinking of him, when she said in the same interview, ''This business is intimate. And it's essentially feminine. What male executive will throw away a whole batch of powder, because the shade's off an indiscernible fraction? Sniff a half-dozen sachets daily for months to be sure the odor chosen is the most wonderful smell in the world? Or spend weeks mixing nail polish to get the right color—the one women will adore—that will make her look like a lady instead of a slob? I've been doing it every day of my life—and I adore it.''

Wellington Cross remained, but most of the old inner circle was going. Lanie and Genevieve Cliff Daily were retiring. Wonnie had gone back to England. Maria Hugo was also gone. Elizabeth had outlasted them all—and so many others. Rather than recall old times and old friends, she was busily gathering a new group of faithful attendants to serve her until, as she was convinced she would, she outlasted them. They were all much younger in years, but few were possessed of that sense of urgency, that spark, that driving vitality that kept her younger than most people had ever been in all their lives.

There were Jack Treat, and Lanfranco Rasponi, and Florence Owens, and Julia Brokaw Lowell, and Mary Dendrammis, her old friend, Carl Gardiner and, most of all, there was her niece, Patricia Young. Pat had been through two marriages and had one young son. Her life had not been a very happy one, and she was beginning to lose a sense of direction when Elizabeth swept her up and changed all that.

She moved in with her aunt and became her companion, her guardian, and, in a sense, her shadow. Where Elizabeth went, Pat went. She suffered her small cruelties, her whims, her outbursts, and her enormous kindness. Like Georgia Reed, so many years before, she was another who would never have to worry for as long as she lived. All she needed to be was faithful, and Elizabeth would look after the rest.

That was always the rule. Serve me well, and you won't have to wait until heaven for your reward. Those, who did not or could not adhere to it, saw the other side—the vindictive, sadistic, and often very petty other face of Elizabeth Arden.

She began to travel at an even more furious pace. If there had been no air age, it would have had to be invented just for her. There was so much to do, so many places to visit, and, suddenly, she could be anywhere in the world in a matter of hours.

Elizabeth and Gladys were flying West. Elizabeth glanced over at her sister. She was so thin, not thin in the way of fashion, painfully thin in the way of hunger and suffering. The new dentures were giving her trouble, and she was pushing against them with her tongue. The stewardess passed the trays, and Elizabeth's gesture was almost a warning, jabbing finger. "Eat something."

Gladys smiled. People were forever telling her to eat something. It was the only pleasant change that had resulted from Ravensbruck. No need to starve herself into the latest styles. She studied the antiseptic airline meal with dismay. A short while ago she would have sold her soul for it, but a return to Paris gastronomy had revived taste buds that she thought had been killed by the North German chill. The new teeth would give her an adequate excuse to ignore Elizabeth's admonitions and reject the plastic-looking food.

She turned and stared out the window. Beneath the clouds were mountains, and plains, and rivers. Five years out of her life, and she had come back to a different world. She wondered if she would ever get used to flying these great distances. Elizabeth adored it. She took to the air as if born with wings.

It had been so long since Gladys had last seen her son. She had

The two sisters made an unbeatable business team. Gladys and Elizabeth en route to Paris after opening the Madrid salon.

At the Belmont Ball, held at the Waldorf-Astoria on June 1, 1966, Mrs. Elizabeth N. Graham (Elizabeth Arden) is seen with Ambassador John Davis Lodge (left) and Admiral John M. Will. Seated next to her is Mrs. John Davis Lodge.

never met his wife. What were they like? Would there be a show of love? There would surely be kindness, after what she had been through, they could not help being kind.

While Gladys ruminated on her family, Elizabeth's thoughts were on what she held nearest and dearest. I'll show them that Elizabeth Arden doesn't need them, she thought. I'll show them that Elizabeth Arden doesn't need anybody but herself. The San Francisco salon had been located in I. Magnin's. The store was moving into new quarters, on Union Square, and wanted her to pay for her own installation. Rather than do that, she would build her own salon, and what a salon it would be. She had already chosen the site, a divine house on Sutter Street. Everybody told her that it was off the beaten track, too far from the heart of the shopping section. What nonsense! A few blocks, that was all, and if it was now off the beaten track, Elizabeth Arden would put it right on it.

With Daily gone, she would put that nice Lillian Macmillan in as manager. She smiled as she recalled their meeting. The old intuition had been working just fine. She had gone to Denver to do the commentary for a fashion show at Neusteter's. Macmillan was the assistant buyer at the store, who had been assigned to work with her.

Elizabeth had a lot on her mind. The first group of dresses came out. They were in different shades, but all she could think of was Mediterranee, the newest color in the collection, and that was how she identified the lot. Macmillan asked—what color is this— Mediterranee—and this—Mediterranee—and this—Mediterranee. Alarmed by getting the same response each time, she signaled to Bettie Hamilton to do something. Bettie hastily wrote the colors on a slip of paper, wrapped it around a rose, and slipped it to Miss Arden. From then on, things went beautifully. She read the colors, and Macmillan carried the whole thing off to perfection.

Former Ambassador to Spain and Turkey Stanton Griffis often escorted Elizabeth to charity balls.

On the dais and attending the Philharmonic luncheon Elizabeth Arden flanked on the left by William Randolph Hearst, Jr., and on the right by New York City's former Mayor Robert Wagner.

On the way to the airport, she said, ''Get that Macmillan. I want her.''

''She's just taken a new job.

''I don't care. Top the offer. Get her.''

At first, Gladys had not been overly impressed with her daughter-in-law, Patti. Her open American simplicity was not to the French

:[262   ]:

taste, but as time passed, she grew to value and love her. Any reservations she had about the marriage were completely vanquished by her two adorable granddaughters.

Flying was one of John Baraba's big passions. When he was released from the Air Corps, he had joined Lockheed as an engineer. He was happy in his work, but it did not satisfy his mother. She wanted him in the business. There was an empire, and it belonged exclusively to the Graham sisters. With a greater perception into fatality than Elizabeth had, she knew that they could not live forever, that somebody would have to take over after they were gone.

He was the only male heir. It could all belong to him. She hammered away at the subject until the easygoing John relented and admitted that he might be interested. That was all Gladys had been waiting to hear. She called Elizabeth and convinced her to start him under Bert Chose. The West Coast territory was one of the most lucrative, and Chose would soon be retiring. She looked at her son and had visions of a giant rising out of the golden California sunset.

The next thing was the matter of name. Baraba would not do. They were Grahams. It was a Graham corporation. He would have to become a Graham, and at length, John changed his name. From then on, he was to be a beleaguered pawn, pushed up by his mother and down by his aunt, until he could take it no longer and retired from the business.

In the middle of the visit, word came from Paris that De Maublanc had died of a heart attack. Gladys wept and clung to her son. He had come back into her life at the right moment, the moment when she needed to have somebody to absorb the love that had been Henri's.

She asked only one thing of her son. ''Promise me. When I go—I'll be buried next to him.''

She needed an activity, and turned her attention to the way her family was living. It might have been satisfactory for an aeronautical engineer, but it would not do for the next head of Elizabeth Arden, and she began to decorate. When she was finished, Patti Graham observed, ''Our house was done in Early Grandmother period.''

While Gladys was refurbishing the Pacific Palisades, Elizabeth was ensconced in a suite at the St. Francis, in San Francisco, going over plans for the new salon. One of the innovations was to be an indoor exercise pool.

Bettie Hamilton was summoned to a breakfast conference. When she arrived, she found the blueprints scattered all over the floor, and Miss Arden crawling over them, too engrossed to greet her. She waited quietly and, after a few minutes, Elizabeth asked, "My God, you don't think anybody could drown in that thing, do you?"

She made the Sutter Street salon the most beautiful in the chain. In front, there was a rose garden, and a snack bar and garden were installed on the lovely slate roof. Artists painted ivy up the walls of the adjoining building to serve until the real plants had a chance to grow. The bar was housed in an orange and pink tent which, pretty as it was, proved a most unsatisfactory arrangement. Elizabeth had not counted on the San Francisco climate. There was a lot of rain, and the

John B. Graham of Elizabeth Arden in Paris was the son of Madame de Maublanc and nephew of Elizabeth. Here he is photographed in the hall of the Ritz Hotel with Fraulein Elfie Maerki of Elizabeth Arden in Düsseldorf, Frau Ile Steinboch of the German magazine *Constanze* and Comte Jacques de St. Phalle.

tent was some distance from the roof entrance. The girls had to be very fleet of foot if they did not want to get soaked.

After the lavish press reception, Sutter Street was like a tomb. The doubters had been right; it was too far away from things. Arden ordered Bettie Hamilton in off the road. "She's a very lively little thing, and she knows a lot of people. She'll drag them in, even if she has to use a fish net."

Elizabeth was passionate about yellow, and the last thing she did before leaving San Francisco was to buy some potted lemon trees for the roof. They were her pride and joy, but they died almost immediately after her departure. Lillian and Bettie did not dare to tell her, for they knew it would be blamed on their negligence. Miss Arden had mellowed some with age but, when provoked, she could still blow up a mighty storm.

Elizabeth was due to return to San Francisco on a Wednesday and leave again on early Friday. Miss Macmillan knew that she had to do something about the lemon trees, and she rented some for the period of her stay. It was fortuitous, for the first thing Miss Arden did was go to the roof to look at her trees. She cried delightedly, "Isn't all the rain marvelous? Why, I do believe they've grown three inches since I left."

On Friday morning, the truckers were already there to remove the trees, when Miss Arden unexpectedly appeared. Bettie Hamilton shrieked, "You're supposed to be on your way to New York!"

"I've decided to extend my stay over the weekend. I want to see the contractor. I'm not happy with the color of one of the treatment rooms." As soon as she was out of sight, Bettie sent the truckers away and made arrangements to keep the trees for a few days longer.

Later that day, Miss Arden was walking across the roof with the contractor. She paused to tear a limb from the rented tree and, brandishing it at the man, said, "This is the shade of yellow I want."

Hamilton raised her eyebrows, and Macmillan shrugged. The trees were there to stay.

The trip to Los Angeles had been to see how another of her intuitions, Mary Blakely, was getting along as the new manager of the Sunset Strip salon. Mary was the daughter-in-law of her good friend and former buyer, Grace Kaiser; and Elizabeth had known her socially for years. As Mary Carlisle, she had been a very successful ingenue with Paramount Pictures, playing leading roles opposite stars that included Bing Crosby, Bob Hope, and Lloyd Nolan. Petite, blond, and extremely pretty, she was rather like a much younger, idealized portrait of Elizabeth Arden.

With the passing years, Elizabeth had hired so many women who were merely youthful versions of herself that entering her salon was like watching the television game on which the leading question was "Will the real Elizabeth Arden please stand up?"

When Becky McGrevey went to work in the publicity department, she said, "Why, you know, all the executive women looked alike. Everybody was small-boned, blond, and pink and white. It took me six months, before I knew which was Miss Arden."

Julia Brokaw Lowell worked in the fashion department. She was constantly being amazed by Miss Arden's overwhelming personality and sales ability. She would start talking color and line, and before the customer knew what was happening, she would have ordered ten dresses. The woman would invariably call later to cancel all or most of the order. Weeks would pass before Miss Arden asked, "Did that nice Mrs.——get all those lovely clothes she bought?"

Julia would reply, "That nice Mrs.——canceled."

"The whole order?"

"Yes."

"What a nasty bitch!"

Clients would take all sorts of things from her because she was Elizabeth Arden, and because she had a way of telling them the most dreadful things and making them sound as if they were for their own good. To a plump lady, who was viewing the couture collection, she said, "Why don't you reduce? These clothes look better on thin people. I'll put you on a diet and sign you up for daily exercises and massages."

Elizabeth's great friend, Mrs. Humphrey Statter, the former Mrs. James Russell Lowell, who became the directress of the famous second-floor fashion salon at Arden's Fifth Avenue establishment. Mrs. William Woodward, Jr., is at right.

—Bert and Richard Morgan Studio Photo

It worked. The woman not only bought the clothes, but also paid for the treatments that would enable her to fit into them.

When things at the salon were running smoothly, and all appeared to be serene, Miss Arden would come in and stir them up. She hated tranquillity and believed that people functioned best under pressure. "There's nothing like a little flying fur to keep people on the *qui vive*, dear."

Working for her could be a great trial, but there was always the compensation of the exciting trips. The companion was always given charge of paying bills, tipping, and keeping her passport. On the passport, Miss Arden warned, "Don't you dare to peek inside. They've made a dreadful mistake about my age."

On tipping, the instructions were, "Tip very well, so that the next· time I come, they'll be glad to see me."

Elizabeth's friendship with the British royal family dated back to the reign of King George V and Queen Mary. The queen was a great believer in divine right, especially where her creditors were concerned. She was so famous for not paying her bills that when she opened antique fairs, the dealers would hide their best wares for fear that she might take a fancy to them.

Queen Mary was a client at Elizabeth Arden. On one of Elizabeth's visits to London, her manager asked what she should do about the queen's vastly overdue account. She did not know how to ask her sovereign for payment. Elizabeth said, "Let me handle it, dear."

The next time that the queen was in the salon, Elizabeth asked to be presented to her. After the usual exchange of courtesies, Elizabeth brought up the question of the bill. She had no sooner mentioned it than the queen interrupted, "My dear, you must come to tea at the palace."

The teas became ritual everytime Elizabeth was in London, and her daughter-in-law, the present queen mother, continued the tradition after her death. The result of all this tea drinking was that it completely washed away any question of payment on the part of the royal family.

The policy extended to Mary's other daughter-in-law, the Duchess of Windsor, who was the only person never to pay for treatments or purchases at the Paris salon. There were many shopkeepers who complained bitterly that the late duke had instructed his duchess only too well in the financial attitudes of his mother.

Because of Elizabeth's generosity, it was only fair that Mrs. Lowell and she be invited to one of the queen's parties, while they were visiting England. These annual receptions were such enormous crushes that traffic was stalled for blocks around Buckingham Palace. Miss Arden's invitation was special. Before the other guests arrived, she was to have a private audience with that other Queen Elizabeth, the one who sat on the British throne.

There were some problems that had to be resolved at the North Acton factory and, at the last minute, Elizabeth called and canceled the honor. Much as she loved the pomp and ceremony of royalty, business always came first.

They were very late in getting to the regular garden party. The footman asked what name he was to announce, and Julia automatically said, "Mrs. Elizabeth N. Graham," which was how she preferred to be addressed on social occasions. The man was singularly unimpressed. Elizabeth whispered, "No, dear. Tell him it's Elizabeth Arden."

When she corrected herself, the footman's attitude changed to one of servile respect. Elizabeth smiled. "You see, there are many Mrs. Grahams. But there's only one Elizabeth Arden."

During the late forties and early fifties, she kept popping up all over Europe almost as frequently as she did in America. She reopened her salon in Rome and built a new one in Milan. She was in the German village where her factory had been bombed out, and the people had asked her to rebuild at their expense.

The descent on Madrid took place on the Saturday before the Monday press opening of her first salon in the Spanish capital. The manager proudly took her on a tour of the new premises. The only comment was, "The colors are all wrong. I'll be here tomorrow. Get the painters in."

"But, Señora Arden," the manager protested, "tomorrow is Sunday. This is a Catholic country."

"Something wrong with your little ears, dear? I said—get them in here."

"Si, Señora Arden."

When the painters arrived the next day, they were a surly, unhappy crew. Elizabeth turned the charm on full force. She ordered a magnificent lunch with the best Spanish wines. Afterward they were fascinated with the idea of mixing colors to match mascaras and lipsticks. She even performed her favorite trick of beating egg yolks into the paint to get the right shade of yellow. Palm Beach was the only place where this had gone awry. The eggs had been rotten, and the salon had to be closed for fumigation and repainting. "You can't win them all, dear. No wonder the women in Palm Beach won't even boil eggs.''

By five in the afternoon the Spanish workers adored her and, laboring right through the night, redid the entire place in time for the opening reception.

Castillo got into an argument with one of Miss Arden's pets. He issued an ultimatum that either she went or he did. It was the height of the designer's popularity, but she let him go. Nobody took precedence over one of her girls. It was only later that she exclaimed, ''Damn it! I fired the wrong one!''

She had just returned from Italy and, with the phenomenal facility for anticipating vogues, knew that it would soon rival or outdistance France as the European fashion center. Word went out that she was looking for an Italian designer.

Carmel Snow saw the work of Count Ferdinando Sarmi at the 1951 fashion exposition in Florence. He was working for Fabiani, for whom he had designed some of the most popular dresses at the show. Mrs. Snow wired Elizabeth that she had found her man.

Though Elizabeth adored the combination of an aristocrat and an Italian, she didn't forget about business. When she brought him over, it was on a visitor's visa which meant that, contract or no contract, if he did not suit her, she could get rid of him at the end of three months.

Sarmi did not speak any English. Shortly after he arrived, Elizabeth invited Virginia Pope to lunch with them at the Colony. It was a shrewdly calculated move, for Miss Pope was the influential fashion editor of the New York *Times,* and she fancied that she spoke Italian fluently. Flattering her on her fashion sense and linguistic agility, Sarmi completely captivated the reporter. It might have been said that he kept his job through the New York *Times.*

Elizabeth would call her designer every morning and rattle away in English. For the first few weeks, he did not understand one word, but he already had learned the only necessary response. At every pause, he inserted a bright, ''Yes, Miss Arden.''

Count Ferdinando Sarmi and Miss Arden, who believed that designing for her salon went hand in hand with escorting her to charity balls.

His first collection got a rave review from Virginia Pope, who gave all of the credit to the charming Italian and only mentioned Miss Arden in passing. The fact that she had set it up did not deflect her fury. It was another Jamesian betrayal. This was an Elizabeth Arden collection—not a Sarmi collection. Orders were sent out to all of her advertising and public relations people to play down his name.

She made her point in anger and then completely forgot about it. A few months later she innocently asked Sarmi why he was getting no mention in the press. How could she make him famous if nobody knew who he was? He had to be famous, or clients would not pay Arden prices for his creations.

Her fury was rekindled. This time it was directed at her *stu-u-pid* press department. Word went out again. This time they were instructed to make certain that Sarmi got all the credit that he deserved.

As his English improved, she began to call upon her attractive designer to act as an escort. He was dubious about accepting, afraid that, by becoming one of the beaus, he might compromise his position with the company. He asked the advice of one of the old-timers. She said, "It's easy. There's only one thing you have to know about Miss Arden. If she says come—you come. If she says go—you go."

Sarmi was that rare Italian who hated the opera. He had an equal aversion to the races, but he found himself spending night after night at the former and day after day at the latter. One evening, they were having dinner before the opera. He was terribly proud that Pope Pius X, a first cousin of his grandfather, had just been canonized, and he excitedly told her about it. She became very girlish and said sweetly, "My dear Sarmi, you must forgive me, but I hate Catholics."

On another evening, when he thought he was not on call, he accepted an invitation to a dinner party that Frances Brooks was giving in honor of the Duke and Duchess of Windsor. Mrs. Brooks was acquainted with Elizabeth but had not invited her. Sarmi regretted mentioning it to her. He thought that she would be both hurt and angry, but she did not say a word about it, and he admired her for having the dignity to rise above the slight.

About a half hour before he was due at the party, Elizabeth telephoned. "Where are you? You're late."

Sarmi was confused. "I don't understand."

"We've got a dinner date."

"No. I'm going to Mrs. Brooks."

"You're coming to me. Cancel Mrs. Brooks."

"I can't do that. It would ruin her table."

"Cancel her—or I'll cancel you." So he dutifully went to her.

Mary Dendrammis was the wife of the Greek consul general in New York. The position did not confer affluence and Elizabeth, who enjoyed surrounding herself with wellborn people, gave her a job as a sort of general assistant. Mrs. Dendrammis was terrified of her, and each morning, she would stop at church to pray that she could get through the day without a mishap. The moment Miss Arden began to scream at somebody's inefficiency, Mary would begin to write furiously. The offenders were frightened that she was taking notes that would be offered in evidence against them. What she actually was doing was writing her own name over and over again, hoping that if she looked busy, Miss Arden would not next turn on her.

When Queen Elizabeth made her only visit to New York, Elizabeth was among the prominent people invited to lunch with her at the Waldorf. She had Sarmi design a suit especially for the occasion. An hour before the luncheon, the jacket was still not ready.

Miss Arden's office was in its usual chaotic state. Assistants were bustling in and out asking for approval on this, that, or the other thing. Elizabeth was racing about wearing only her brassiere, hat, and the unfinished skirt. She was answering three phones and doing her own nails, shouting gleefully, ''I can't take a manicurist away from a client.''

A production man came in to show her a new eyebrow pencil. It was the length of a fountain pen and projected to retail at a dollar. She cried, ''No, no, no! It's too long and too cheap. It'll last forever. And nothing that costs only a dollar is worth having.''

She put down the nail polish, grabbed the pencil, and broke it in half. ''That's the length to make it. And the price will be two dollars.''

She went back to her nails and shouted, ''Get Dendrammis in here.''

Mrs. Dendrammis entered on the double, and Elizabeth said, ''Rehearse me, dear.''

Part of Mary's job was to act as social secretary, instructing Elizabeth in the niceties of diplomatic behavior. Elizabeth would have to curtsey to the queen and wanted to make certain that she did it perfectly.

Hat plopped on head, in bra and skirt, polishing her nails, and juggling three phones at once, Elizabeth gracefully sank to the floor in an exquisite obsequity. She murmured, ''Your Majesty.'' This was immediately followed by a roar into one of the phones, ''Tell that bastard he ordered the shipment, and he's going to damned well keep it.''

She was approaching eighty, and frenzy was still the natural milieu of Elizabeth Arden. As she entered her building, a telephonic alarm system warned the help of her approach. Everybody got frenetically busy, even when there was nothing they had to do. Next to idleness, she hated cigarettes. When word came that she was on her way, cigarettes were dowsed and ashtrays emptied.

Becky McGrevey recalled, ''If we were caught still taking that final puff, when the elevator doors opened, the cigarette would be tossed, still lit, into a desk drawer. Then, we'd shut it fast, take a deep breath, and hold it until she passed. Why there was never a fire, or why Miss Arden never admitted that she could see smoke curling from so many desks, nobody will ever know. Maybe, like old Mr. Hearst, who never admitted that Marion Davies drank when she was an out-and-out alcoholic, Miss Arden believed only in those things she chose to believe.''

When the Dendrammises were reassigned to Athens, Miss Arden invited people to a farewell luncheon for them at her apartment. As usual, she was late. She rushed into Sarmi's office and grabbed him by the arm. He was in the middle of a fitting and almost swallowed a mouthful of pins as she pulled him toward the door. ''Come on. We've got to hurry. The car's waiting.''

The street was crowded with midday Christmas shoppers. She elbowed through them with all the dexterity of a football player rushing the opposing line. As they started off, she cried to the chauffeur, ''Faster! Faster!''

He replied, ''Shall I use the whip, madam?'' Charles Noble was a crusty Englishman who had been her driver for years. He coddled her, pampered her, adored her, even named his daughter, Ardena, for her, but, no matter what her exhortations, he would not speed for her. Charles was faithful and so, it turned out, was Elizabeth—how magnificently faithful to him was known only by those who had seen her will.

As they passed La Vieille Russie, the very elegant shop supposedly dedicated to selling the heirlooms of the Russian aristocracy, she cried, ''Pull up for a moment.'' She dragged Sarmi into the store. ''I need your advice.''

She asked to see their men's cigarette cases. A brilliantly crafted, jewel-encrusted assortment was set out before them. ''Choose one.''

Thinking that it was a gift for Dendrammis, he selected a very expensive gold case with a sapphire catch. As they returned to the car, she tucked it into his pocket. ''It's your Christmas present.''

He became embarrassed and tried to explain that he would not have chosen such an extravagant one had he not thought it was for Mr. Dendrammis. "Dendrammis!" she roared. "Who on earth should I give him a present when I've overpaid his wife all this time?"

Sarmi often wondered what Elizabeth would have done had he given up smoking. The cases were her wordless way of expressing gratitude or offering apologies.

Bows had become a Sarmi trademark. He liked to use them on as many frocks as possible. Before one of the shows, Elizabeth went around snipping them off. "It's enough I've got to use his label inside the dresses. I don't need it outside, too."

They had a tremendous row, and she struck him, catching him off-guard and tumbling him to the floor. He would not speak to her for the rest of the day. That evening she thrust a Cartier cigarette case at him, mumbling, "They seemed to like the collection."

The years since winning the Derby had been crowned with great triumphs in her public life and deep sadness in her private life. One by one, she watched her friends pass away. Maud Eily was gone. Elizabeth had overcome her dislike of hospitals to visit her every day, bringing along a flask of scotch. Maudie had smiled. "No ice."

"Better for you that way. Whiskey's bad enough for your complexion. Ice is disastrous." And the two old women toasted a future that one would never see.

For years, whenever she was in New York, the morning had begun with a telephone call to Katie Cross. She was the only wife of an Arden executive with whom Elizabeth shared an intimate friendship. They gossiped, and giggled, and compared notes on the vices and virtues of Duke Cross. One morning, in 1955, the call came from Duke telling her that Katie was dead. It had been a dreadful illness and, perhaps, it was for the best—or so they told each other, but somewhere in the depths of these perennially youthful characters, Katie's death had engendered a swift and frightening perception of the passing of time, the swiftness of time, the sere inevitability of age.

Katie had been Elizabeth's darling little pink-lipstick girl, and

:[275]:

Irene Hayes was instructed to deck the coffin with an enormous blanket of sweetheart roses. On the next day, they did not look fresh enough, and Miss Arden ordered another blanket, and so it went on each day until the interment.

Not even her best makeup artists could disguise the ravages that had distorted the once fragile and lovely features. Elizabeth ordered, "Bring me pink tulle, the best available."

She draped yards of the stuff around and over the face, and then she had the coffin's glass lid lowered. Viewed through the gauzy fabric, Katie was once again lovely.

On the drive to the cemetery, Elizabeth patted Duke's hand and murmured over and over again. "Don't worry. Don't worry. You'll have nothing to worry about. I'll see to that. I promise."

That winter Cross was her guest for the Hialeah racing season. She asked him to take her to a big party on the last night of their stay and introduced him to the host and guests as her vice-president. He assumed that she was only trying to make him important enough, in the eyes of the others, to be her escort.

They took the plane north the next day. During the flight, she asked, "Did you hear what I called you last night?"

"Yes."

"I meant it."

"Thank you. Before I accept, I think you ought to do the same for Jack Treat. He deserves it as much as I do."

"If you think so—certainly. I'll tell him as soon as we get back to the office."

What was one more or less vice-president to her? There was only one real boss—Elizabeth Arden.

Carl Gardiner understood this. That was how he had remained her general manager longer than any other man, including Tom Lewis. Some people dismissed him as a "yes" man, but he was much more than that. He had a gift for making her do exactly what she wanted to do, even when she quixotically protested that she was against it. He also could prevent her from doing those things she had agreed to do for the sake of others, but did not basically want for herself. He was

At the Arden Sales Salon in New York. Carl Gardiner and Miss Arden
discuss sales strategy with three members of the Arden staff.

—Walter Curtin

one of the few people who understood her and, in understanding,
never underestimated her.

With Gardiner, Treat, and Cross in New York, Gladys in Paris,
and Gordon Yates succeeding Haslam in London, the business would
be protected for as long as she lived. It was questionable as to how

long it would survive her—for always, over them all, there was Elizabeth Arden.

Public tributes began to crowd in on her. It was as if the sometimes ruthless, always driving ambition had become the lovable eccentricity of a venerable old lady to whom respectful recognition had to be paid. Elizabeth took it all in her stride. She observed, ''If you live long enough, you find you've either worn out your enemies or outlived them.''

She was the only representative of a cosmetics firm and the only woman, aside from Edna Chase, to be named to the Distribution Hall of Fame, by the National Conference of Distributors.

Syracuse University gave her an honorary Doctor of Law degree for ''enriching American standards.'' After more than sixty years, she had finally got a diploma.

She was invited to Canada for the dedication of Dalziel Pioneer Park. She planted a ceremonial tree on the park site that had once been the Woodbridge farm where she was born and grew up. It was suitable that there should be some sort of memorial. Florence Nightingale Graham was buried there, although she so often refused to stay in her grave and returned to haunt the strange, glamorous creature who was inhabiting her body.

In Los Angeles, she was given a ''Great Lady'' award at the biennial fashion spectacle of Theta Sigma Phi, the national honorary sorority of women in journalism. The ladies of the press cited her ''For having made beauty attainable to all American women.'' Her college career was complete. She not only had a diploma but she had also been pledged.

She was even asked to be one of the judges of the 1952 Miss America contest. In those days, it was a great honor, and no other person from the beauty world had ever been selected. The other judges, that year, were actress-writer Cornelia Otis Skinner, theatrical producer Vinton Freedley, and music critic Deems Taylor.

Elizabeth arrived in Atlantic City with an entourage including her personal maid and her publicity man, Emmett Davis. The contest was sponsored by a group of companies including some who manufactured beauty preparations. The first thing that the promoters did was to instruct her never to mention her business.

At the first luncheon, the master of ceremonies introduced the judges to the girls. All the others said, ''Thank you,'' or, ''So pleased to be here,'' or some similar brief and innocuous phrase.

Not Miss Arden. She took over the microphone and the audience. She told them how wonderful it was to see all those pretty little girls from small towns, but she thought it was a pity that they had never had the opportunity to obtain the professional beauty treatments that were available to their big-city sisters. So that everybody would have a fair and equal chance, she was going to bring down her staff to give treatments to and make up each and every one of them before the pageant.

While the promoters were having fits, Elizabeth was having headlines. She got still more press coverage with the photographs of her girls making up the contestants. When accused of being rather unethical, her eyes opened wide, and her little girl voice whimpered, ''I don't know how you can say such a terrible thing to me. I was only trying to help all those sweet youngsters.''

A box at the Atlantic City track was put at her disposal, and she gathered all the other judges and took them to the races. She explained, ''We're all the guests of Jack Kelly—whoever the hell he is.''

Davis whispered that he was the father of the new movie star Grace Kelly. She nodded. ''He's the father of Grace Kelly—whoever the hell she is.''

When she had an audience with Princess Grace, of Monaco, a few years later, she executed her best Dendrammis curtsey and knew who the hell she was.

Davis never had known anything quite so exhausting as traveling with this little lady of seventy-five. She loved to play cards until all hours and was up an average of eighteen hours a day. The secret of her energy was the little catnaps she could take anywhere at anytime. She could be riding in her car, close her eyes and be asleep im-

Elizabeth Arden being presented with the Golden Cup of the Comite du Bon Gout Francais awarded by Ambassador Bayens, while M. Rodel, the president of Comite du Bon Gout Francais, looks on.

Elizabeth with her pet dog, Pee-Wee,who, true to his name, christened the Golden Cup she had just been awarded.

mediately. She was known to do the same in the middle of a dull business meeting.

At two one morning, her maid, who kept normal hours, was asleep, and she asked young Davis to unzip her dress. She wagged a flirtatious finger, ''But, first, dear, close your little eyes.''

She slipped into a dressing gown and insisted he have a snack with her. He did not get back to his own room until three. Less than four hours later, he was awakened by a call from Miss Arden demanding the time. He squinted at his watch and told her. She sighed impatiently. ''Not here. I know that. In Buenos Aires.''

''I have no idea.''

''Find out.''

''Why do you want to know?''

''It just occurred to me. I have to fire my manager down there—I want to make sure she's in the salon, so I don't have to waste money calling person to person.''

''Miss Arden, your bill is being picked up by the contest people.''

The lady, who had almost ruined their promotional setup by gathering headlines for her own products, responded in a shocked tone. ''I'm surprised at you. I thought you had better manners. One shouldn't take advantage of one's hosts.''

One of the more memorable tributes was the Golden Cup of the Comité du Bon Gout Français, presented in Paris for the creation of her French perfume, Mémoire Chérie. It was the first time that it had ever been awarded to an American woman and received tremendous press attention.

A mob of reporters were waiting when she returned to New York. Pee-Wee was also waiting. Pee-Wee was a mongrel that had come with a cottage she once had rented in Saratoga. At the end of the racing season, she returned the house and kept the dog. He slept on one of Elizabeth's mink coats and was named for his famous resistance to any form of housebreaking. He was equally famous for his taste for caviar. He was once sent a pound with the request that he share it with his mistress.

:[281]:

Catching sight of Elizabeth descending from the plane, Pee-Wee broke free of his lead and raced toward her. She put down the Golden Cup and opened her arms to embrace him. The dog saw the cup, got up on his hind legs and did the one trick he knew, that for which he was named, all over it.

A gust of laughter burst from Elizabeth. "So much for Elizabeth Arden's soon-to-be-tarnished tributes."

Elizabeth first met Mamie Eisenhower, when the general was president of Columbia University, and she came into the New York salon. Mrs. Eisenhower had been a client at the Paris salon during the years when her husband was stationed in Paris as American Chief of Staff. Upon being introduced to Miss Arden, she smiled and said, "So you're Gladys' sister."

It was the first time that Elizabeth had ever received that sort of billing, but she had the good grace to be sufficiently amused to tell the story on herself at dinner parties.

The two women liked each other immediately, and Elizabeth became an early supporter of Eisenhower for President. After he was elected, she was given the unofficial title of beauty maker to the Republican administration.

She asked Sarmi to create a very special gown for her to wear to the inaugural ball. "I want to look thin, and beautiful, and—young." She laughed embarrassedly. "And I want to stand out from the mob."

He designed a column of black velvet with a voluminous matching cloak. At the first fitting, all her associates agreed that it was perfect. It made her skin look translucent, and her figure slim, and she would certainly stand out in it. None of the other guests at that party would be wearing black velvet.

Sarmi studied her reaction and, without her saying a word, knew that she would never wear it. She went through the collection and selected a chiffon in many shades of blue. It was pretty, but she did not look especially slim, or young, or different—she only looked like another Arden girl.

:[282]:

It was during the Eisenhower years that she acquired a reputation for being old-fashioned and conservative. It was not altogether deserved. She was only catering to the tastes of the group of extremely dowdy women who were the wives of the Republican heirarchy.

They were beginning to say that she was an old woman who had fallen behind the times. It was true in the sense that the chaotic times were breeding a fashion look that was very distant from the refined good taste for which she had always been famous.

It would be a mistake to think that she was unaware of what was happening. She saw where the trends were leading early enough to have set them—had she so chosen. At a conference of beauty editors, the question arose of where to find a new look in makeup. Women were getting bored with the faces they had been wearing since the war years. They wanted something new, something daring. Elizabeth suggested, ''Bring your models over from Europe. The young girls in England, and Italy, and Scandinavia—they've got just what you're looking for.''

The next few years proved how sound her advice had been, but she was one of the few who did not take it. She questioned the wisdom of changing her entire point of view to suit the fancies of a youth-oriented society. She was doing very well by remaining one of the few places catering to the tastes of the many middle-class, middle-aged women who had no desire to look like caricatures of their grand-daughters. Ironically, she was playing Eleanor Adair to Charles Revson's Elizabeth Arden.

When Tom White's daughter, Nancy, took over the editorship of *Harper's Bazaar,* she wanted to change the dignified format to one that recognized and kept abreast of the revolutionary new ideas in fashion and beauty. Partly out of sentiment, Elizabeth was one of the first of the old advertisers to go along with her, but there was also an element of genuine curiosity about new trends. She noticed everything. Her favorite question was, ''What's new, dear?'' And she really wanted to be told.

One of Miss White's early layouts was a series of photographs, taken by Richard Avedon, of an unmistakably Eurasian girl. It was before the vogue for exotic and black models, and bearing an Arden makeup credit, it had to have the approval of her executives. They turned it down and even threatened to withdraw all advertising if it was run without a credit.

Avedon was certain that the rejection was inspired by Miss Arden and began to fume about her bigotry. Miss White was not so sure. She had Elizabeth's confidence and decided to take the photographs directly to her, bypassing Gardiner and the others, who had been so positive that she would never approve that they had not bothered to show them to her.

Elizabeth saw the potential as an attention getter. She loved the look and approved the series. She even went so far as to send hearty congratulations to the startled Mr. Avedon, who, like her staff, had been so certain that she would not go for anything that was not straight WASP. The staid Mrs. Graham might not have approved of the passenger list, but Elizabeth Arden was still willing to take the trip.

During this period, when she was supposedly no longer ''with it,'' she also anticipated the male peacock of a decade later. She had been advising men to use her preparations since she first started manufacturing them. There were specially packaged variations for men, that were given as Christmas presents. In the early fifties, she became the first major manufacturer of women's cosmetics to put out a line for men. She also opened the first men's boutique ever to be attached to a beauty salon.

Her relationship with the Eisenhowers led to a minor scandal occasioned by Mamie's first invitation to visit Maine Chance, Arizona. An invitation to Mrs. Eisenhower meant an invitation to a party of fifteen, including her secretary, her sister, her companion, Secret Service people, and even her own cook.

Mrs. Jascha Heifetz was evicted from the cottage she had been occupying, and several thousand dollars were spent to bring it up to Elizabeth's notion of First Lady standards. When this was added to the average of $1,000, per person, that Elizabeth was losing on the

At a Blue Grass party at the St. Regis roof Elizabeth Arden and Nancy White, who was then editor in chief of *Harper's Bazaar.*

space taken by Mrs. Eisenhower's party, the total cost to Miss Arden was nearly $25,000. Never had she spent money so wisely. The visit brought her millions of dollars' worth of free publicity.

Nobody could criticize Elizabeth's generosity to her guests—that was her own affair—but the means of transportation became a controversial issue. The group was flown to Arizona in the Presidential plane, and the liberal press made a great fuss over the question of who paid for it. When it was discovered that the government did, there were critical reams of space devoted to why the poor taxpayers should be forced to foot the bill for the First Lady's pleasure jaunts. The next time that Mamie visited Maine Chance she arrived by train.

Elizabeth ended the Eisenhower years by being innocently involved in another minor political controversy. When John F. Kennedy was running for the Presidency against Richard Nixon, there was a great deal of adverse comment on the amount Mrs. Kennedy was alleged to spend on her wardrobe. Jackie replied by pointing an accusing finger at her opposite number. She said, ''I'm sure I spend less than Mrs. Nixon on clothes. She gets hers at Elizabeth Arden. Nothing there costs less than two-hundred dollars or three-hundred dollars.''

Elizabeth leaped to Pat's defense. Conveniently forgetting the 1956 inaugural gown that Sarmi had designed and made for the Vice President's wife, she said, ''Mrs. Nixon has been a client for the past four years. She has always paid her bills. She has a wonderful figure and can wear ready-made clothes.''

She neglected to mention that the ready-mades did cost the estimated two-hundred dollars or three-hundred dollars, but she did recall that the bills were paid which was always sufficient to win Elizabeth's favor—even with other customers who were ''damned Demmies.''

Her love of horses remained the only deep emotional involvement in her life. In the decade following the Arlington fire, her stable earned $2,517,153 and still lost money, because she was more interested in racing than breeding. It cost a small fortune to buy and condition horses that had a potential of winning. Formidable as some of the prize money was, the real profits came after the horse's racing days, when, depending on gender, it was either put out to stud or used as a broodmare. This was the part of the game to which Elizabeth was almost indifferent. She loved beautiful and swift horses to the exclusion of the more practical aspects of owning them. Even in the stable, sex was never an Arden motivation.

A few years after winning the Derby, Elizabeth decided that the time had come for her darlings to have a home of their own instead of being boarders at Leslie Comb's Spendthrift Farm. She leased and later bought a 750-acre property outside Lexington, Kentucky. The living quarters were as comfortable and unostentatious as her Belmont cottage. Miss Arden may have lived ostentatiously, but Mrs. Graham preferred an understated simplicity.

At last, there was an actual Maine Chance Horse Farm. The revolving door continued in operation, and in the first five years, there was a turnover in farm managers to rival the one in horse trainers. Elizabeth was ruthlessly determined that it would be one of the most beautifully run and maintained farms in the country.

She succeeded. When Captain Boyd Rochefort, trainer for the Queen of England, visited America in 1955, he declared that Maine Chance Farm was the finest present-day stable in America. That year Elizabeth wistfully commented, "If a woman has a nice, comfortable man, it can be a great help to her. But I seem to have had much more luck with the horses than the men in my life."

It never occurred to her that this might well have been because she devoted much more love and attention to them than she ever had to any mere male.

She had another fire in 1957, when a large barn was destroyed at the farm. An alert employee saved all twenty of the valuable horses that were being housed in it. Elizabeth observed, "As long as the babies are safe. I always knew there'd be a third fire. I've been waiting for it. Now, the suspense is over."

Her favorite horse of the late fifties was a beauty named Jewel's Reward. When he was still a colt, she had been advised to put him up for auction at the Saratoga summer sale, because his front legs were straight, which was supposedly bad for a racer. The bidding only went to $3,500, and she refused to sell. After he won his first big race, Elizabeth crowed, "He may have straight legs, but he doesn't know it."

He developed into a great champion. It was because of this darling baby that Elizabeth had not been on hand to welcome Mrs. Eisenhower to Maine Chance. Jewel's Reward was entered in the

Elizabeth Arden Graham and Jewel's Reward with Willie Shoemaker up being led to winner's circle at Belmont Park, October, 1957.

Even baby talk and Miss Arden's Eight Hour cream didn't deter one of Elizabeth's darlings from biting the tip of her finger off.

Widener Cup Race at Hialeah and would have felt dreadful if she had not been there to cheer him on. As it turned out, Mrs. Graham would have felt much better had she stayed away.

Molly Collum, who had managed Maine Chance, Arizona, for two years and had been Elizabeth's adviser on horses for many more years than that, was her guest at the Florida event. Calumet Farm's Tim-Tam gave Jewel's Reward a very close race. Molly noticed that there was a great deal of bumping on both sides. The Maine Chance horse came in first, but she wondered what the judges' final decision would be. Before she could voice her doubts, the track ushers descended upon Elizabeth and whisked her away to the winner's circle.

She was already being congratualted by the governor of Florida, when the numbers came down. The judges had called a foul. Jewel's Reward had been disqualified, and the Calumet horse declared the winner.

Elizabeth rushed through the light rain to her limousine. The incident was particularly humiliating, because Mrs. Gene Markey, the owner of Calumet Farm, was feuding with her. They had once been close friends, but after Tom Smith left her, Elizabeth had tried unsuccessfully to hire away Calumet's fine trainer, Ben Jones. Mrs. Markey learned about it, and that was the end of the friendship.

The Florida episode brought about a change in racing etiquette. From then on, it was ruled that neither horse nor owner would be permitted into the winner's circle until after the judges announced their final decision.

Jewel's Reward, darling that he was, did his indulgent owner another injury. He loved oranges, and while Elizabeth was feeding one to him at Santa Anita, he bit off the tip of her finger. She calmly picked it up and had it stitched back on, without a word of recrimination against the darling. No matter what they did, the babies could do no wrong.

When Helena Rubinstein heard about the incident, she asked, "What happened to the poor horse?"

In reply, Jewel's Reward died of colic six months after biting the hand that fed him.

On New Year's Eve, 1958, Elizabeth was one of the most vivacious women in the room. She was charming and flirtatious, the fluttering belle of the ball. In plunging décolletage, her soft blond hair bouncing to the beat of the music, she danced almost every dance. Midnight came and went with no surcease in her gay energies. The observers would indeed have been startled to discover that, with the hour, she had passed her eightieth birthday.

One of the novelties that the hostess provided for her guests was a fortune-teller. Elizabeth queued impatiently. She was so very anxious to learn what exciting things the future held in store for her.

CHAPTER SIXTEEN

Octogenarian

Eighty. Was it true? Elizabeth would never admit it to others or face it to herself. Florence Nightingale Graham had been born eighty years before—not Elizabeth Arden, not Elizabeth Graham. Florence could slow down, could stop, could come to an end. Never Elizabeth. Elizabeth would go on forever. Her pace intensified, her incredible energy drove her relentlessly forward. Elizabeth could not stop. Elizabeth could not slow down. Elizabeth could not come to an end.

The temper rejected the mellowing of age that had begun to tame it, and the rages once more sent tremors through salon and stable. Let others stop for reason and explain. She did not have that kind of time. It was do it her way or be gone, and there was so much still to be done—her way.

The great days of the Sunset Strip were over, and she decided to move her salon to the heart of Beverly Hills' smartest shopping center, on Wilshire Boulevard. Nicholai Remisoff was again commissioned to do the decor.

Elizabeth came to inspect the premises just before the official press reception. Mary Blakely was so proud of the place that she fairly sang its praises. She was particularly pleased with the spacious blue and white reception room on the second floor. The dominant area was composed of two lovely sofas with a mirror hung between them. Elizabeth paused at the reflection.

She beckoned to Mary and asked her to describe what she saw in the mirror. The reply was, "Why, a very beautiful room."

Miss Arden nodded. "Exactly. You couldn't sell a damned thing in here."

Too impatient to wait for the handymen, she pushed up her sleeves and started to shove around the heavy furniture. One sofa was removed to another part of the salon, and the rest of the pieces were rearranged. When she was finished, she returned to the mirror. "Now, you can sell. You can see yourself in the mirror."

Mary agreed doubtingly. "Yes. But now the room looks so large."

"Don't worry about that, dear. We'll just put up a little wall. It'll hide the offices and provide a passage without coming through here. I hate the clients to see the business end. It spoils the magic."

After the press party, everybody was preparing to leave for home. Mary was pulling on her gloves and called out to ask Miss Arden if she was ready to go. A voice from below her replied, "In a minute, dear."

She glanced down to see her employer, still clad in her Sarmi suit, on her hands and knees cleaning food spots off the carpet. She pulled herself up and gestured to her work with a smile. "There! If I couldn't do a better job than those cleaning women, they'd be where I am, and I'd be where they are. That's the little secret, dear. Always be better than anybody you hire."

Elizabeth had originally purchased an enormous corner lot for the new salon but had decided to build on a smaller property adjacent to it. The original property had cost $500,000, and she thought that she might as well sell it. She told Mary, "I'm not in the real estate business, dear. You keep an eye out for a buyer."

Shortly after, Mary was approached by the Security National Bank, which wanted to know if it was for sale. Mary replied tentatively, that it was—for the right price. The bank offered $750,000.

Mary thought that provided a very nice profit and called Elizabeth to tell her about it. There was a moment's hesitation at the other end of the phone, and then the lady who was not in the real estate business said, "You know, dear, if they're offering seven-hundred fifty-thousand dollars, it must be worth a million dollars. Why don't we see if we can get it?''

With her heart in her mouth, Mary told the bankers that Miss Arden wanted $1,000,000. They replied that it was out of the question, and she left thinking that was the end of it. A week later, they called her back and said that if Miss Arden would really sell for $1,000,000, they would manage to scrape it together.

Mary was elated and telephoned to tell her employer the good news. There was another Arden pause. ''You know, dear, they gave in just a little too quickly. I think we can get $1,250,000.''

Mary thought that Miss Arden did not want to sell and was ready to forget all about it. She relayed the message to the outraged prospective buyers and put the transaction out of her mind. A short while later, the bank bought the property at Miss Arden's figure.

People were beginning to whisper that she was no longer able to think as quickly as she once had but, in her slow way, the little old woman had managed to clear a 150 percent profit on a $500,000 investment in less than a year's time.

Word went quickly around the salon when William Graham had died. Elizabeth stopped on the fashion floor to look at the toiles for the new collection, Sarmi began to offer his condolences. She quickly cut in, ''Let's get down to business. It's going to be a difficult day. My sister's brother passed away.''

That was the only comment she made. After all the years, she still had not forgiven him for conspiring with Tom Lewis.

It was not long after that her sister, Lollie, died and also her nieces, Virginia and Beatrice. Pat Young was the only other member of the Graham family in America. The girls had each had a son, but Elizabeth was only perfunctorily interested in the young boys. It was to Pat she turned in her need never to be alone.

Mrs. Young still shared the apartment with her, and she began to rely more and more upon her. Somebody had to fill the emptiness—somebody had to be there *always,* and it had to be a younger somebody. Most of her contemporaries depressingly reminded her of

The castle in Ireland. Elizabeth's last acquisition and the first to be sold from her estate upon her death.

The entrance hall to the castle in Ireland. It was decorated by Michael Scott.

her age, and the few superficially youthful ones did not possess the energy to keep up with her.

Life with Aunt Elizabeth could not have been easy. Pat had to be ready to hop on a plane at a moment's notice. Elizabeth was spending so much time flitting around the globe that she kept wardrobes at the places she visited most frequently to save the time and effort of packing. Recalling the terrific pace, Mrs. Young later said, ''I don't go anywhere anymore. I stay home. I guess I'm all traveled out.''

Elizabeth did not need much rest and, consequently, did not think it was necessary to anybody else. A good night's sleep was often interrupted by the arrival of fresh flowers, by air freight, from one of the Maine Chances. Elizabeth awakened the whole household to deal with them. All the stems had to be cut. If one blossom so much as grazed another, there was hell to pay. Arrangements were made in every vase. The bath tubs were filled with those flowers for which there were not sufficient containers. The job took hours.

The poor woman also had to serve as guinea pig for new products. What Elizabeth did not try on herself, she tried on Pat. One evening a sample of a new bath oil arrived just as Pat was stepping out of her tub. Elizabeth rushed in, crying, ''You've got to try this. It's wonderful. Turn on the water.''

''I've just had my bath.''

''Have another. It'll make a new woman of you.''

Mrs. Young once sneaked off for a week's vacation in Germany without telling anybody where she was going. She only wanted to rest and be blessedly alone At the end of it, she called Gladys who informed her that Elizabeth had flown over in search of her. Pat said, ''I'll be on the first plane to Paris.''

''Too late. She's gone. On her way home, she stopped in England just long enough to have tea with the queen mother and buy an old Irish castle.''

She raced into the 1960's with no remission in her enormous vitality and appetite for work. She refused to recognize the existence of age. Her attitude was—''Father Time, you don't bother me, and I won't bother you." But time was relentless and refused to make a bargain. It never appeared in her mirror. She could look at her reflection and be pleased that she had won. It was in the harshness of photographs that time made its most telling appearances, and that was worse than a looking glass, for eternal youth was her image to the world.

Every picture was closely scrutinized by her publicity department, and long lists of suggested retouches were submitted to photographers. It was not surprising that only Miss Arden received this careful attention. As a result, she often looked like the one ironed piece in the wrinkled mass of her acquaintances.

The vast majority of American citizens can do nothing about the way they look on their passport pictures. Miss Arden insisted that this was nonsense and had some powerful friends exert a little influence to arrange for hers to be touched up. It must have caused a bit of confusion in the minds of some immigration officers, when they were presented with the passport of a woman closely resembling, but clearly twenty years younger than the one who stood before them. The confusion must have been compounded by the fact that the picture looked forty-two, the woman looked sixty-two, and her age was listed as eighty-two.

The tender loving care that she bestowed upon her photographs and herself did not immunize her to the small ailments to which a person of her years was prey. When she was summoned to the French Embassy, in Washington, to receive the Légion d'Honneur, she was suffering from both a broken wrist and a severe case of gout, but she insisted on going. She said, "I'm not going to disappoint Ambassador and Mme. Alphand."

Roughly translated, that meant that she was not going to disappoint herself. Gladys had received the Légion several years earlier, and Elizabeth felt that it was high time that it was also accorded to her.

She had her dressmaker cut the sleeves out of her dress and substitute a cape of the same fabric with a hidden sling for her arm. The pain of the gout made her wince, as she squeezed her tiny feet into the elegant, newspaper-lined shoes.

Florence Owens accompanied her to the embassy. When the ambassador bestowed the honor, Elizabeth was all solemn smiles. Her charm never wavered during the reception that followed. Only Florence knew what agony she was experiencing. On the way home, she said, ''Elizabeth, I never thought you'd make it.''

Elizabeth Arden being congratulated by the French Ambassador Hervé Alphand and his wife, Nicole, after receiving the Légion d'Honneur in Washington.

Miss Arden slipped out of her shoes, sighed with relief, and replied, "You ought to know me better than that."

At the end of each day of the Belmont season, she would grab her office manager, Barbara DeBrul, or Florence Owens, who had replaced Lanie as manager of the New York salon, or Pat, or whoever else of the inner circle was around, and would dash out of the Fifth Avenue office into the waiting limousine. As they crossed the Fifty-ninth Street Bridge, she would cry, "Faster! Faster!"

"We ride to win, madame!" Charles would respond without ever accelerating above fifty miles an hour.

She was off to spend the night at the Belmont cottage. No matter what hour they arrived, dinner was kept waiting, while Elizabeth bustled out to see her darlings. There were massages, and kisses, and words of endearment for the animals, and scowls and complaints for the trainer and stablehands.

After dinner, she was into the books that the trainer kept on the horses. These detailed the careful schedules that had been set up in advance for each of them. If she thought one of the babies was tired and should not be exercised, or another had the sniffles and should not be entered in a race, she blithely changed the dates. The trainer would get furious, and she would return fury for fury, shouting, "You are working for me. They're my horses."

Exit the trainer. Business disposed of, it was time for cards. No matter how late they stayed up playing canasta, a game Elizabeth loved and at which she consistently lost, they were awakened at four thirty in the morning. Elizabeth had already prepared the coffee and cheerfully shouted, "We'll have a nice little cup and then go and watch them water the darlings."

By eight thirty they were on their way back to New York and the start of another business day. Her guest would have trouble keeping awake, while Elizabeth peacefully napped, gathering her strength in slumber.

The meeting was to set policy for the coming season. Carl Gardiner was making an important point, when Elizabeth glanced at her watch. It was two fifteen. She rose, and grabbed Mrs. Debrul by the arm. As they rushed out of the door, she called back, ''Everybody remain where you are. We'll return shortly.''

It was a scene repeated, whenever one of her horses was running at a nearby track. A private plane was waiting at Butler Field to fly them to Monmouth. From her own box, she watched the race in which her horse was running. He lost, but it did not matter, for it was not his fault. It was that stupid little jockey. How often did she have to tell them not to use the crop except in dire extremities?

She went down to the paddock. A few pats and caresses for the horse, a few expletives for the rider, and they were back in the plane headed for New York. When she went back into the meeting at seven thirty, everybody was waiting and prepared to resume where they had broken off.

The force of her will seemed to increase with age. Mrs. DeBrul rushed in breathlessly. Rudelheimer, the man who made special leather products for Arden, had collapsed in the men's room. Elizabeth sprinted past DeBrul over to where the man was stretched out. She tore open his shirt and went to work on him with her healing hands. While she massaged his heart, she hissed insistently into his ear, ''You will come out of this! You will get up! You will be well!''

He did not dare to refute her. She revived him and sent him home in her car. She probably had saved the man's life, but she had insisted that she would, so it did not surprise her.

The close relationship with Barbara DeBrul ended in a slander suit, in 1962. Mrs. DeBrul sued Miss Arden, asking $185,000 for seven alleged acts of slander. In addition, her husband, a dentist, wanted $50,000 for loss of his wife's services, plus $150 for medical expenses for her.

Mrs. Willette Brown, who also had worked for Arden, testified that the day after Barbara left her job, Miss Arden went through some papers in the office containing Barbara's possessions and said, ''Look at this. This is how people steal. Barbara DeBrul is a thief. She was stealing all the while, and she will pay for this.''

:[299   ]:

Mrs. Brown said that when she told Mrs. DeBrul what had happened, Barbara was so upset that she became ill.

Mrs. Sara Pennoyer, who worked for an advertising agency and happened to be in the Arden office at the time of the alleged slander, testified that she heard Miss Arden say of Barbara, "Anybody who took her word would be crazy. Her judgment is poor. She is certainly not a person to hire."

Through her attorney, J. Howard Carter, Miss Arden entered a denial stating that the alleged slanders occurred after Barbara was "discharged for good cause." She added that any remarks made about Barbara were without malice and part of the legitimate business operation.

A settlement of $2,500 was made after Miss Arden took the stand. It included a stipulation that this did not mean she was admitting any liability. Whatever the truth of the matter, the language did sound strangely like the sort Elizabeth would use in an unreasoning fit of anger over what she considered a betrayal. After the trial was over, her only comment was, "I'm rather disappointed in that little girl."

Elizabeth fired Sarmi in 1959, after hearing a rumor that he was going into business for himself. She was furious that he had not mentioned it to her and asked no questions of him. She simply gave him five minutes to get off her premises. He was forced to leave so quickly that his staff had to pack his personal belongings and bring them to him on the following day.

She decided to do without a designer. The boys were all too troublesome. There were too many disputes. They insisted on their own artistic expression, and she insisted that her expression was more valuable, because she was a woman—and because it was her business.

The custom-made clothes, which had always lost money, began to slip so badly that there was the possibility that they would have to be eliminated. This was disturbing news to Lanfranco Rasponi. He was her fashion publicist and only had a job for as long as there was fashion to publicize.

Miss Arden and her public relations man Lanfranco Rasponi on one of their European jaunts. Rasponi lasted longer than most with Miss Arden, and she had respect for his judgment in more than just PR.

Elizabeth Arden with Oscar de la Renta, another designer she started on the road to fame and fortune. They are shown at her shop in Palm Beach.
Bert & Richard Morgan Studio Photo

After leaving Arden, Antonio Castillo had joined Lanvin and had become one of the most successful couturiers in France. Elizabeth was constantly lamenting, "I should never have let the little Spaniard go."

His assistant, Oscar de la Renta, had heard the legend of her temperament, but he had also heard how well she paid. He wondered if given a chance, he would be able to work with her.

He examined his prospects in France. *Haute couture* was dying in Paris. It was beginning to depend on the gimmicks of a Courregès. After St. Laurent, there would be no more big names made there.

With Norell, Trigère, Galanos, Sarmi, Blass, and Beene, American high fashion was still very much alive. He decided that he wanted to work in New York and, if possible, for Elizabeth Arden. She might be difficult but, look at Castillo and Sarmi, she made names.

He gambled on his luck, took four weeks off, and journeyed to America. He knew Rasponi and asked him to arrange an introduction. Rasponi had a better idea. He would let Elizabeth discover de la Renta.

He was doing publicity for the Spoleto Ball. He decided to seat them together, knowing that De la Renta would be charming, and that Elizabeth would ask what he did and, when told that he was Castillo's assistant, would take it from there by herself. It all worked out exactly as the publicist thought it would, and De la Renta went to work for Miss Arden in 1962, thereby saving both the custom line and Rasponi's job.

At first the two got along splendidly. Not only was De la Renta a first-rate talent, but he had the one thing that Elizabeth found indispensable in her employees—time to spend with her. He was single, a stranger in New York, charming, and good-looking. He also learned early that, at Arden, one designed Arden-type clothes. The innovations would have to wait until he was on his own.

The oddly incongruous couple spent many evenings together in her apartment. De la Renta, who was an excellent amateur chef, prepared meals that they would eat on the terrace. In the flattering shadows cast by the waning sun, Miss Arden turned a becoming and girlish pink. She often wore a pale-pink tea gown that she had bought in Paris years before. She loved the frock so much that she refused to discard it even after it began to show its age.

As a special surprise present, De la Renta made a new adaptation of the cherished dress. She claimed to adore it, but she never wore it for him. When he asked why, she replied, "I'm saving it for a very special occasion."

De la Renta never saw her in the dress until the day he went to pay his final respects at the Campbell Funeral Home.

It did not take De la Renta long to discover that the profit, as well as the future, lay in ready-made clothes. He suggested that Miss Arden try going into it. She became very enthused but later abruptly changed her mind. It was the beginning of the deterioration of their close friendship. To the designer, it seemed like a very arbitrary decision. But she was a very arbitrary woman and, by then, a very old one. When he finally decided to leave, she called to plead with him to stay. He begged, "Don't plead with me. You'll make me cry."

She said dryly, "No. Let me do the crying. You stay."

He relented for a little while but, soon after, left for good. He commented, "I worked for her for two and a half years. It seemed like ten."

When she knew that there was no way of getting him back, Elizabeth remarked sadly, "He left too soon. There was still so much I could teach him."

The doctor said, "Miss Arden, you'll have to give up your horses or your business. You haven't the strength to handle both."

She cried, "How can I choose between them? They're my life!"

All week long, her horses had performed marvelously well. The Jewel's Reward incident was forgotten, and she was enjoying the racing season in Miami. The gentlemen from Chicago were delightful and, when they started to discuss the possibility of buying her business, she glanced from them to the winner's circle and back again. She said slowly, "I think that might be a very good idea. I'll speak to my manager. Now, if you'll excuse me, I've got to see my babies."

Before the meeting with the prospective buyers, Carl Gardiner went over the figures with the Bank of New York. The magnitude of the profits was revealed for the first time, and one of the staid and dignified bankers could only repeat with awe, "I had no idea. I had no idea. Good Lord, I had no idea!"

All the interested parties were gathered in the conference room, awaiting the arrival of Miss Arden. The representatives of the Chicago group were in very good spirits. They had met every condition and were confident that they would leave New York with the Arden Company in their possession.

They waited, and waited, and waited, but she did not appear. At length, she sent word that she would not appear, the deal was off. That was all the explanation that she gave the people in the room. She later told her secretary, "I've provided for everybody who means anything to me. I don't have to worry about anybody. And I'm not going to give up my business. It's mine, and it will remain mine until the day I die."

She stopped buying horses on a grand scale, started to use unqualified trainers simply because they did not challenge her, sold horses that should have been used for breeding. The choice had been made. It would be the business, and the stable winnings dropped from $359,856, in 1962, to $243,104, in 1963, to $64,249, in 1964, to $24,595 in 1965.

Elizabeth changed her mind about the youth market. She decided that, to keep her position in the cosmetics world, she would have to woo it. She brought over Pablo, the daring makeup artist from her Rome salon, who had made fashion headlines by sprinkling glitter on women's eyelids.

There was conflict from the beginning. Intellectually, she knew that his ideas were right, but emotionally, she clung to the past and to the pink shades for which she had been famous. He would make a new lipstick, and she would say, "This pale beige isn't right for me."

"But it is right for a schoolgirl," he would retort firmly. No matter what color he devised, she kept trying to sneak a little pink into it.

After becoming the first makeup artist ever to win a Coty Fashion Award, he had enough security about his position to shout at her, "Pink, stink!"

He ducked as the makeup palette came sailing across the room. It was her last splendid display of temper. From then on, Pablo changed the colors she ordered behind her back. He was convinced that she knew, but that she chose to blame the chemists. The fight was going out of her.

Only occasionally would the old spirit flare up. When one of her financial advisers suggested that she set up a foundation, like Rubinstein, to protect the business from excessive taxation should anything happen to her, Elizabeth curtly interrupted, "I've a good horse running at Belmont this Saturday, you must come out to see him."

After he left, she thundered, "Foundation, indeed! I haven't worked hard all my life just to give my business to charity!"

In 1964, she bought a choice piece of property in Chicago, on North Michigan Avenue's "Magnificent Mile." She intended to build a jewel box of a salon to replace her old one on Walton Place. The architect drew up plans for a three-story building crowned by penthouse offices. Carl Gardiner rightly protested that the property was zoned for a skyscraper. It was an extravagant waste to erect a building of that size. Elizabeth said, "Don't fight with me. This one's for my old age. Everybody's got a right to have one salon for their old age."

Nicholai Remisoff did the interiors in Regency style. The colors were black and white with accents of pink. The foyer and couture salon were lined with surrealistically painted glass panels. It was rather reminiscent of their first collaboration, but that was the Arden look. He had invented it, and she had made it her signature.

At the annual Blue Grass party at the St. Regis roof in 1965, Miss Arden is handed the mike by "Killer" Joe Piro, who acted as master of ceremonies. Lady Georgina Coleridge is seated on right.

After the opening, Remisoff said, "I'm getting old. I think this will be my last salon."

She nodded wistfully. "Mine, too."

Helena Rubinstein died in April, 1965. The reports were on the radio and television all day long. The only thing Miss Arden said was, "Why do they have to keep on giving her age?"

Society had, at last, accepted Elizabeth as one of its own. It was that rare event, when her sense of timing was off. She had gained the position she had so long sought, at a point when the value of society was being questioned on all sides. Even the descendants of the older leaders, whom she had so long worshiped, were thinking of society as stuffy, dull, and not worth the effort. They gladly relinquished the shallow shell of that old game to the *nouveaux riches* who did not realize that it had died, leaving only the ridiculous, moribund posturing for photographs only they looked at and columnists only they read. In large measure, Elizabeth presided over a sad company composed largely of the brand new tycoons of the industry that she had helped to create.

As a party giver, her most successful achievements, the annual Blue Grass parties, were reserved for those connected with her business—the press, clients, buyers, and employees. On those occasions, she was the *grande dame* of the St. Regis roof, and nobody was permitted to forget it. A raucous man once came up to her, slapped her on the back, and cried, "Hiya, Lizzie."

She turned to Duke Cross and icily ordered, "Fire him!"

Duke shrugged. "He doesn't work for us."

The interloper owned a string of pharmacies in the Midwest. He was never again permitted to buy the Arden products.

In March, 1966, Elizabeth underwrote the annual Flamingo Ball, staged in the paddock area of Hialeah. She was stopping at the Sea View Hotel, in Miami. Before the ball, she sat at her dressing table. The hairdresser was busily pinning on false pieces to thicken her thin and wispy tresses and to hide the bald patches on her scalp. Miss MacEwen had come down from the Palm Beach salon to do her face. The manicurist was stoically suffering the abuse hurled upon anybody who did her nails.

Elizabeth studied herself in the mirror. She said softly, "Why, I'm just an old woman. I won't be here much longer."

Mackie, who had been with her for forty years, burst into tears. "Don't say that. Please—don't—"

Elizabeth drew herself up. "Why not? It's true." She took her hand from the manicurist, grabbed a tissue, and thrust it at her old employee. "Now stop that blubbering and get on with it. I've got to look lovely tonight." She glanced down at the smeared, newly polished nails and started to shriek, "You call that a manicure! God—you're stupid!"

Like most of her undertakings, the Flamingo Ball was a great financial success. The New York *Times* called it, "The most lavish barn dance in history."

Elizabeth wore a pink evening gown embroidered with crystal beads. To the casual observer, she appeared to be in perfect health and amazingly youthful-looking. Those who knew her well could see beneath the surface image and realized that she was not at all well. She lightly excused her reluctance to move from her table as the result of a game leg that would soon be mended. She had suffered one of her many falls and could not move without severe pain.

The crowd circled around her, paying homage to the queen, but when she attempted to introduce her guests, she could not remember their names. A close friend justified this by whispering to all and sundry, "She's had a series of small strokes, you know. But she's doing magnificently."

The more she was forced to an awareness of age, the less inclined she was to put her affairs in order. It was almost as if she thought that by procrastination, she were postponing death. Surely, God would not take her before she had finished her business on earth.

That summer she was accompanied by Pat Young on her annual trip to Europe. It was in the nature of a long farewell. She spent ten days at the Irish castle she had bought and completely redecorated a few years earlier. It was the only time she ever had actually been in residence. As if she had already accepted the fact that she would not live to enjoy it, she spoke of turning the place into a retreat and vacation home for her employees. The heads of the European branches came to stay with her. She kept saying, "Won't this be a lovely place for my girls?"

The London staff came to dine with her at Claridge's. She was unfailingly gay and charming, but it took a great effort. By the time they settled at the Ritz, in Paris, she was not feeling good; it did not prevent her from attending all the fashion openings.

A serious kidney infection developed, and Pat moved into her

One of the last photographs taken of Elizabeth Arden before she died was at the Flamingo Ball at Hialeah, 1967. She is seen there with Alfred I. Barton and her niece, Mrs. Patricia Young.

Bert and Richard Morgan Studio Photo

Miss Arden, photographed on the grounds of her Irish castle with two of her fillies — Canticle by Sovereign Path out of Lunestone and Honey Fun by Alcide out of Honey Flower.

room in the hotel to be with her night and day. She had ordered several dresses from Castillo, the most important of which was the gown she was going to wear to the opening of the new Metropolitan Opera House, and she insisted upon having them.

Castillo arranged for his staff to come to the Ritz. Supported on either side by Pat and a nurse, she patiently stood up through the long fitting sessions. She did not complain when the pain became acute. Instead, she gasped, "This one will stand them on their ears. Oh—I can hardly wait to wear it."

She improved and promised the doctor that she would rest. After he left, she bounded out of bed and cried, "Let's start packing. We're going back to Ireland. I've got a horse running in the Derby."

There was no sign of slowing down even after she returned to New York. She went to the opera looking radiant in the Castillo creation. She immersed herself in plans for a trip that would take her to San Francisco, Los Angeles, and Chicago for big charity fashion shows. There were endless business conferences spaced by luncheons with old friends.

She was at Twenty One with Henry Sell, savoring the chicken pot pie that she always ordered. She gestured with her fork and said, "I know my will is all wrong, and my estate is in dreadful shape. But I'm going to fix that. As soon as I get back from the coast, I'm going to have Carter in and go over everything."

As they were leaving, she stopped in the doorway. She clutched his arm and murmured, "Oh, oh—so little time, Hanque, so little time."

She embarked on the tour with Serge Obolensky, Pat, and an entourage of models and staff. The first stop was San Francisco. They placed a special bench in the elevator of the Sutter Street salon, so that she could ride up in comfort. She said to Mary Yee, the operator, "You know, it wasn't so long ago that I started in a hole in the wall not much bigger than this elevator."

Her old friend, Mrs. Ambrose Diehl, moved out of her own home and into the St. Francis to be with Elizabeth. They chattered away long into the night, girlishly giggling, and reminiscing about old times. At the luncheon fashion show, Elizabeth charmed many of the ladies into placing orders on the spot.

That night Alma Spreckles was giving a big party. Elizabeth's gown was laid out on the bed, and she was having her hair done. She kept repeating, "I'm going to have such a good time."

Somebody looked out the window and remarked, "It's going to rain."

MISS ELIZABETH ARDEN

"It wouldn't dare!" Miss Arden cried, and it didn't.

There was a great bouquet of white roses displayed in the window of the Beverly Hills salon. She shuddered visibly and ordered, "Get rid of those. It looks like you're getting ready for a funeral."

Elizabeth and her party were staying at the Beverly Hills Hotel, where the benefit fashion show and supper dance was also to take place. Tonny Duquette, who had decorated the Irish castle, was giving a party for her on the night before the show. While she was dressing, she accidentally slammed her knee into the bedspring. It was very painful, but not wanting to miss a party, she disregarded it.

The knee was very seriously swollen by the next morning, and a doctor was summoned. He advised her to stay off it, but she was determined not to disappoint all the guests at the fashion show. The ugly swelling did not diminish, and just before she was to dress, she again called the doctor and instructed him to administer a shot of novocaine right into the injured area.

In the ballroom, Mary Blakely and some of the others waited, wondering if she would be able to make it. Suddenly, Elizabeth was in the doorway, looking absolutely lovely in a simple white gown with tiny red satin slippers peeping out from beneath the hem. She swept across the room, giving no indication that anything was wrong with her. The warm, enchanting smile was bestowed upon strangers and friends alike. During her procession, there were the usual murmured estimates of her age. The more conservative placed her in her sixties, while others, incredulous at their own calculations, averred that she could not be older than somewhere in her mid-fifties.

In her opening address, Elizabeth declared her pleasure at seeing so many beautiful women, and her greater pleasure at seeing so many beautiful men. She flirted outrageously, complimenting them on taking the time to come over to select their wives' clothes. "You men have such gorgeous taste. One look at your wives—I hope they're your wives—tells me that."

By the time Lillian Macmillan took over for the fashion com-

:[312]:

mentary, the audience was in the palm of her hand. Afterwards, Elizabeth told her, ''You were very good, dear.''

Miss Macmillan smiled appreciatively. ''Not as good as you in that opening speech.''

The next day, the knee was still in terrible condition. Like a little girl desperately unhappy about missing a party, Elizabeth plaintively told Pat, ''I don't think I'll be able to make Chicago. You'll have to go in my place.''

She flew directly home to New York.

EPILOGUE

A young reporter once asked Elizabeth Arden about her will. Miss Arden winked and said, "When the time comes, dear, there'll be a few little surprises."

There were.

Some intimates, who were certain they would be remembered, were overlooked, and others, expecting nothing, were happily surprised. The will was explicit about the disposal of everything except the most important item of all—the empire. The regal Miss Arden's last words were a paraphrase of those attributed to Louis XV of France. *"Après moi le deluge."*

She was most specific about the disposal of $11,000,000 in legacies. Four million dollars was to go to Gladys, $1,000,000 to her son, John, and $2,000,000 to Patricia Young, plus her jewelry, valued at $1,000,000, all her personal effects, and the bulk of her estate after taxes and bequests were paid.

She left $4,000,000 to her employees and servants, including $200,000 to her lawyer, J. Howard Carter, and $250,000 to her manager, Carl W. Gardiner. There were gifts ranging from $5,000 to $200,000 to the others. Large sums were to be divided among those with ten years or more of service in the salons in London, Paris, New York, San Francisco, Chicago, Boston, Washington, and Los Angeles, as well as those employed in the Long Island City factory, the Elizabeth Arden Sales Corporation, and Elizabeth Arden, Inc.

Epilogue

There were special instructions for the disposal of her stable. Those horses in training were to be sold first, the mares sold last, and those with foals, together with them.

About the business—nothing. During the last years of her life, many of her assistants thought that they could run it more efficiently without her. Very well. She was giving them the opportunity to have at it.

There was one small handicap. They had to raise $48,000,000 before they could start.

By not setting up a foundation, she had done precisely what she had sworn never to do. She had turned her business into a charitable institution with the United States government as the only recipient of its generosity. The government had a claim to $37,000,000 in estate and corporate taxes. The larger total came when the personal bequests were added to it. No business in the world is so liquid that it can readily come up with such an enormous sum, but the money had to be amassed without endangering the company—and as quickly as possible.

The parade of sales started. First, the Irish castle, then her New York apartment went. It was bought by Charlotte Ford Niarchos, who was then in the process of divorcing her husband. Mrs. Niarchos never lived in it, because her former spouse gave her a rather magnificent flat on Sutton Place. She later sold it to its present occupants, Mr. and Mrs. Cornelius Whitney.

Next, the horses were sold for much less than their estimated value. The University of Kentucky bought the Maine Chance Farm for $2,000,000. This led to the first of several extravagant lawsuits. A California horseman, Rex Ellsworth, and a Lexington veterinarian, Arnold Pessin, brought a $30,000,000 antitrust action against the University of Kentucky Research Foundation and the Bank of New York. The result was that the company could not touch that money until after the action was settled.

The old factory and warehouse on East Fifty-second Street was sold for $650,000, and Elizabeth's private estate, adjacent to the Maine Chance, Maine, resort, went for $110,000. As can be readily adduced, the company was somewhat short of its financial goal.

:[315]:

The executors of the estate were the Bank of New York, J. Howard Carter, Patricia Young, and Gladys de Maublanc. Gladys was immediately disqualified, because she had retained her Canadian citizenship. Amazingly, after fifty years in France, she was not, nor had she ever been, a French citizen.

There were sixty inquiries into buying the business following Miss Arden's death. All the problems would have been solved had the executors accepted any one of them, but they were vetoed in favor of going it alone.

Carl Gardiner was appointed president with a six-man board including three bankers, J. Howard Carter, Patricia Young, and himself. Pablo was to act as the public voice of the company and, subsequently, its creative director.

Gladys listened to all the great plans and drew her own conclusions. She wondered what a lawyer and three bankers knew about face cream. She knew that her niece had never taken an active part in the business. As for Gardiner, he was a questionable factor. He had been efficient enough with Elizabeth to guide him, but how good would he be at running the show all by himself?

Sister thought about it from every angle and finally made her evaluations. She sold her $4,000,000 legacy back to the corporation for $2,000,000 in cash and returned to France. She died two years later and, as she had requested, was buried alongside her husband. Her ambition had turned her son into a Graham, but she rested eternally a De Maublanc, next to the man she had loved so deeply, despite all that she had found repugnant in his actions and attitudes.

One of Gardiner's first acts was to discontinue the losing custom-made department. He announced that the company was going to seek a new appeal and expected to serve a "much broader group of customers."

The Arden ready-made collection was like a class reunion of her designers. Except for James, who was no longer in business, they were all represented—the lads whose reputations she had helped to make—Antonio Castillo, Ferdinando Sarmi, and Oscar de la Renta. The dominant shade was green, a color Elizabeth had always disliked, but the aura of her quiet good taste still pervaded. Perhaps, after all, they had learned something from her.

Maine Chance, Maine, had a fire in 1969 and another in 1970. Including the burning of the original edifice, on which Elizabeth first built, that made another three fires. The company decided to close its doors forever.

By the middle of 1970 neither the legatees nor the government had received any payment, and Carl Gardiner resigned as president of the Arden Company. His duties were taken over by Charles Bliss, who was also chairman of the board of the Bank of New York.

On September 30, 1970, there was announcement, in the New York *Times*, that the American Cyanamid Company had been approached to buy the Elizabeth Arden Company. Cyanamid was already in the beauty business through its Breck Hair division. The announcement continued that no decision had yet been reached.

Actually, Cyanamid had first been approached during the previous April by Sidney J. Weinberg, Jr., a partner in the investment banking firm of Goldman, Sachs, and Company, which was allegedly acting as authorized agents for the executors of the Arden estate. In May, it was supposed to have sent a descriptive memorandum on Arden to stimulate additional interest. As a result, Cyanamid undertook a detailed and costly investigation of the company.

By August a deal for the purchase of the Arden Company, all its assets and liabilities, was being discussed. The price was $35,000,000—$28,000,000 in cash, $4,500,000 in stock or notes, and $2,500,000 in a contingency payment.

Cyanamid learned in early September that it would expedite things if the contingency payment went exclusively to Miss Arden's sole residuary legatee, Patricia Young. Cyanamid did not agree to the arrangement, but that did not stop the forward motion of the deal. Supposedly, the Arden executors were anxious to sell to Cyanamid, because "it had the ability to rebuild the business."

On October 1, 1970, there was a meeting at the Cyanamid offices attended by J. Howard Carter, and Charles Bliss. The written agreement for purchase was read aloud and, with one modification, approved. As they were leaving, a Cyanamid representative quoted Carter as saying, "You people have a great deal; you'll see that in a couple of years."

It was alleged that on the same day the vice-president of Eli Lilly and Company called Bliss and told him that the investment banking firm they had hired to evaluate Arden had delivered its report, but that Lilly still wanted to do its own investigating before deciding to make a bid. Bliss cautioned him that negotiations with Cyanamid were moving rapidly.

The next day the written agreement with Cyanamid was approved by its executive committee and hand delivered to the Arden offices. On the same day, the executors were informed that a special meeting of Cyanamid's board would be held on October 7, formally to approve the terms of the agreement. The executors mailed back the original of the executed agreement with a covering letter, from Bliss, containing a handwritten postscript: "I, personally, am very happy about this and will do everything I can to speed the finalization of the agreement." It was signed informally, "Mitch."

October 2 was a very eventful day. Bliss was informed that Lilly would forgo its own investigation and would like to meet with him on October 8, or thereafter, to discuss Arden.

It was alleged that on October 3, Lilly was informed that it could only obtain Arden by tendering a substantial down payment and bettering Cyanamid's $35,000,000 offer. Supposedly, Goldman, Sachs had agreed to meet with the Lilly people, on October 5, in their offices to discuss the matter.

It would be logical to assume that Goldman, Sachs was interested in making a better deal. Its fee was dependent on the total amount received for Arden by the estate.

On the evening of October 5, Cyanamid's president was informed, by Bliss, that the executors were likely to sell to a third party. It was alleged that by 3 A.M., on the morning of October 6, Lilly and the Bank of New York had executed a memorandum of understanding, purporting to sell Arden to Lilly for a purchase price of $38,500,000, and that Lilly turned over a $20,000,000 check as down payment.

Later that morning, Bliss met with a representative of Cyanamid. He said that he had initially refused to conduct negotiations with another purchaser because, as far as he was concerned, the agreement with Cyanamid constituted ''a deal.'' However, his counsel had informed him that he had a duty to accept a better offer, and the executors decided that they were free to accept another purchaser so long as the cash down payment was made by that purchaser before Cyanamid's board of directors' meeting on the next morning.

On October 20, 1970, Cyanamid tied up the estate by suing for $60,000,000 against the estate and another $60,000,000 against Lilly. In February of the following year, it also sued Goldman, Sachs for $120,000,000.

It was said that the sole beneficiary of the increase in purchase price, under the Lilly agreement, would be Patricia Young.

Four years had passed since the death of Elizabeth Arden, and none of the lesser heirs had received one nickel of their legacies. These were the little people, like Georgia Reed, whom Elizabeth had always looked after, the old girls she kept on long after they would have been disposed of by a more sensible employer. They began to lose hope that they would live to see any of the money.

Pat Young and Mala Rubinstein, Helena's niece, met at a luncheon. Mala said, ''Isn't it a pity our aunts never met? I think they would've liked each other.'' She smiled. ''At least, they would've understood each other.''

Echoing Hemingway's famous last words, Pat replied, ''Yes. Isn't it pretty to think so?''

The heirs received a Christmas gift, on December 24, 1971, when American Cyanamid settled its case out of court for an undisclosed amount. They could again look forward to receiving their money. It came just in time, for they were beginning to need it very badly. Many of them had been recently retired by the Lilly Company.

Lilly was a very efficient organization. They got rid of everything that did not function perfectly. The beloved salons, in San Francisco and London, were moved to new and more convenient locations. The entrance areas that Nicholai Remisoff had designed for all the establishments deliberately wasted space in elegant ambience. They were soon cluttered, like bargain basements, with racks of overstyled medium priced garments. A rumor started that those salons that did not begin to carry their own weight would be closed, as the Rubinstein salons had been closed after her death.

The simple home offices were redecorated to impress visitors with the importance of the company. Elizabeth had always felt that it did not matter what the offices looked like. The important thing was to impress clients with the grandeur of the salons.

A Lilly executive was showing Duke Cross through the new offices. He said, "How do you like them? I think we've given Elizabeth Arden a little class."

Pat Young fished into her handbag and brought forth a tiny tube with an enameled top. Holding it up for inspection, she said, "This is their latest lipstick."

She hunted in her bag again and found an exquisite thin gold case that looked as if it had been designed by Van Cleef & Arpels. "This is the last one my aunt brought out, before she died."

In May, 1972, Prince Michael Evlanoff died, at the age of seventy-six, an ill and lonely old man who had spent his last days in a nursing home ironically named Florence Nightingale.

By the sixth anniversary of her death the darling horses were a fading memory, recalled most vividly by stablehands swapping wild tales about Mrs. Mud Pack. Her lovely homes were occupied by strangers. Her concept of the business had been altered into something that she would not have recognized as her own. All that remained was the name—Elizabeth Arden—and that, too, had been a dream.